Sketches from the Ranch

Also by Dan Aadland

HORSEBACK ADVENTURES

TREADING LIGHTLY WITH PACK ANIMALS

WOMEN AND WARRIORS OF THE PLAINS:
THE PIONEER PHOTOGRAPHY OF JULIA E. TUELL

Sketches from the Ranch

A Montana Memoir

Dan Aadland

Illustrations by Nik Carpenter

Howell Book House
New York

Howell Book House
A Simon & Schuster Macmillan Company
1633 Broadway
New York, NY 10019

Macmillan Publishing books may be purchased for business or sales promotional use. For information please write: Special Markets Department, Macmillan Publishing USA, 1633 Broadway, New York, NY

Text copyright © 1998 by Dan Aadland. Illustrations copyright © 1998 by Nik Carpenter

MACMILLAN is a registered trademark of Macmillan, Inc.

Library of Congress Cataloguing-in-Publication Data: available upon request.

ISBN 0-87605-078-X

Manufactured in the United States of America

10 9 8 7 6 5 4 3 2 1

Book Design: Nick Anderson

Cover Design: Michael J. Freeland

The following publishers have generously given permission to use quotations from copyrighted works:
From *The Poetry of Robert Frost,* edited by Edward Connery Lathem, © 1958 by Robert Frost,
© 1967 by Lesley Frost Ballantine, © 1930, 1939, © by Henry Holt and Company, Inc.,
© 1997 by Edward Connery Lathem. Reprinted by permission of Henry Holt and Company, Inc.
Lines from "Fiddler Jones" from *Spoon River Anthology* by Edgar Lee Masters.
Originally published by the Macmillan Co. Permission by Hilary Masters.

To Magnus and Kristine and Nora and Elmer

Contents

CONTENTS

Acknowledgments

T. S. Eliot told us that it takes a great deal of history to make a little literature, and a book that attempts to reflect a collective ranch experience, indeed, a culture, must drink from many springs. There are the tales told during my half-century under Montana's big sky by family and neighbors, by parishioners of my father who sat with coffee in the parsonage living room, Stetsons on their knees, and by the first ranchers for whom I milked cows and moved cattle. There are tales told by the land itself, in wagon tracks across a range of bunch grass and yucca and prickly pear, and those told in sign left by people who were here on the ranch before even the pioneers, "The Children of the Large Beaked Bird," the Absaroka, the Plains Indians known as the Crows.

And then there are the many individuals who have contributed to this book in some more direct way, a long list of them from which I will mention three: Nik Carpenter, whose efforts to create the artwork for this book were both Herculean and enlightened; Madelyn Larsen of Howell/Macmillan who was her usual strong, soft voice from New York during this, the third book for which she has been my editor;

and Emily, my wife of more than thirty years, my ranch girl, my homefront editor, who furnished the support and understanding without which none of my books could have been written.

A Note to the Reader

Although the word "Sketches" in the title of this book may suggest light, unrelated episodes and may seem an invitation to browse as you wish, I really would prefer you read this book from beginning to end, just as you would a novel. For a story is told. The thread of narrative resembles a small stream, trickling its way down the valley, detouring beaver dams, meandering around digressions. But viewed from far above, the stream would be seen to progress steadfastly down the valley to a resting place, and its journey is one I would like you to take with me in proper order.

THE RANCH

On a fall day flooded with sunshine, on a sagebrush-covered flat overlooking a valley, a stocky man rode a galloping Indian pony in pursuit of a dozen loose horses. The sheen of sweat on the animals' coats and their easy lopes suggested they had already run a long way. Suddenly the group slowed to a trot and stopped as if on signal. The lead horse dropped his head to graze, the rest followed suit, and the man muttered, "Good." He slackened his reins so that his own mount could graze, then swung off to check the cinch and stretch his legs.

The horses had stopped at a fortunate place, on a knoll allowing Magnus a clear view of the valley and of the vast space surrounding him. To the man's left were the Absaroka mountains, a blue wall named after the Crow Indians, the tribe that still occupied the ground on which the ponies picked bunch grass from between clumps of sage and yucca plant. There was new snow on the mountaintops, caught by the morning sun. A bank of clouds floated below the peaks. Behind the man, to the east and close to the Crow's new agency, were the Pryor mountains, bearing the name of a soldier with the Lewis and Clark expedition. To the northwest, sixty miles away but looking close, sharply peaked and stark, were the Crazy Mountains, named after a woman who broke under the stress of frontier life. And far to the north, appearing like distant white clouds, fully one hundred miles away, was the range called the Snowies.

The snow on the peaks spoke of things coming soon, and so did the clear air, warm, yes, but with a trace of bite around the edges. Even now, late in the morning, the man had resisted removing his heavy wool sweater and tying it to its accustomed place behind the cantle of his saddle.

Directly below him, down a steep coulee lined with scattered fir trees and blood-red buck brush, on the still-green valley floor, were the buildings of the abandoned Crow Agency. He knew the place from previous horse-trading trips, knew the adobe mill and the smokehouse and the fort itself, and even from this distance he could see that the buildings had begun to deteriorate. The agency had moved east. The Crows, skillful in their negotiations with the white man, had originally won a reservation larger than many states of the union, too large a tract for a small tribe to hang onto, given the press of white immigration. So the reservation (though still imposing, compared with those of other tribes) was being reduced in size.

It was this movement of the agency headquarters east and the scheduled opening of a portion of the reservation to white settlers that made the man on the knoll rest himself and his horses longer than he would normally allow. He was studying the valley floor, nodding with appreciation at the green fields around the agency buildings, watered by the irrigation ditch dug by the Crows and their agent. He would dig more irrigation ditches. He would make the whole valley floor as green as Denmark.

It was nothing for a man with muscle who wasn't afraid to work, he thought. The valley floor sloped down in grade, so you made a long measuring board and put two legs on it, one slightly shorter than the other (using dimensions you'd memorized) and placed a carpenter's level on the board. You set the measuring board on the ground like a long sawhorse. When the bubble centered, the drop in grade for the length of the board was the same as the difference in height of the two legs, just right for a ditch used to flood-irrigate the land below it. You chose a place up the creek well above your land, a place where the willow-lined bank was low; you surveyed your ditch with many placements of the measuring board, staked it out, then dug it with a team of horses and a slip. The slip looked like a wheelbarrow with no wheel, just a steel box with a flat sharp edge on the bottom to dig into the ground and two han- dles projecting to the rear, between which you walked.

Handling the slip, raising the han- dles for more bite, lowering them for less, was a man's job, dangerous when the slip caught a rock. Magnus had learned the skill from miners. Finally, when the ditch was done, you went back to the creek, took off your clothes, and waded into the icy stream, piling river rocks into a diversion wing to raise the water level and fill your ditch. Then, by God, you could turn things green. And that is how this ambitious young man summarized several months of back-breaking labor. He knew of the sweat, the blisters, and the bruises involved in digging a ditch a mile long through rocky river-bottom land, the mornings when every muscle would ache. But none of this bothered him in the least.

The ponies looked up from their grazing as if wondering what this white man would demand of them next. He had let them run for miles, just as they wished, cor- recting their progress only when necessary to keep them running approximately north. Wild as they were, there was no point in attempting more control until they were tired. Now they were again showing signs of restlessness, sniffing the air with noses high pointing south toward their home range. He would have to move them along. He would corral the horses by the agency buildings, where the soldiers had kept theirs until recently, then go back upstream to talk to the squatter who had built the barn and hut a half mile above the agency buildings. He had business to attend to.

The man's name was Magnus Jensen. The year was 1892. Custer and his troops had died on a terrible Sunday two days' ride to the east just sixteen years earlier. The wagon tracks Magnus paralleled as he herded the ponies were remnants of the Boze-man Trail, a supply route for mines to the west. A war had been fought over that trail, a war that ended just twenty-four years before Magnus rode this route, when the United States admitted it had lost the fight to a brilliant Lakota leader named Red Cloud.

Born three-quarters of a century after him, I never met Magnus Jensen, nor did my wife, his granddaughter, for she was the baby of her family and Magnus had died of complications from diabetes before Emily was born. Yet I know him. I fix fences he built, repairing the remaining single-strand barbed wire he used, replacing occasion-ally the cedar fence posts he cut and trimmed and tamped into holes dug by hand. My cattle graze the ground he claimed, and my children have played in the yard around the same house, much enlarged, that he bought from a squatter. The log barn he used no longer survives—we knew it well but could not save it, for the logs had rotted out and it had become a danger. Daily, my life as a rancher intertwines with his, and the day when he first saw the ranch on which he would spend the rest of his life seems very close to me.

Magnus was an immigrant, a dairyman, a cowboy, and a rancher. Coming to America from the Danish island of Bornholm in the 1880s, he had worked his way to Montana, settling near the mining town of White Sulphur Springs. He rode the range as a cowboy for several years in that central Montana country, the land of Charlie Russell. Then he teamed up with relatives to mine an entirely different kind of wealth than that being dug by those around him, to mine it from the very miners who worked the claims nearby. They were hungry, those miners, hungry and thirsty for something fresh, for the sweet home taste of milk, the tang of sharp cheese, and real butter on their biscuits in the morning. So this young dairyman from Bornholm built his nest egg quietly, through the hard work that comes with milking by hand a band of cows twice daily, of growing the hay and grain they require to produce well, of feeding, fencing, and shed-building.

He had become a horseman along the way, a good one. In my favorite photo he sits a dark-colored horse. Although now portly, in middle age, Magnus's erect, proud figure exudes power, the right arm which holds the reins big under his long-sleeved shirt. Only his hat and boots are stereotypically "western," for he is clad in bib over-alls. His saddle is the A-fork roping design, popular with cowboys of the time, and his bit is a United States Cavalry officer's model. (I know the bit well for I own it now and use it.) Behind him in the photograph is the log barn the squatter built.

Family lore is rich with stories of Magnus's prowess with horses. His son Elmer put it bluntly. "If Dad could get one foot in the stirrup and his hand on the horn there wasn't a horse in the country that could get rid of him." His grip and his grit were legendary. "He told me once his idea of a good horse was one you could ride for sixty miles that still had the gumption to try to kick you when you got off," Elmer said.

To further supplement his dairy income, Magnus made trips to the Crow Reservation to buy unbroke horses. He would travel east by rail to the reservation boundaries, then purchase a band of young, wild horses from the best of all horse traders, the Crows. Fashion at the time was for solid-colored animals, most cowboys believing pintos and paints were the result of inbreeding. (They also felt white hooves did not hold up as well as black ones.) From the band he bought, Magnus would pick his own horse, one with a single-foot gait if possible (not rare in those days), spend a day or two training that one, then use it to herd the others two hundred miles back home. To one who knows livestock and horses, that feat seems almost unimaginable. Because the instinct to run with the herd is so very strong in horses, chasing a band of wild horses is dangerous. To herd horses one's mount must be well-trained enough to have overcome all the natural tendencies to run with the pack or, at least, the rider must be skillful enough to deal with some wild consequences. To tackle such a task as Magnus did, on a horse that only days earlier was an untrained member of the band, speaks of great skill and courage. Once Magnus had the horses home, he would saddle-break the rest of the band, selling them to nearby cowboys and miners.

And so it was on a trip to buy horses that Magnus found his ranch. The valley floor below him would raise hay for winter, while the hills above furnished summer pasture. He could see it all superimposed on the scene below in his mind's eye, and now he would begin to make it his. The wild ponies watched him swing into the saddle. They had their wind now, but after their initial stampede they had begun to learn to be moved by a man on horseback. A game trail led down the side of the coulee toward the valley bottom. Magnus eased his horse around the bunch, gently pushing them, until the bay that led the band spotted the trail and headed down it at a trot.

The rest lined out in single file. Magnus's horse, herd instinct still intact, gave two stiff crowhops, which his rider countered with a jab of the spurs and a pull into a 360-degree spin. Then they all dropped down the trail.

At the mouth of the coulee the ponies skidded to a stop, stared ahead and snorted. Alone among the scattered fir trees and stumps from recent logging was a single, huge, long-needle pine. In it was something large, lying horizontally. At first Magnus thought it might be a garment hung in the branches of the tree. Then the smell of death colored the sage scent in the breeze, and he realized he was looking at an Indian tree burial. The ponies shied around it, heads cocked sideways, Magnus following them. Just what this young Danish Lutheran immigrant thought of the burial is uncertain, but we know it received his respect, for the site was never molested.

The corral at the agency buildings was still serviceable, and the ponies, unsuspecting, ran along the pole fence and through the gate. Magnus took time for a short rest. In his saddle bags were bread and cheese from his own dairy, along with a little jerky. He ate standing. Then he jumped back on his tired pony and headed south up the creek. The colt, stubborn about leaving his companions, zigzagged, trying to swivel back toward the bunch. Magnus controlled him by skillful use of rein and spur. *Frem og tilbage* (forth and back) thought Magnus, like a boat without a keel. When the horse's back went tense under the saddle, when Magnus felt him "hump up," the man knew a buck was on its way. He spun the colt in two tight circles, then lined him out and spurred while reining in, finally smiling for the first time all day as the colt dropped into a swift, smooth single-foot. "I knew you could do that," he said aloud in Danish. Three days earlier in the Crow camp, he had noticed the colt come down from a lope into the single-foot when the Indian ran the ponies in among the tepees to assemble the bunch and make his best trade. And he had noticed also the trader, in his first sort of the ponies, attempting to exclude this brown one from the deal.

The squatter was bearded and dirty and tired-looking, but his blue eyes were honest, and he stood beside the new barn with obvious pride. His speech was a combination of broken English and Norwegian, understandable as long as he went slowly. Magnus understood English at this point in his life, but could speak little. Norwegian sounded to him like Danish with an accent.

The barn smelled of new peeled pine. It was a good barn, the squatter told Magnus. He had used some fir logs, but preferring the easy-working pine, he'd cut every tree of that kind in the coulee, excepting, of course the one "with the Injun in it."

"The fir will last longer," Magnus said. It was this fir, he knew, that was the closest wood in America to the kind from which Scandinavians built their boats. It was a wood that, once soaked with tar, lasted almost forever.

Yes, the squatter planned to file on his little spread as soon as the government would let him. Indeed, the papers were already prepared. Magnus looked at the tired face, then to the old Jersey milk cow in the crude corral, finally to the collar-marked mule team grazing in the meadow. He fished in his saddle bags and brought out a small leather bag. Poking into it, he counted out a handful of gold coins. "Here are five hundred dollars. Put my name alongside yours on the homestead papers, and give me a receipt. File the papers the very morning they open the office this fall. When I come back I'll give you five hundred dollars more. You can stay here till spring and keep the mules and the cow, but your 160 acres will be mine."

He saw the squatter hesitate, running his palm over his beard, but he had seen as well when he produced the money the sudden shine in the eyes of the woman who sat on the porch nursing her baby. Then she looked down at the child but stayed alert, he could tell, listening breathlessly to every word they said. "Yah, that's fair. I can do that," the squatter said.

"Then get the papers. And tell your neighbors that Magnus Jensen from White Sulphur Springs wants to build a ranch, and that he can use several more homesteads, and that he'll pay them fairly. I'll be back by Christmas."

Magnus turned to go, but he was stopped in his tracks by a female voice that said, "There's coffee." To fail to stay when a Norwegian offered you coffee black as pitch with a piece of crude but sweet cake alongside would not be just unfriendly. It would be hostile. And so he stayed for a tin cup of coffee, sitting on an empty nail keg by the table of rough-cut cottonwood planks as briefly as he dared. He left the people the rest of his cheese. Then he turned his pony north.

So Magnus built his ranch. He phased out the dairy business over several years, traveling periodically to the site near the agency, buying out several more squatters. He prepared in other ways, too. His search for a wife was by mail to his native Bornholm, where he located a young girl named Kristine. He had distantly known her family, remembered a quiet little girl, tried to imagine how she would be grown up, then arranged for her passage. The agreement was less binding than "mail-order bride" implies. Magnus would pay for her passage. If Kristine did not like him, she could work as ranch cook until he was repaid. Otherwise, they would marry. The verdict was apparently a quick one, for they were joined in a ceremony at White Sulphur Springs in 1895 by a circuit-riding Lutheran pastor. So Magnus was ready. He had a wife, and his ranch was waiting.

The term "ranch" connotes many things. More than a century of romanticization in western dime novels, and nearly that long in the cinema, has imbued the word with an aura beyond its dictionary definition. Thus it is important to point out that Magnus's ranch was not a "Ponderosa" or a "Southfork." By Texas (or eastern Montana) ranching standards, the spread was small indeed. Conversely, to homesteader mentality, the ranch was comfortably large. It began as a few hundred acres and grew, particularly during the 1920s. During that decade homesteads crashed on the rocks of the reality John Wesley Powell had tried to pound into Congress back when homestead laws were being debated. The reality was simply this: 160 acres of western land, in years of normal rainfall, would not support a family.

This was a hard sell for Powell. Eastern congressmen who were wealthy farmers had accumulated their means on farms much smaller than 160 acres. Not make a living on so much land? How could that be? But these congressmen had never seen the prairie wind blow dust, had never seen the ground crack and parch, had never watched tumbleweeds roll and hills turn brown. So in even south-central Montana, relatively lush by western standards, small, dryland homesteaders had to say goodbye to their dreams when the rain quit in the 1920's, and sell out to those who had been a trifle more successful.

Magnus's ranch eventually comprised about sixteen hundred acres, straddling an irrigated valley running north and south with hill pastures on both sides. Land above the ditch is called "dryland," meaning that it can't be irrigated, and late in most summers the irrigation ditches form a bold border between green and brown. The hills may look sparse to a Midwesterner's eye. (The Iowa term for any land that cannot be farmed is "wasteland.") But the native grasses are high in protein and, if not overgrazed, will give mother cows the nourishment to raise calves that are fat and sleek by weaning time. The irrigated land in the valley was the key to survival in hard times, for irrigated hay can grow even when summer rain does not come, and after haying the watered fields spring back green to furnish fall feed for the stock to eat once the ranges have given out.

The county road eventually moved down from the base of the hill to the valley bottom. Thus a highway and a river split the land near the sheds Magnus built and the house, which he continually enlarged. Magnus and Kristine had a child who died as a baby, followed by others who lived, until five children came to share the ranch with them.

Those few around me left alive who remember Magnus seem to have considered him solid and comfortably prosperous, but not wealthy. He was known for his civic pride. He furnished land for the first organized church south of the Yellowstone River in Montana, Immanuel Lutheran, was a charter member of its congregation, and tended the church building on the ranch for twenty years until a larger structure was built in the town four miles north. He also furnished land for the first post-reservation school. He was known as a magnificent host.

Although Magnus does not seem to have made enemies, he was the sort who took matters into his own hands. Among his five children was an adopted girl, a lone Norwegian among Danish brothers and sisters. When very small, she was being raised alternately by two aunts, neighboring homesteaders, of questionable mental stability. The two would fight over the little girl, kidnapping her back and forth. At a certain point, Magnus had heard enough. He rode to the homestead which was at that particular moment in possession of the child, reached down from horseback and picked her up, placed her on the saddle in front of him, rode home, and adopted her. End of problem. The girl, Aunt Gert, died a few years ago at age eighty, the good humor never having left her eyes.

And what of the girl from Denmark, Kristine? Those who remember her always use the word "kindness." She was kind and she was gentle and, like Magnus, loved company. When the county road relocated to pass her house, Kristine would spot travelers coming from up the road, rush to fix them coffee and cake, then walk out to intercept them and ask them in. My aging neighbor still refers to her as *Mrs. Johnson*, while he recalls the ranch lady of his own generation (Kristine's daughter-in-law) with her first name, Nora. Why *Johnson*? Magnus and Kristine had followed the common Scandinavian immigrant practice of changing their names. Magnus apparently chose Johnson to differentiate himself from other Jensens (and Norwegian *Jensons*) to whom he was not related, while Kristine Americanized her first name to Christine.

Another sort of Americanization took place as well. In those early years of our century one's level of assimilation was measured by his or her command of English. (*No one* wished to be a "hyphenated American.") Magnus, like most farmers and ranchers of the time, kept a simple ledger, expenses on one side of facing pages, income on the other. In addition there were notes of mundane details. Magnus's earliest journals are completely in Danish. Later, there is a mixture of Danish and English, and finally, the writing is completely English. The ranch children were admonished to learn English well and to help their parents learn it. To this end, the children were sent to a boarding high school, Billings Polytechnic Institute, sixty miles away, where they worked at the school farm for tuition. There were no closer secondary schools. And so in the matter of language the children became the teachers, and they became so in other ways, too. Elmer, the oldest son, became the family chauffeur when Magnus found, like many of his generation, that his first automobile did not respond to "whoa," or to "gee" or "haw" or rein or spur.

Though financed chiefly through the children's own labors, the boarding school education was a touch of class. So was the purchase of a cabinet grand piano, delivered from the railhead with team and wagon by a salesman and family friend named

Bauske, an Orthodox Jew, musician, peddler, a man so skilled, we've been told, that he could weld cast iron. We own a faded snapshot. There is a small, solid wagon with flat bed, the piano in wooden crate aboard, the ranch house in the background. There is snow on the ground, and next to the team of horses, on his own pony, is an excited small boy. The boy was Emily's father, Elmer.

The story of Magnus Jensen-Johnson is an American story of land-taking, of achieving the dream so impossible in Europe, where farms were tiny and so often controlled by someone else, where wars often soaked an entire decade of a man's young life, too often taking it in the process. Per Hansa, in Ole Rolvaag's book *Giants in the Earth*, reflects on the 160 acres of Dakota prairie he has claimed: "Was he really to own it? Was it really to become his possession, this big stretch of fine land?" And he asserts often that the land is *his*, that no "prince in pantaloons" can take it away from him or tell him how to manage it.

World War I came and went. (Magnus's sons were too young to serve.) The Twenties were prosperous, then tough, as was the whole next decade, survived with food and meat grown at home and a bit of cash flow from the cream cans and eggs that went with the mail carrier to town each morning on a vehicle now motorized but still called the stage. (The driver left the empty cream cans off by the mailbox on his return trip with a check and, if requested, a pound of butter inside.)

Eventually that time came when health began to fail Magnus and Kristine, when during winter it was too much to load daily with pitchfork a huge wagonload of loose hay for the cows. It took not only much skill but great strength to gather a hundred pounds of hay on the end of the fork, its handle bending to an arc with the weight, then placing that forkful perfectly to build the load; and then, of course, unloading it all to the impatient cows an hour later. Twice, since Magnus assembled the ranch, it has passed through the generations. Neither time has it been inherited outright; in each case the ones who stayed with the land having purchased portions of it from an estate that included other heirs. Two of Magnus's sons became ranchers, each buying part of the ranch before Magnus died, during World War II, a year after Kristine.

Elmer, born in 1903, the oldest of the boys, a small, wiry, blue-eyed horse-man, bought the largest share. With his wife Nora, a German girl raised on a dryland farm north of Billings, he saw the ranch through transition from team to tractor, through cycles of relative prosperity sandwiched between disasters. Twice he had to completely liquidate his cattle herd, once because of a new, mysterious illness nick-named "bangs" but known now as brucellosis, a silent sickness without symptoms that took the calves out of the cows and brought them empty to the calving barn the next spring. Regular pregnancy testing of the cows at fall weaning time was not done in those days. When the big Hereford bulls ran through the summer with healthy cows, when Elmer checked regularly to keep them out of the neighbor's pastures and with their own harems, he had a right to assume the cows were pregnant. When he culled questionable cows, kept the animals supplied with good grass and minerals, and fed them well when the snow flew, he had a right to expect calves to arrive in the spring. And now something new and insidious sneaked up on the herd and slipped away the unborn calves, so that for a year's work and worry Elmer came up empty, the yearly paycheck evaporated, stolen by an unseen thief.

And then there was the incident with Brownie. In the lifetime of a horseman an animal like Brownie comes along probably just once, if he's lucky, and maybe never. Brownie was the last offspring of a gaited mare Elmer might not have bought from the man with the checkered reputation, had he known the whole story. The mare was named Lady, which she wasn't. She was crazy, crazy enough to go over backwards with Elmer in the middle of the river. But oh, could she move, and Elmer, like Magnus, could not resist a horse that single-footed (or racked or performed a running walk), that could cruise ten miles an hour without trotting or loping, the rider feeling as if he were floating on a magic carpet. Lady could do this, her neck arched, her rear end tucked, the *rat-tat* of her hooves in perfect four-four tempo.

So Elmer bought the mare. Years later he was told that she was the result of an act of silent revenge, an act by a poor man who resented the dominance of his wealthy neighbor, a neighbor who owned a magnificent stallion reputed to be a Kentucky Whip (a family of saddlebred). During darkness, on a moonlit spring night when his mare was in season, the man sneaked her into an irrigated pasture where the stallion ran with his mares. He held the mare by her lead rope. The stallion dashed over to first inspect, then tease, then breed the new arrival. Afterwards, the man and his mare fled in the night.

The result of that surreptitious union was Lady, and Lady gave birth first to Tommy, who made a coarse but useful gelding. Then Lady refined the act, and had a nut-brown foal. This colt, a generation farther from his illustrious grandfather, had his mother's gaits, but they were less natural—the rider had to work harder for them. No matter. He was that rare saddle horse that felt vibrantly alive no matter where you touched him, his pasterns like shock absorbers no matter how rough the terrain, his beautiful neck and shoulder shaped like the mount of a Confederate officer.

There is always, when that special stud colt comes along, a resistance to making it a gelding, even though one's head tells him it is best to do so. Geldings, after all, unbothered by a huge segment of nature's distraction, are more tractable. There was, as well, until recently in the West, the belief that a male horse should not be castrated until he had his full growth. To keep him the arch-necked beauty Elmer wanted, he delayed cutting him until the colt was fully developed.

It happened on a September day, the very first day in Emily's memory. She remembers her dad teasing and chasing her around the table, both of them giggling, before he went on his morning ride. Emily knows it was September because there were boxes of apples on the round oak table, and in short-season Montana, September is the month for apples. Then, in starkest contrast, she remembers the rest of it, her Uncle Art coming back to the house in answer to Nora's request that he check on Elmer. Art tied his Appaloosa saddle horse to the back gate. Emily remembers the look on his white face as he stood at the kitchen door telling of finding his brother, then the precipitous leaving of the two adults in the automobile.

On the west side of the river, up on the range, there is a long, relatively flat, dryland hayfield. On Brownie, now four, and still a stud, Elmer had cantered into the field, discovered the herd of neighboring horses that did not belong there, and had given chase. The green-broke stud, galloping headlong through the gate, chasing the herd with stallion instinct intact, his rider probably loving every moment of it, did not gauge his clearance through the gate next to the massive cedar post, did not know to allow an extra six inches of space for the knee of his rider. The sledge-hammer blow stunned Elmer, sent the landscape wavy in his vision, sickened his stomach.

But still he did not know the extent of it, did not know until he got off his horse to close the gate, and the shattered bone exploded through his leg and the blood gushed. So that is how his brother Art found him after discovering Brownie wandering saddled but riderless, the horseman lying on his back near death from loss of blood, his leg mutilated.

Elmer survived. He survived the ex-army doctor called out of a tavern for the emergency, who set the leg with bones not touching. He survived the gangrene that invaded his leg because of the doctor's folly, and he survived the required bone grafts, then the six months in the hospital followed by another six lying in bed in his own house, a prisoner there, the sounds and sights and smells of the ranch around him but untouchable. But all things on the ranch did not survive.

The neighbors were all that neighbors can be. They helped Nora with chores, even put up all of Elmer's hay the following summer. But the accident had happened as tints of yellow invaded the leaves of the cottonwoods and hinted of snow to come, and the cow herd could not be brought through the winter without a strong man to feed them. So the cows were sold. Rebuilding the herd would have to wait until Elmer recovered, heavily in debt because of medical bills and loss of income.

The cow herd was not the only thing sold. To keep the ranch intact all superfluous mouths to feed were sold also, including several of Elmer's work teams, the decision to let all work horses but a couple favorites go probably influenced by the coming of the tractor at this time (the late 1940s). It was better that Elmer lay flat on his back in the hospital when the Percherons Dan and Daisy trotted into the sales arena at the Billings Livestock Commission, better that he did not have to watch the lifelong partners proudly make their entrance, perfectly in step on their accustomed sides, as if invisibly harnessed and hooked to a wagon, ready to work with nowhere to go in this time when mechanical marvels stood ready to replace them. They sold for peanuts.

Elmer recovered, his "good leg" slightly shortened because it supplied bone to graft to the shattered one. He forever wore boots altered by Connolly brothers, the saddle makers in Billings, one heel built up higher than the other. He recovered with a limp and an aversion to walking long distances, a limp that disappeared when he sat a horse, his old proud manner intact. I remember watching him get on a plug, a sorry critter that held its nose in the dirt as if ashamed to be a horse. When Elmer settled in the saddle and took up the reins the horse rose in stature, picked up its head, arched its neck, its entire demeanor altered all because it felt a true horseman on its back and it knew there would be expectations.

Brownie also survived. He was quickly gelded after the incident. Elmer knew better than to blame him. As rider, it was his job to be in control, to not cross a certain unwritten line known by good horsemen, a line that alters daily while a young horse is in training. Brownie could not be faulted for acting the part of a spirited, half-trained stud horse being asked to perform the ultimate call of the wild, that of chasing headlong a herd of horses, for he was doing what instinct told him to do, and his training had not progressed enough to overcome that instinct.

As a gelding Brownie retained plenty of pizzazz. He and Elmer taught Emily to become a horsewoman. I have heard sailors say that one best learns to sail with a quick, responsive, sensitive craft, not a tub. And, if supervision is adequate, a rider learns more quickly on a horse that is responsive and sensitive. Brownie vibrated with life until his dying day, and Emily mastered him.

Emily was riding Brownie next to the preacher's kid, mounted on a new mare named Rosie, when she showed her friend "Indian Coulee" the tree that had held the burial. Most of it was gone, of course. There was no trace of the blanket-wrapped object Magnus had seen seventy-five years earlier, but among the massive branches of the long-needled pine there was still a single horizontal stick, grey and gnarled, but pointedly telling its history. And the town kid on the mare, the boy who had

worked on ranches since he was fourteen, who was drawn so strongly toward horses and her, took interest too, and lowered his voice as he asked questions, then did not speak again until the horses had climbed out of the coulee and onto the sagebrush flat.

And so the third generation on the ranch began. There would be schools and war and three boys born. There would be many cycles of life in the valley, many trips of the trees through new leaf, full-ness, color, and cold. Barn kittens would be born, get old, and die. Boys would be babies, then little ones attempting inde-pendence but walking beside you holding your hand, then alien creatures with cracking voices, and then men. Again, a couple would purchase part of the ranch from heirs with a bank mortgage, yet never pretend they owned it, for you do not own a ranch—it owns you. All this would happen before the year of the story this book will tell.

And why have I begun to tell of this year in the 1990s with stories of Magnus and Kristine, of Nora and Elmer, of days before tractors, when the tracks of Indian ponies were still fresh? I have done so because when one works on a ranch he never lives a day without interacting with those people of the past who worked the land before him. There is not a day when I do not touch the things they touched, when I do not see the rise and fall of the ground made by the furrows of their plows, when I do not look over my shoulder for their approval of the job I am doing and either joy in having lived up to the task or despair because I haven't. The hills and the rocks and the woods on this ranch outlived Magnus and Elmer, and they will outlive me. And my story, which you are about to read, is equally their story.

SPRING

I

Calving • The stud colt • A new "snipe hunt"
The nature of the cow • A close call • Lion bait

Spring in Montana is green grass, but also stinging ice balls whipped by wind. It is warm days when the ground gives up its frost and the pasture sinks gently under your boot, but also days of wet, heavy snows that confound four-wheel drive, days of cruel blizzards to frost your budding green-grass dreams. On one of those days when the weather is having an identity crisis alternating hourly between January and May, on a day I have cabin fever and prefer my horse to the pickup truck, I catch Major and saddle him. I will check the calves on horseback, the best way really, vaccinating and ear tagging the new one I saw on the edge of the woods while I was feeding, the black one with the white face, still down, its mother licking off the afterbirth, not yet taking its first staggering steps toward the back end of the cow to teats of warmth and life.

I'm going out to fetch the little calf

That's standing by its mother.

It's so young

It totters when she licks it with her tongue.

I shan't be gone long.—You come too.

Mr. Frost, I have a love-hate relationship with your poem. Yes, it *can* be that way and sometimes is. It can be that way when you find a newborn, cute, up and sucking, its wiggling rear end telegraphing delight with the milk and impatience for more. It can even be that way when it's difficult, when you corner the laboring cow in a stall, secure her head, then help her with the calf puller, timing your efforts to her contractions, the spring-smell of placenta water spilling around you. First come the two front feet (you know they are front ones because the hooves are pointing down—up would mean they are rear ones, a breech birth). Then you find the nose, the head not turned back dangerously, but pointed in the right direction. Sometimes, though still in the womb, the calf's mouth finds your finger and tries to suck, so you know it is alive. And then, after the straining (both yours and hers) it is there, wet and slick at your feet, taking its first choking breaths. And you drag it, so slippery you can hardly get a grip, around to the front of the cow, where she can bond with it by smell and lick it into life and know (if a cow can know) that she has done well.

Yes, it can be that way. It can also be bad. There are years when scours, white and evil-smelling, runs out of the calves' back ends and they die no matter how many pills you shove into them. There are cesarean sections when the calf (if it's still alive by the time the operation is performed) starts life with a vet bill on its head nearly as big as its worth will be at weaning time. There are days you drag through your feeding, numbed by the birthing efforts you've spent between two and four a.m. rescuing a hypothermic calf, warming it any way you can, with heat lamps, the wood stove in the house, and a tubing of hot colostrum, heated up from its storage in the freezer. Some years calving is easy, and some years it is a marathon, when real spring never seems to come.

. . .

Today I have saddled my big, steady, gelding, Major. He and I will cruise through the trees looking for anything amiss. I hear a crack and look over to the corral where the stud colt snorts after sending a sharp kick the way of the Australian Shepherd pup, who has gotten careless. The colt's ears are not back. His hind foot has knocked a big chip out of the corral pole behind him, but he is not mad, has not really targeted the pup, has simply renewed a "no-trespassing" sign.

I study the colt, coming-three now, started last fall under saddle just enough to tell me that my work would be cut out for me, even if it weren't for my leg. He is not wild. He accepts my advances, my touching and currying and picking up of feet casually enough. But there is something indifferent about him, something suggesting a pledge to a higher calling and somehow above this messing with ropes and cinches, longeing and driving, my usual early steps in training a colt. His back is short, his withers high, his chest deep but not wide, with the inverted "V" between the front legs the old timers prized for endurance. His disposition may be questionable for a breeding stallion, but I already have an excellent breeding stallion. Although I will probably breed this colt to a few mares, he really has a different mission. He is my Pegasus, I his Bellerophon. Before him the mountains will shrink, and the rocky trails will be velvet under the glide of his running walk. Some crystal day we will leave early and crest the 11,000 feet of Sundance Pass while the morning sun still kisses the summer frost on the alpine grass.

But this work morning I will ride the more mundane Major. I brace the bad left leg for the moment when it will bear my weight alone, insert my foot into the stirrup, and swing into the saddle. He turns to my neck rein and steps smartly toward the job at hand. I must not sell Major short, for he is a fine horse. The first few rides on the stud colt have spoiled me a little, they've been as my middle son says, "scary but fun," for the stud colt is a Ferrari. Major is an Oldsmobile. But there is something to be said for the steadiness and strength of Oldsmobiles.

During the past week we have had a chinook. I am told the word means, in one of the Indian languages, "snow-eater." A warm south-west wind that sweeps through the cuts in the Beartooth front of the Absaroka mountains to my south, the chinook has done its job. Snow remains only in the shady places. On the south sides of some of the cottonwood trees there is fresh-smelling earthy grass, a tint of green visible through the old brown growth, preliminary green, for there will be much hard frost before winter gives up. But its smell, mixing with those of the thawing manure and the first inch of mud over the frosty footing now felt carefully by Major as we pick our way toward the woods, its smell awakens stirrings in both me and Major, who presses into the bit. The dog has felt it too. He has spent two days pointing his nose into the wind, his ears sleeked back and his eyes half closed, soaking it in, reading its shades of scent.

Most of the cows are on the feedground, where I have earlier fed thirty bales of hay, chopping the strings and flaking the bales off the bed of the pickup as it idled driverless in its lowest gear. A few, those with very new calves, maternal devotion epitomized, stand instead at the edge of the woods, their calves noisily sucking, forgoing the chance at their share of hay. When the calves are finished, their mothers will eat what the other cows have left.

The new baldy calf is just where I spotted him earlier, between two cottonwood trees next to the tiny stream that flows from the spring. He is on his feet but staggery. Every lick of his mother's rough tongue, the tongue that stimulates blood to the surface of his skin, the tongue that removes the red remnants of his earlier life inside her, pushes him nearly to the ground. He is shivering, his body having given up much of its heat to the south wind and the wet ground. There is a large bare spot in the middle of a patch of remaining snow, a spot where he was born, that is muddy, melted by the calf's precious heat. But he is motivated. His nose points steadfastly toward its target no matter how convoluted the motions of his body. If he can get to the teats and suck he will live. If not he will die. The milk will be both nourishment and warmth in the middle of his body core. And the first milk, the colostrum, is life itself, packed with the antibodies the calf needs in its fight for life.

The calf gets confused momentarily and thrusts his head between the cow's front legs. He tries sucking on tufts of hair before his mother, totally on task, rudely shoves him toward her hindquarters, still with stimulating tongue. Then he gets there. There is a mad thrusting of his nose into her bag, two or three misdirections, then the first nibble, finally the flood as the calf hits pay dirt. There are sucking sounds. White milk runs out the calf's mouth, down his face, and onto his black throat. His tail goes up into the air and wiggles.

Only then does the cow notice Major and me, who watch from a respectful distance. She gives just one slight shake of her head, so small it would not be noticed by one who does not live with these animals, just a double nod, really. But Major and I notice it. Major takes a half step backward and keeps his eyes riveted on the cow. I rein him down the line of feeding cows in temporary retreat. She has said to me in cowish, "Come closer and I will make mincemeat of both of you." She has the size, the strength, the speed, all the tools to do it. But a calf's capacity at first feeding is small. He will soon fill, overcome his hypothermic shivering, and lie down for a nap. I know this particular cow to have a fairly gentle nature. She will leave her sleeping calf and go to the feedground. I will then snatch it for a moment, do my thing, and retreat.

There is nothing eventful going on among the rest of the herd. Many of the cows are within a few days of calving. On these, the entire area under their tails is swollen and dripping with mucous. Most of the calves have already reclined on their temporary beds on the hay the cows will eventually eat from under them. I ride to each calf and watch it get up. If unhurried, a healthy calf will *always* take a moment to do a full stretch after it gets up. If it does not stretch, raising its head and elongating its body for a moment of comfort, making its back into a concave curve, it is sick. There are no exceptions I know of.

All the calves stretch. I see no serious signs of the diarrhea we call scours. A few calves do show the yellow runniness that comes from gluttony on the teats of a productive cow, but none show the white, evil stuff that must be treated immediately lest the calf dehydrate and die. I cannot think of scours without shuddering, without remembering the spring I helped Elmer fight a terrible epidemic that invaded the herd. We doctored and doctored, shoving the big antibiotic capsules down little calf throats with the tools we carried for that purpose. The dilemma was that some calves had scours but were not sick enough to be caught on foot, and those sick enough to run down and grab were already too sick to save. We brought the whole bunch into the corral, separated them from their mothers, and pilled them all. But by the time we were done with that calving season there was, on a remote section of the ranch, a terrible pile of dead calves, heads and feet sticking out everywhere, a sight that has many times haunted me.

This is a happier time. The last brief spate of sleet has passed, and a startlingly warm sun has come out. I stop Major on the south side of a big tree in a patch of sunshine and get off for a moment. We both soak sun. Seldom do I wish I still smoked, but standing in the sunlight, leaning back on Major, the cows and their still-healthy calves in front of me, a patch of the blue, snow-capped Beartooth mountains peering at me through an opening in the trees, I feel the rare exception.

I take off my heavy canvas coat, roll it up, and tie it with the saddle strings behind the cantle. The light down vest and long-sleeved shirt are enough right now, though certainly this will change. I watch a red cow leave the feedground, a cow that has not calved, note that she heads not toward water but into the nearest cottonwood grove. As her rear end swivels toward me I can see a football-sized, light-colored bubble. Alone, she is going to a place she can give birth and defend her calf if necessary.

Meanwhile, on the other end of the feedground, the baldy cow with the new white-faced calf is ambling toward her hay ration, pausing periodically to look back to where her calf, full of milk, has bedded. I mount Major and ride nonchalantly into the woods, not directly toward the calf, trying to look innocent. The cow stares at me from a hundred yards away, then, satisfied I'm up to some other business, begins to gulp hay. I tie Major out of sight of the feedground and pull my loaded syringe and ear-tagging tool out of the saddlebags. Then I proceed on foot, just as if I were stalking an elk. Were the cow one of my more aggressive ones and were she closer to the calf, I would probably lead Major along and plant him between the calf and cow, then work quickly with the big gelding as decoy. But this situation is more tactically friendly.

I find the calf, deep in his baby sleep. *He* turns out to be a *she*, a heifer calf. The syringe comes out of my shirt pocket, I slip the needle under the skin on the neck, and, presto, she is vaccinated against at least eight life-threatening maladies. Now to give the little girl an earring. The ear-tag tool both pierces the ear and installs the tag, locking the stud on the tag into a little plastic button. When I press the handles of the tool the calf awakens with a bawl so loud that you could probably hear it in town. She isn't in all that much pain, but she is definitely awake and in the company of a strange two-legged creature instead of mamma cow. Her bawl has done the trick. With an attack-moo the cow heads my way on a dead run, a few of her more aggressively protective colleagues following in trace. If there is going to be a fight, they want in on it. The baldy cow, however, is slowed by brush. Besides, as long as the calf is between her and me, she will stop at the calf. Almost always. She does, licking it back to its feet, throwing my way an occasional cow-curse in the form of shakes of the head and paws at the ground which toss up spray of old leaves, twigs, and mud. I smugly return to Major, pull out my notebook, and log in the calf with her mother's number and "H" for heifer. I take a quick tally. With the birth of this baldy heifer, I am half done calving.

Now Major and I discreetly track the cow we saw heading into the brush. She is an older cow, an old hand at giving birth, and she is wasting no time. We find her down already, pushing mightily, and we watch from fifty yards, the cow too intent on what she is doing to notice us. The calf's front feet are out, hooves properly pointed down. There is a mighty push, and the nose, then the entire head emerge. The cow

rests. She pushes and rests in succession, each time gaining a few inches. The calf's head has broken through the placenta, so that hurdle is cleared. Two more pushes and the body has all but emerged, with only its hips and hind legs yet to be born. The cow stands up and pushes once more, and the calf is suddenly in a steaming liquid heap on the ground. We watch for signs of life, see the head moving, watch the cow turn around to start licking. All is well in the maternity ward. We will go home, give this new one some time, then return to treat it as we have the baldy heifer.

Suddenly the sun is gone, and huge snowflakes fill the air. So fast do they come that the bare, melted spots on the ground freckle with white immediately. I turn in the saddle, pull the quick-release knots with which I've tied my coat, swing it from behind the saddle, and put it on. By the time we get to the pasture gate, all is whiteness. I tie Major to the hitching rail at the tack room, replacing his bridle with a mesh nosebag into which I've poured a coffee can of grain. He munches while I unsaddle. The stud colt comes up to the corral fence and sticks his nose over for a bite, which I give him, holding a bucket up until he fills his mouth completely. I turn toward the house, anxious for the coffee and lunch, *my* ration, which Emily will have prepared.

I turn once to look at the stud colt. We face each other twenty feet away, joining eyes through the falling snow. Had the sun lasted, in spite of the poor, muddy footing in the corral, I might have ridden the colt today. Then my left leg, irritated by the morning's work, gives me a twinge, and I remember the quickness of the stud colt. Half glad it has started to snow, I walk to the house.

Emily and I have a quiet lunch, just the two of us, a rare thing, for like most modern ranchers we do not *only* ranch. More on that later. Steve, the rear guard of the Aadland boys, the last one home, is playing his trumpet at a basketball tournament today. But Emily and I are too tired for sparkling conversation, the calving activities of the night before having taken a chunk from our rest. It had been pretty routine, actually. I had set the alarm for 2:30 a.m., made the night check along the feedground with pickup and spotlight, and seen nothing worrisome. Then I checked the heifers in the corral. First-calf heifers need special attention, for the first birth is more likely to be troublesome. Sure enough, a black heifer had feet sticking out of her behind. She was lying down with two others, trying to rest, but her mud-covered hide suggested she had been through a struggle. Sometimes a cow, particularly an inexperienced one, will try hard to give birth but quit when she can make no progress.

This heifer was a gentle one and all went well. I got her into our maternity pen, a steel box stall with head catch. Confused, she walked right in, tried to get through the head catch, and was caught. By this time Emily's built-in sensors had detected I had been gone too long, so she rose, dressed, and came to the lights in the shed. I took off my coat, rolled up my right sleeve, and grasped the obstetric chain in my right hand. (The chain looks exactly like a husky version of a dog's choke collar.) The two front feet I saw protruding from the heifer's vagina had receded back into her now, chased back into the womb by all the activity she had been through. I found the front feet with my hand, pushed in still farther until I could feel the nose and tell that the head was in position, properly pointed toward me, not back. Then I looped the slip end of the chain around one front foot and took a half hitch with the chain around the other front foot, in both cases working the chain up above the pastern joint to the lower leg bone. All this is more difficult than it sounds. The reason it is necessary in the first place is that the birth canal is too tight for unassisted birth. Your hand works

under constant pressure while adjusting the chain, and it soon aches.

Then I put the calf puller in place, a long jack-like device, and gently began to work the handle. As I pulled, Emily guided, inserting her hands along the sides of the calf's front legs, working them out, then holding the nose down so it could follow the legs. The head was difficult, and so were the hips, but soon the calf came in a rush and lay at our feet steaming. Emily cleared its mouth. It was breathing and shivering. Then it let out its first garbled blat, and the heifer, hearing this hitherto unknown part of herself, mooed back and became agitated. Getting a grip on its slimy black hide, I skidded the calf around to the front of her, let her study it a moment, which she did, bright-eyed, and then, from a safe position behind her, I released the head catch. This expensive maternity pen, which we've shelled out for only relatively late in our ranching careers, is a good outfit, much safer than what we once had.

This pull was easier than some. We watched the heifer nose the calf. Confused at first, she kept looking at us back over her shoulder. Then something clicked. A light turned on. This was *her* calf. She madly began licking, the calf responding by lifting its head and making its very first moves to get up. We decided there was no need to watch longer. It was barely above zero in the shed, yet I was sweating at the effort. We left the pair in the shed, lights on (probably unnecessarily), and went back to our bed.

. . .

Now, in our easy chairs after lunch, we lean back and try for a quick nap to make up for lost sleep. Rascal, our twenty-pound Siamese cat, jumps to the back of Emily's chair and lands behind her head, rocking the chair back, then settles in, a supplementary pillow, purring. Emily, always most comfortable in the company of cats, quickly dozes. For some reason, though my eyelids have drooped during lunch, I can't. I stare at the blank screen of the television across the room, then realize what has been nagging me. I see what was on that screen last night, just before I made my evening run with pickup and spotlight around the calving cows.

Oh, she was cute enough all right, blond, in a tiny red skirt that required her meticulous attention before she could curl decently on the couch next to the talk show host, her legs crossed. She flashed her million-dollar smile, the two exchanged pleasantries and compliments, and then the host asked, "Well, what have you been doing out there in Colorado?"

"Oh, just hanging out. I really needed a hiatus after the stress of that last film, and I can kind of be myself out there on the ranch."

"Well, what do people do for excitement out there?"

"Lots of things. It's not like I'm in the sticks or anything. I can see Denver from our deck. Anyway, I visited some friends up at University last week, and they got me in on something that's sooo hilarious!" She began to giggle, unable to get any more words out for a few moments, the talk show host looking joyfully tolerant. "You won't believe this, but they have a thing they call cow tipping!"

The host tightened his eyes and said, "Cow tipping? What the hell is that?"

Again, she had to overcome giggles before she could speak. "Well, you take a bunch of beer and go out in the country until you find a cow pasture. That's not hard in Colorado. As soon as you find lots of cow doodoo you're in the right place!" (Hilarity from the audience at the face she has made.) She continued, speaking each phrase with a rising inflection on the end, as if each were a question. "You sneak into the bushes until you locate a cow. Well, cows sleep standing up, you know. You didn't know that? Anyway, they're kind of zoned when they're sleeping, so you sneak up, then dash toward them, and push them over. It's soooo funny! Even though they're big they don't have much balance when they're asleep, and it doesn't take much to tip them right over." She absolutely shrieked with the hilarity of it all, and the amused audience joined in.

The host looked a little skeptical. Hailing from the country's heartland, he should have been considerably *more* skeptical. He looked at her ninety-five pound body, the tiny thigh peeking from under the dress, which she pulled down one inch, the same inch, for the twentieth time. "You actually did this? *You* actually tipped over a cow?"

"Well, no," she simpered. "I was back by the beer keg most of the time!" Again, an explosion of laughter from the studio audience. "But lots of them did. There was a commotion out in the bushes you wouldn't believe when all the cows ran away!"

The talk show host sensed that the audience needed a change at this point. Perhaps they were disappointed to hear the actress had not done the cow tipping herself. He changed the subject to plans for the blond's next movie. I made a change at this point too, pushing the off button on the television remote control and tossing it over onto the couch. Emily and I sat staring at the blank screen, almost too incredulous to speak.

It is always hard to analyze one's own feelings, but with a night to think about it I have decided my reaction to the actress has been twofold, first anger, then incredulity. The anger stems from hearing of animals being treated as toys. A ranch is like a big extended family, in our case a family containing horses, dogs, cats, and cows. In the past it has also contained goats and rabbits. All have their roles, and all have their natural dignity. We do not expect the cats to act like the dogs, the cows to have the intelligence of the cats, or the horses to have the mannerisms of the cows. And we do not expect any of them to be humans. To us it is not wrong to eat animals, but it is wrong to mistreat them, to belittle them, to take away their natural dignity. So the actress and her friends have set out to convert animals to toys, and that is offensive to us. Even though I realize laughter is contagious and know that television studios are adept at extracting it from audiences, I was still surprised at the audience's positive reaction. Would they have laughed as hard if the actress's wild outing had featured knocking bird's nests out of trees or torturing cats or substituting a squirrel for the ball in a game of touch football? Where were the howls of protest?

My incredulity, however, is even stronger than my anger. How could these people know so little about cows? The actress seemed to actually believe the activity occurred as she described it. So did the host, after being initially skeptical, and so did the audience. Wasn't there even one farm kid in the studio who knew that cows *do not sleep standing up*? Horses sleep standing up, at least part of the time. Cows lie down! I've never seen scientific proof that cows never approach a state of sleep while standing, but they normally bed down at night, even if the ground is covered with snow. Horses occasionally lie down to sleep, but apparently can rest quite well in the standing position. The only thing more difficult than pushing over an 1100-pound cow when she is on her feet is doing it when she is lying down.

Cows have senses that are incredibly acute. They hear better than any human, and their sense of smell is comparable to that of wild animals. Bovines were prey on the original food chain. That gave them a range of vision of nearly 360 degrees. While it might be possible to sneak up on an unusually sedate cow, a herd always has its most watchful members. At night, making calving checks, I can sometimes walk among my *bedded-down* cows, but not because they do not detect me. They know me and are gentle enough not to take flight.

Physically, cows are herculean by human standards. No person can run as fast as a cow. Arnold Schwartzenegger is positively puny compared, even, to a 600-pound weanling steer. The incredible reality of a grown cow's weight, the unyielding static inertia of 1100 pounds, does not really strike one unless he has tried to roll over a sick (or dead) cow. None of these things seemed to occur to the host and his studio audience. Oh, what I would have given to see two college jocks attempt to tip over the mamma cow that shook her head at me on the feedground that morning.

The reality, of course, was that the actress (if we can trust her sincerity) had been "had." She had bought into the 1990's version of the "snipe hunt." That extracurricular activity, cherished by an earlier generation of college students, involved arming freshmen with gunny sacks and sending them out to collect a creature called the snipe. Usually the freshman was taught a ridiculous call or whistle that was supposed to attract the critter. Donning freshman beanies (required equipment), the poor innocents would traipse about the woods, emitting the strange sound, while the upperclassmen at the edge of the woods rolled in their scheduled hilarity.

(So widespread became knowledge of this scam, that I have had trouble convincing people there is actually a bird called the snipe, and that Southern gentlemen with double shotguns and pointing dogs actually do, indeed, hunt it.) I always suspected that the college snipe hunt and now, no doubt, the cow-tipping idiocy, are more than anything excuses to get coeds out into the woods.

· · ·

But what has happened to America's knowledge of and empathy with the cow? Neither respected like some species of wildlife nor revered like family pets, the cows referred to by the actress on the talk show were somehow exempt from the American affinity for animals. This is ironic, because if any one animal raised and nourished America it was the cow. There was a time when most Americans owned one. First there was the segment of America that farmed or ranched by profession, fully one-third of the population at the time Magnus Jensen rode his pony onto what became our ranch. Then there were the town-dwellers all across America, in days before zoning and interstate highways. Such town families often had large yards or a dab of pasture on the edge of town where they could keep a milk cow. Typical was a family with a father who worked at a job outside the home while Mom worked at everything else needed to raise and nourish. In addition to duties within the house, her jobs often included milking the family cow, superintending the garden, and minding the chicken coop.

These three typical components of the family's economy—milk cow, garden, and chicken coop—furnished nearly everything the family needed to eat. The chicken coop provided fresh eggs and fryers. The garden, and the canning effort that followed its harvest, furnished both fresh and preserved vegetables. And the milk cow raised her own calf (and perhaps several others) for meat or cash. Sometimes there was also a pig pen, with weaner pigs raised on a slop mixture of fermented milk and grain. In addition, the five gallons or more of foamy, rich milk the cow gave each day raised rosy-cheeked children. The milk had a host of additional uses. It was made into cottage cheese. The cream was skimmed off (only farmers who owned several cows had cream-separating machines) and whipped as a topping for the cakes and pies produced on the wood-burning kitchen range. Odd, isn't it, that these delicacies—whole milk with no fat removed (and no additives), real whipped cream (which many of today's Americans have never tasted), angel-food cakes delicately baked with egg whites, flaky pie crusts baked with lard, actual butter on hot bread Mom pulled directly from the oven—odd that these things didn't simply kill families outright, drowning them in seas of cholesterol. Even more odd, isn't it, that experts tell us today's youth, after twenty years of bombardment with health information and regulation, can do fewer pull-ups, are weaker, slower, and fatter than those inveterate milk-devouring children of past generations? (But those are subjects for another book!)

So most families in the American past either had a cow (which they called by name) or knew someone who did. Most children grew up with chore time twice a day, with watching the family cow being milked (and soon doing so themselves). Most children watched the barn cat sit on her haunches during milking time, sit patiently until Dad or Mom aimed a teat away from the bucket and skillfully sent a stream to the cat's mouth ten feet away, shooting with the accuracy and aplomb of a naughty child with a squirt gun. Afterwards, the inch of foam on top of the bucket, hot foam produced by vigorous milking, was usually scraped off and taken to the chicken yard, where frenzied hens dived into it. And the cat and her kittens got their full share in a bowl.

It was not all pleasure, of course. Milking a cow is hard work. The old farmers who milked a dozen cows apiece, twice a day, developed forearms and grips like King Kong. (They've about died out now, but shake hands with one of those old surviving farmers, and you will feel the power.) Cows can be contrary, and a familiar scenario was to have one's bucket nearly full only to have an impatient cow, a cow you trusted enough not to hobble, kick over the bucket or place a manure-soiled hoof right in the middle of it. That meant, of course, that all the milk went to the chicken coop and the hog pen rather than into the house. There was hard work and frustration, and many farm children first learned their parents could curse during a particularly tough evening in the milk barn.

Yet chore time, as Emily remembers it from her childhood, was a special time, a time for interaction with her parents and all the animals in this food-producing micro economy centered around the milk cows. The whole farmstead waited for that hot, creamy, life-giving liquid. There was always a cat with a litter of kittens in the loft of the barn, kittens Emily could mother while the milking went on. It was, she says, the best time of the day. And later, when she was a mother of small sons, she milked two different Brown Swiss cows in succession, the first a matriarch named Swiss Miss, the next a heifer named Chocolate. For a brief time I had the boys half-fooled into believing that if I mixed cocoa with Chocolate's grain ration she would give chocolate milk. The obvious question, of course, was why I did not do so. My protestations that we couldn't afford to lavish expensive cocoa on a cow were not convincing, so the story never went over the top.

But while the milk from Swiss Miss and Chocolate did for the Aadland family exactly what it did for families in past generations, nourishing children, providing delicacies, feeding additional animals, we too butted up against certain facts of modern life. The milking was only possible while Emily, stubborn about being a stay-at-home mom during her boys' youngest years, was able to be home for weekday chores. (That eventually changed.) My long commute to the job that kept the ranch afloat made helping with milking in the morning impossible for me. And, like most modern families, we enjoyed an occasional camping or vacation trip. The problem of finding someone to cover milking chores for us if we left was first difficult, finally insurmountable. Milking is relentless. It must go on twice a day every day, including Sunday and the Fourth of July. (One-family dairy farms are operated by people with unbelievable endurance. One such couple I know went ten years without missing a milking of their fifty-cow herd, then missing only because the man and woman were so ill they could not rise from their bed. Only then did they call for help.)

Well, things have changed since the years when cows were central to the lives of so many Americans. Few families daily milk a cow. Only two or three percent of Americans live on farms, and many farmers are specialized, raising only grain; their farm yards, which once teemed with chickens, geese, dogs, cats, and kids, now golf-course-scale lawns; their fences, no longer needed, bulldozed and buried. The actress on the talk show can be forgiven for some of her foolishness. There are reasons she has little respect or affection for cows, besides simply her lack of personal contact with them. She has probably been told cows are ecologically incorrect, responsible for the decimation of the rain forest. She probably has not downed a glass of milk for years, fearful of losing her nearly anorectic figure. After all, a major health organization recently classified milk, the *only* food produced naturally by mammals for their young, as an "unhealthy food." (Simultaneously, another health organization sounded the alarm that young American women had dangerous deficiencies in phosphorous and calcium, that their bones were less dense than those of young women several generations ago, and that they would be in greater danger of osteoporosis after menopause.)

I can do little about some of this. But I can fairly assume that if you picked up a book entitled *Sketches from the Ranch: A Montana Memoir* you have some interest in cows. I can assume this because the word "ranch" brings to most people's minds a picture with three elements: a cowboy or rancher, the horse he sits, and a herd of cows somewhere on the landscape. So I can at least do my small part in countering the many current myths about cows. Here goes:

MYTH #1—*Cows are tropical creatures, ill-suited to northern climates, misplaced here by humans.* This one is easy: balderdash. Cows are bovines, and bovines of one kind or another flourish in the wild from the Equator (water buffalo) to the Arctic (musk ox). Further, as domestic animals, cattle have been selectively bred by mankind to suit whatever climate the humans occupy. Humans have bred dogs ranging from Mexican hairless Chihuahuas (which would be hypothermic in minutes in the wilds of Alaska) to Malamutes (which would lie panting in a puddle of saliva if they tried to function in Panama City). Cattle reflect similar diversity. The small, thin, light-colored cows I saw in Vietnam would have difficulty surviving in Montana. They reflected their climate as assuredly as the young Vietnamese army officers who trained with us Marines at Quantico, Virginia, many moons ago, who, shivering, donned their second suits of long underwear when the leaves had barely turned and who disappeared altogether, excused from training, in November.

In Montana the British breeds have been most successful. In early homesteading days, a typical family had shorthorns, good all-purpose animals, perhaps Jersey and Guernsey cows for milking and, later, Herefords for beef. (Emily remembers from her girlhood a trip to the railroad depot in Columbus, Montana, to pick up two Guernsey heifer calves, shipped from Oregon.) All these breeds hail from the raw and rainy British Isles. Angus cows, along with "black baldies," the black, whiteface cross between Angus and Hereford, predominate today. They are extremely tough animals. The inside of a barn or shed is alien to many of those that run in Montana, and their newborn calves usually rise successfully from the snow. Native wild animals in Montana do no better.

MYTH #2—*Cows are stupid, the brains and survival instincts having been bred out of them by mankind.* This one is more complex and more subjective. Let's take the second part first. It is true that all domestic animals have been bred and conditioned to have greater reliance on humans. Sometimes the line is thin, however. Your pampered domestic cat, if released into the wild becomes, I am told, one of the most relentless predators in nature and does very well for itself. Among cows, milk breeds seem most gentle (though this is *not* true of the other sex, the bulls), and they do seem to be less capable of surviving on the range, of calving unassisted, of fending for themselves. Part of this is because they have been selectively bred to produce far more milk than a single calf requires, so their metabolism is demanding and productive, and they need high-quality feed. If not properly fed, such a cow will not readily breed back, either. Her system will not cycle (go into estrus) and she will come up empty the next year.

Unfortunately, the nice dispositions selected in some breeds seem to have an inverse relationship to survivability. Many is the cattleman who has wanted to cull a particularly aggressive, even vicious cow but has not been able to bring himself to do so. "She always has a huge calf at weaning time, and she never loses one," he'll say. She'll fight that calf to its feet, work on it until she drops to get it breathing, then feeding. And so, as a breeder, you attempt to keep a balance in your herd of range cows, culling the true killer (and a few do exist) but being tolerant of a fair amount of "fight."

In building our own herd Emily and I sought nice dispositions and particularly liked some of the mellow animals that were mainly Angus but with a dash of Brown Swiss blood. But domestic or not, cows are capable of dropping their domesticity entirely and reminding you that they share genetics with Spanish fighting bulls and even, some think, with the animal knowledgeable African hunters fear most, the Cape buffalo. I've been threatened by cows many times, chased a few times, and caught once or twice. The safest way to tag and vaccinate newborn calves is not on horseback but with my pickup truck, the calf snagged by a hind leg and pulled up to the door. I have had protective cows get their noses up to the steering wheel as I shrunk into the cab, an iron grip on the calf with one hand and a syringe in the other.

. . .

But I've really been mauled just once. It happened before we bought the modern maternity pen, and the event was a large factor in our decision to spend the dough on that contrivance. We had just a few heifers to calve out, because our work schedules make it difficult to cope with first-calf heifers. All the ones we had saved back seemed to have nice dispositions. But the line between civilized and primitive, social and savage, can be a thin one indeed, in animals just as in people, and pain and stress can push an individual over it. The heifer, a red Angus, had a calf in her, a calf that was too large. She had tried hard to give birth, but had exhausted herself. I put her in a box stall, the inner one of several in-line stalls, roped her, snubbed her up to a corner post, and commenced pulling the calf.

The pull was a tough one and the calf, unfortunately, was dead. The cow, exhausted and partially paralyzed by the pressure on her spine (not uncommon, and usually correcting itself in a few minutes) lay on the stall floor. I loosened the lariat from the post to relieve her of any pressure, then opened the gate. She seemed completely immobile. I reached down with my left hand and worked the lariat loose from her neck. Just as the loop cleared her nose there was a tremendous roar, she leaped to her feet and into me, and I went down. I remember very little of what went on for the next few moments. Emily said later it looked as if I were moving in slow motion. I got up, free of the cow, and walked, Emily said, as if there were no urgency at all toward the outer steel gate, to open it and let the cow out. The cow, meanwhile, had collapsed in pain for another moment.

The truth is, I was out on my feet, a stubborn KO'd boxer, with no referee to see the vacant look in my eyes and stop the fight. I only remember two things, both sounds, the first Emily screaming at the cow as she regained her feet and knocked me down again from the rear. Then there was a strange ringing or clanking noise. It sounded far away. Slowly I realized, slowly it dawned, that the sound was being made by my head ramming up against the bottom of the steel gate, the cow smashing me from behind with repeated blows.

Three things saved me. First, the cow had no horns. Most of our cows are "polled," that is, genetically selected to have no horns. Second, the cow's paralysis was spasmodic. Emily told me afterward that the heifer would rise, attack, then fall down again. Last, Emily herself, screaming to bluff the cow, timing the opening of the second gate just right, then half pulling me out to finally put a stop to the situation. When she got a good look at my face she quit asking why I was moving so slowly. "How much are you hurt?" she asked, taking my hand.

"Just my head. And it's pretty hard."

I must have smiled, for she said, "Thank God you're a Norwegian." I am thankful she was there, and I shudder at the many similar tasks I've performed when I was alone.

I escaped this event with bruises and an improvement in my education. All close calls are sobering, but this one became even more so when we heard, two weeks later, that the husband of a childhood friend had been killed in, apparently, a similar incident. He had gone to check the calving barn at daybreak, had not returned in a time frame our friend considered reasonable, and she had gone down to find him lying on the shed floor, the cow now calm.

I "canned" the heifer that attacked me, took her to the livestock auction the next week. She would go to slaughter rather than to a career of raising calves, truly "natural selection" at work. But I did not blame her. In her bovine mind another animal, a human, was causing her great pain. She had no way of knowing that the pain was over. In her perception the only way to stop the pain was to take out the critter causing it. That was me, and she just about succeeded.

· · ·

None of this answers the question of whether cows are stupid or not. Animal intelligence is a tough call. We tend to judge it with human standards. Canine intelligence is so obvious to us, we rate it highly. Anyone can read a dog's body language. A cow's body language is less obvious, but it is there. Every summer a few tourists get worked over, gored, tossed about, and sometimes killed by bison in Yellowstone National Park. Normally the bison are giving off every normal bovine signal that would tell any farm child used to cows and bulls to stay away. Indeed, to anyone who knows cattle the bison might as well be holding up neon warning signs, but the tourist, blissful behind his single-lens reflex, just keeps coming like a lamb to the slaughter until he is charged.

We live in an age of anthropomorphism, an age when the media, chock-full of Disneyism, has encouraged people to see animals as little humans with motives and emotions identical to our own. Hard-headed animal behaviorists discourage this, but it goes on anyway. All animals do things that by human standards are "stupid," but all, it seems to me, occasionally exhibit beautiful, primitive traits that show an intelligence almost akin to our idea of wisdom.

Cows certainly do many stupid things. They will stand at a fence and bawl, ignoring an open gate just a short distance away, a gate they could walk through. One would not expect to be able to train a cow to subtle commands, although a team of oxen (steers trained to work) is trained to turn right on "gee," left on "haw," and is in every way as controllable as a good team of horses. But for all that, most of us do not look to bovines for subtle response to our version of intelligence.

That said, cattle have many wonderful senses and instincts. Caught in a barbed-wire fence, a cow will normally just shake herself loose, not panicking and tearing herself to pieces as some horses will do. If she must cross a bog, she takes her time and feels her way and is less likely to become mired than a horse, which again, often panics. But I suppose the side of cows I most admire is the side I see while calving. Commonly, a two-year-old heifer will give birth by herself to her first calf, clean it off, get it to its feet, and juggle it back to where it belongs so that it can nurse and live. She does this totally without instruction. (Emily and I took Lamaze classes to get to the same grade level.)

And once the calf is born, the quality of the average cow's parenting is something to admire. The cow is totally dedicated to her calf. Never is it neglected; never, if she can physically avoid it, is it harmed or hungry. Her willingness to defend her calf seems noble by human standards, and it makes some of nature's most awesome predators steer clear.

Several years ago a woman we know called, voice shaky, to inform us that she had hit a mountain lion with her automobile just up the road from our house. "He was sitting on his haunches right there in the middle of the highway. I slowed down almost to a stop, but I did hit him, and I'd hate to think you've got a wounded mountain lion around the buildings. That could be dangerous."

Yes, it could be. I was not that surprised at the closeness of a lion. Mountain lion populations are proliferating through the country, both in the West and in states outside their traditional range. Although they are hunted (under strict regulations) in Montana, they are on the increase here as well. I knew I was not legally empowered to take this matter into my own hands, so I called Jeff, the game warden. "Go ahead and check it out, Dan, and take your rifle. You can't have a wounded lion around. If one's dying in the barrow pit, put it out of its misery and then call me. But I'm betting that if the car didn't kill it outright, you'll never see it. They're tough as nails, and probably this one just got some fortunate instruction in staying away from highways and cars."

"I've got a whole field of cows and newborn calves right by the road, Jeff. Sure hope it didn't bother them."

"Oh, don't worry," he said. "Mountain lions like to chow down on sheep and an occasional colt, but I've rarely heard of them bothering cattle."

I thought about that as son Steve grabbed the flashlight, I the rifle. We walked gingerly up the highway. Jeff had been right on all counts. We found skid marks, a small spot of blood on the pavement, but no lion. With foolish bravery we dropped down into the trees below the road toward the river. There was an inch or two of snow on the ground. Our flashlight beam showed the lion's tracks heading into the darkness, but no further sign of blood. We gingerly felt our way down the lion's trail, breathlessly listening. There was no sound but the gurgle of the water under the ice, and we could see where the lion had crossed it, dragging wetness onto the ice on the far side. He was not seriously hurt, and he was long gone. We climbed back onto the highway and flashed our light into the pasture to the east. We could see the lion's tracks, see that he had walked the fence line next to the bedded mother cows so quietly they had not heard him. He had chosen to avoid the cows completely.

So why had the mountain lion, an amazing cat bigger and stronger than an African leopard, passed up a chance at veal for supper? Deer, of course, are a mountain lion's bread and butter, and there were plenty of those. In weakened condition from fighting through snow for feed, the deer were probably vulnerable enough to keep the lion content. But were the lion an old one, his joints a bit rusty and his teeth worn down, or a very young one, recently weaned, domestic stock might have appeal. It is easy to see why his choices would be those the game warden explained. Sheep run when riled, and they haven't the physical tools to defend themselves against predators, so mutton, available on the next ranch, would be appealing if the lion could not find a young deer to kill. Jeff said lions took colts as well, and I knew of that. Friends during the last summer had stitched up two nasty claw wounds, one running down each side of the back of a yearling colt. A lion had jumped on its back, "ridden" the colt for a distance, then been shaken off. Horses are big and strong like cows, but horses are flight animals. Some mares will defend their foals, but when the chips are down they will run. The lion knows this, knows that while the herd runs he can jump on a colt and bring it down. (Its usual method of killing is to sink its claws into an animal's nose and jerk sharply upward, breaking the neck.)

But cows are a different critter. Had the lion grabbed a calf it would have bawled, and he would have had to fight both the mother and her friends. True, other predators could handle the job. A grizzly can take a cow simply because it is so immensely powerful, and wolves can do so by gang effort and intelligence, chasing, harassing, wearing down the cow until the strongest of the pack rushes in, bringing the critter down and commencing to eat even before she dies. But the solitary mountain lion, wise as he was, knew to look for easier prey.

. . .

MYTH #3—*Beef cattle are inefficient producers of meat; the grain required to feed a steer to slaughter weight could feed many people.* The second part of this statement is true, but not because of the first part, which is false. Don't sell short man's ability to breed animals well-suited to serving him. The problem is not any inefficiency of the cow, but rather humans' insistence on eating a particular type of beef, fat, marbled, and juicy (in spite of cholesterol warnings).

Drive through eastern Montana (and many other parts of the West) and you will see vast areas of rough, broken terrain, far too steep and rocky to farm. (If one *could* farm it the cost would be terrible erosion of the shallow topsoil.) Although the grass in such terrain looks sparse, it is packed with protein. If not overgrazed, the grass is an infinite renewable resource. On this grass, with no supplements, no grain, nothing extra save salt and minerals, a mother beef cow will raise a calf from infancy to five or six hundred pounds. After weaning, such calves, with modest supplements, can continue to grow and gain on grass until they weigh more than half a ton. An entire economy was built in the late nineteenth century around cattlemen trailing steers up from Texas, steers that had topped out in growth. Brought to eastern Montana to spend a year on this rich grass, the steers actually resumed growing, put on hundreds of pounds, and fortunes were made for cattle investors.

Grass-fed animals, those that are raised with no use whatsoever of the world's grain supply, yield a beef that is flavorful, high in protein, low in fat and cholesterol and, for all practical purposes, identical to the bison meat that is now the rage. However, the beef is not as tender as its corn-fed counterpart nor as marbled and juicy, and Americans (and even more so, Asians), simply have not accepted it widely. (We all talk a different diet than we actually eat, don't we?) So the determining factor is not the efficiency of the animal, but people's palates.

Well, it is time for this interior monologue to end. In my easy chair I relax now, my time on the imaginary docket explaining the nature of one of the animals I raise having finally brought on the inclination to rest. It has not been an idle digression. I could not be good at what I do if I did not believe in it, could not rise in winter when the alarm rings to check on animals for which I did not care, for which I had no respect. But it is good now that I can catch a few minutes rest. The early-spring sun is already low, the shadows cast by the leafless cottonwoods long. It is almost time to make another check of the calving cows.

"Freedom, Heyday," cried Caliban · My breakout · Pronghorns
St. Olaf · Rattlesnakes under the outhouse

Spring on a Montana ranch is not only calving cows. It is also the crocus, the brave flower that picks its way, sometimes through snow, to decorate the still-brown grass of the dryland hills. It is a small boy with a bouquet of pussy willows in one hand, the other hand thrust into his mother's palm as they come up from the woods late in the afternoon. It is the return of the meadowlark and the sandhill crane.

There is for me, most years, a sudden coming out, a sudden breaking free, about half way through the season we call spring. South-central Montana does not have the clearly defined seasons found in much of the United States. High altitude and chinook winds breed erratic weather. We do not have the brutal, humid cold of northern Minnesota or Michigan. Yes, our temperatures drop as far, but our drier air lets cattle winter out, and our chinooks break loose periodically the winter's hold. But we are susceptible to frosts very early and very late and to wet snow storms as early as September and as late as May. It has, on the ranch, truly snowed on the Fourth of July. We dare not plant a garden until the first of June, never pronounce it safe until that month is over, then hope our seed choices, always the earliest variety, mature by late

August when the tops of the mountains often first whiten and frost appears on the chicken house roof.

It is late April. Chances are that our annual "Easter storm," the two feet of wet, heavy snow that fell a couple weeks ago will have been our last one. We came through it quite well: no calves lost, no vehicles buried spinning in four-wheel drive in a mix of wet snow and mud, no panic about the quantity of hay left. The snow has melted down into a thawed, receptive earth, and the hills already show it. I have driven to school along the Beartooth front, my usual route, the mountain snow pink with morning sun, and now at the end of the school day, as part of my own coming-out, will shortcut back home over the hills. My release is a studied and premeditated one. I've driven the pickup instead of the car to better handle the roads on the shortcut home. The spring play I directed is successfully completed (we did *The Odd Couple*), the kids have taken down the set and stowed the equipment until next year, so now play practices are done and I can legally leave at 4 p.m. Daylight saving time has kicked in. It is spring. Gone for another year is the descent of darkness before I can get home to the ranch. Gone is fixing fence in the headlights of the pickup and loading hay under the vapor light in the barnyard to be fed off to the cows the next morning, still in darkness, before I shower, change, and head for school.

. . .

I have savored and anticipated this day. It has been dry since the snowstorm, dry enough to disarm all but the deepest mud holes on the gravel route home. The route is a shortcut in distance, not in time, paring twenty miles off the sixty I drive on the paved route to the south. The paved route nearly touches the bases of the Beartooth Mountains. It is beautiful, but high in altitude and treacherous for the one person I know foolish enough to commute on it daily through the winter. The gravel shortcut goes west over the dryland hills quite directly, rises from the valley of the Clark's Fork of the Yellowstone, descends into the intermediate valley that lies between my job and my other job at home, then climbs again over foothills and winds through coulees. I pass through the little town of Roberts along Rock Creek, cross a paved highway—a second of smoothness between washboards—and stop at the convenience store strategically located to hook anglers headed for Cooney Reservoir.

I park to the side, not blocking the pumps, and go in for a Coke. There is a new proprietor who does not know me. It is Friday, so I am wearing jeans and cowboy boots, another treat for myself I started years ago and which has successfully corrupted any semblance of faculty dress code at my school. I wear a tie once each week, to church, and once during the school year, on the opening day of my spring play. "Heading over for some fishing?" asks the man behind the counter.

"No, just headed home." That's not enough. In rural America it doesn't work very well to be stingy with information. "I teach over in Bridger. This is a shortcut home."

"Yuh don't say? You the coach over there?"

"No." I pick a diet cola out of his cold case. "I teach English."

"English? A big strong guy like you?" He has blurted that out and is instantly embarrassed. Perhaps I have given him my Marine officer look, something I am told I sometimes do. So I soften it for him.

"I ranch, too."

He seems relieved. He tries to make a joke. "Well, I'll be watching my grammar the next time you come in. Have a few cows, do you?"

"A few. Ninety or so. And a dozen brood mares."

He looks surprised. By Montana ranching standards the number of cows is quite small, but it is large enough to qualify me as "real." "Must keep you busy."

"It's a great life if you can stand it."

Then I am back in the pickup, its diesel engine throaty and strong, the Coke balanced between my knees, the little bag of peanuts held at just the right tilt on top of the steering wheel, the bumps in the road making the whole thing a challenge but one I am used to. I flick the radio through a talk show doctor, the Country–Western station (where it could stay if they would just play some Bluegrass), then the local public radio affiliate which, unfortunately for my tastes, has switched already from classical to jazz. Then I turn it off.

The convenience store man has wondered if "ranch" meant hobby ranch. Perhaps he first thought I had bought myself twenty acres and a house and had a couple horses, had given the little place a name packed with instant grandeur, maybe something such as "Eagle Crest Ranch." But he should have been more observant when I pulled in, should have noticed the sprinkles of hay and the steel posts in the back of my pickup and the tired look in my eyes. I have caught a look at myself in the rearview mirror. The image is definitely that of one who has come through a winter with two full-time jobs separated by nearly sixty miles.

In this, however, I am in good company. I read somewhere that nearly half the country's farmers and ranchers have full-time jobs off the farm. Stores that cater to farmers and ranchers, which sell fencing materials, animal health products, seed and so forth, have been slow in realizing this, slow to expand their hours beyond the normal eight-to-five on the five business days. Just what has caused this rather profound change is too complicated for my economically challenged psyche, at least on a Friday when the play is done and the winter is done and the sun is shining. But I do sometimes envy Magnus and Elmer, for they lived in an age when a man could say he was a rancher and not need to add a footnote, not need to add that he could only keep ranching because he worked somewhere else as well.

But to complain today would be sacrilege, for the warm wind blows in through the window and the meadowlarks sing in the sage. A jackrabbit lopes onto the road, plays a dangerous game staying ahead of the pickup nearly in the center, tops out at thirty-five miles per hour, the speed to which I've slowed to avoid him, then disappears into the barrow pit. We rise over minihills, roller coaster humps, and drop off their far sides fast enough to bring that sensual, pit-in-the-stomach surge. (When

Emily was pregnant she said that feeling was doubled, so I'd go as fast as I dared on the roads over humps like these. The child she bore has always been a speed demon, perhaps a pagan connection.)

.   .   .

In our part of Montana there are no neat, mile-square section roads like those one finds in Iowa farm country, for the routes here must follow the contours of the land. Too many hills and coulees intervene to allow the road to go on a surveyor's line. The coulees are too steep to be crossed at right angles, so the roads slant down one side, then turn sharply back where they jump across the bottom, switchbacking up the opposite way. I am driving too fast, am well aware of it, and I realize I'll need to mend my ways when I top a rise and am suddenly in the middle of a herd of pronghorn antelope, grazing across the road. I slam on the brakes, putting the pickup into a semi-controlled slide, finally getting it stopped. The antelope look up startled, their huge eyes confused. Then their white rump patches flash, the hair on them rising and the sun reflecting off it, the pronghorn billboard you can see for miles. I am told antelope have distance vision comparable to humans using eight-power binoculars, that they are farsighted and everything under fifty yards away is a blur to them. That is the reason for their confusion. Then they line out as only pronghorns can, show why they are considered by some to be the fastest land animal over long distance on the face of the earth. In much less than a minute they are easily a half mile away. There is a nice, big buck in the bunch.

I do not get very excited about hunting antelope anymore, though I still partake occasionally. When Emily and I first came back from the Marine Corps and graduate school I taught for a while in eastern Montana. Antelope are extremely plentiful there, brought back from the brink of extinction around the turn of the century by good wildlife husbandry. One could legally take two antelope per season there, still can, and to a new teacher whose take-home pay scarcely covered the propane bill for heating our trailer on its windswept hill, the antelope meat was a staple and a god-send. We would always take one of the animals to the skilled local grocer. He would perform his magic, and the meat would emerge from his smokehouse converted into a lean, hard summer sausage that could be used for sandwiches and fried for breakfast with eggs. The whole town partook of this sausage, and it often appeared on the hors d'oeuvres plate with cut cheese at faculty parties. A bachelor friend made many meals of the stuff, fried in one of the little appliances made for cooking a single hamburger, a popular gadget at the time. I feel a presupper pang at the thought of Mr. Ryan's sausage.

I have pulled up now from the intermediate valley, that of Rock Creek (I'll descend still into several smaller drainages before I hit home), topping out among huge fields of green winter wheat. It is all so unbelievably big. My vision to the south is limited to twenty miles by the Beartooth front, but west, north, and (in the rearview mirror) east it is easily seventy-five miles. A. B. Guthrie gave us a name for it, The Big Sky. Few places I have been on this earth give such a sense of endless horizons.

My high school freshmen have recently finished Jack Schaefer's *Shane*. On the very first page the narrator describes the arrival of Shane, describes his ride into the valley. The narrator judges there is nothing remarkable about the horseman, but notes the reaction of two cowboys Shane meets, notes that they stop and turn and stare after they have passed him. The narrator sees all this plainly in the clear Wyoming air even though Shane is *several miles away!* This is what they came here for, those Scandinavian ancestors of mine, men used to getting away from cramped villages on steep mountainsides in just one other way, by going to sea, the only other place one could see so far.

I skirt Cooney Reservoir. The ice is just out. A few fisherman have arrived with campers and boats for the weekend. They come by a northern route, mainly from Billings, so as soon as I leave the lake the road is mine again. The best is yet to come. There are cows now on this open range section of the road, cows with small calves, so I reluctantly ease off the accelerator as I climb the big hill that will give me the view

I've been waiting for. Then I hit the crest and it is there before me, in a valley where two creeks merge, tiny and white against the new green of spring, still two miles away, the little Norwegian Lutheran church we call St. Olaf. I can't look on it without a rush of recollections. Now my foot willingly slacks off the accelerator, for I have only two miles for many memories.

. . .

When I was a boy living in town, my father, the pastor, had two churches, a larger one in town next to our parsonage home, and this one, St. Olaf. The country congregation was much the smaller, the shrinkage caused by young folks leaving for jobs elsewhere and the first generation of immigrants partly dying off. Most were Norwegian. The roads to the church were mainly dirt, the running jokes about "Carbon County gravel" always popular among the knot of men in boots and hats who traded stories, often with prechurch cigarettes in hand, at the base of the front steps before going in to services. Since getting to the church was often trying and the congregation small, services were held every other Sunday, and as oldest boy I often accompanied Dad. This was strictly optional. Church and all its accouterments were required and unquestioned at home in the morning, but Dad knew the cravings of his brood for playtime on Sunday afternoons. Just the same he typically turned just as he opened the door, his leather valise containing surplice and text in hand, and asked, "Danny, do you want to go with me?" And usually I did.

When dry, the roads were smooth black dirt. When wet or snowy, or worse, when snow overlaid six inches of mud, they were close to impassable. If they were insurmountable even by rancher standards, Dad would get a call not to come at all. But that was very rare. We had a black four-door 1947 Ford armed with snow tires, and Dad kept it revved to plunge us through. We had more than one harrowing experience. Once, on the infamous Redenbo Hill, we first chained up, barely ascended, then stopped dead when a chain broke and went sailing off into a snowbank. We fished for it and retrieved it. Broken, it could only help us if we laid it out in front of the chainless tire. So we ascended the hill as follows: I would place the chain in front of the tire, Dad would pop the clutch, and the car would jump forward four feet or so. Then I'd place a loose hubcap behind the wheel so that the car would not roll back, move the chain to the front of the tire again, and get out of the way of the flying mud. And in this way, four feet at a time, we went the quarter mile up the hill toward home. I remember afterward, the car heater having partly dried my wet, cold, clothes, standing over the floor furnace at home, hot chocolate in hand, and a violin concerto booming through the speaker banks Dad had built for his high-fidelity phonograph.

The people at St. Olaf were protective. Sometimes a rancher in a Jeep would insist on meeting us half way between home and the church to escort us, then repeat the favor on the trip home, even though we were certain we could make it. But it is probably our arrivals at the plain white church, with steeple and cross, that I remember best. Someone had always gone to the church early in the morning to build a fire in the coal furnace downstairs, and the smell of the heat through the vents was pleasant. Before and after there was visiting, people comparing notes on the weather and the ranching. But the service itself was equally formal whether the whole congregation was there or "two or three were gathered . . . ." Dad chanted the liturgy of the Evangelical Lutheran service while Irvin Loftus, rancher/organist, pumped hard on the foot pedals of the reed organ to keep the accompaniment strong. Everyone seemed to like and expect the quiet formality. (No one had told us we needed an infusion of popular music or that we needed to stand and shout to have a Christian experience.)

St. Olaf church had a choir, too. Dad's favorite joke was that when called to be a pastor in Montana he hadn't dreamed the position would include the honor of directing the St. Olaf Choir. (The reference was to the well-known college choir from Minnesota.) He had recruited nearly everyone in the country congregation to be in the choir, so that when it came time in the service for the choir to sing, all but a few of the very old and very young left the pews to stand in front, leaving virtually no audience for their efforts. But oh, could they sing. Bach and Handel were not strangers, and the pieces in Norwegian, especially around Christmas, *"Delig er den himmel blaa"* ("Oh, How Beautiful the Sky") and *"Jeg er saa glad hver julekveld"* ("I Am So Glad Each Christmas Eve") hang in my mind. I can still hear Knute Stratveit slurring up to the high places on the tenor part.

Two miles isn't enough for all this, so I slip the pickup up to the steel gate in front of the church and turn off the engine. Dad's St. Olaf Choir was made up of ranch wives, most of whom knew they could sing, and their husbands, most of whom swore that they couldn't. But Dad tricked them. With a musician's ear for voice quality and pitch, even in the spoken word, he'd identified some diamonds in the rough, bass and tenor voices that rose and fell in inflection like waves in the sea of the ranchers' Norwegian accents. And so, partly because he needed the money, partly no doubt because he was plotting, he hired out during summer to stack hay for some of the ranchers. A middle-aged farmer or rancher cannot look at a man with size and powerful physique (even if cloaked in pastor's surplice) without imagining the work that physique could perform, and those at St. Olaf were not bashful about asking. Dad was a big, strong, man.

So Dad stacked hay one summer, made a little extra money, then asked his employers to show up at choir practice. "Oh, but I can't sing," was the expected reply.

Dad pointed at the straight haystacks in the field, each tier of bales lined up nicely with the next. "If a preacher can stack hay, a rancher can sing in the choir." That did it. The Hoines brothers had bass voices fit for Russian chorales, and once they learned their parts by rote with Mom's help on the piano, they never forgot them or wavered from the pitch. Irvin Loftus, the organist, was already trained, and he got Knute tuned in on the tenor. It became a very fine choir.

I am parked facing the church, the diesel drone gone, the windows lowered to let in the smell of sage and new spring grass and the singing of the meadowlarks, several of which are perched on the tops of fenceposts nearby, their yellow, speckled breasts catching the sun. Their voices are soprano, their one fine song a descent of three notes, then a rise to a trill. There are no trees around the church. Indeed, the only trees in these high dry hills are chokecherries in the coulees and an occasional cottonwood where a good spring flows. To the right of the building is the cemetery, still used. The one fancy grave is for the pioneer pastor, Jorgen Madson, who Magnus knew and for whom he furnished the church space on the ranch, who founded that congregation (which became Dad's town church) and many more, including St. Olaf.

The crown jewel of St. Olaf events for my siblings and me was the country version of Vacation Bible School. We attended the town one as well, but found it a little staid, an extension of Sunday School and even of public school. But the week at St. Olaf was an adventure. There was, first of all, a tremendous meal at noon. (To hard-working ranch families, there were three meals each day called breakfast, dinner, and supper.) Ranch wives took turns cooking for the pastor's family, an appreciation for the extra work he performed that week, and each used her day to serve up a banquet she hoped was superior to that fixed the day before. Then, afterward, in the grassy area behind the church, unbothered by the slope of the hill, there was always a tremendous softball game. We had no equipment other than bat and softball, never dreamed anything else should be required. The game lasted the noon hour and beyond, my disciplined dad having so much fun himself that he let playtime spill into early afternoon.

. . .

But even better than the softball games were the rattlesnakes under the outhouse. The church had no indoor plumbing. There was a kitchen in the basement with wood range (Norwegian church ladies must have a kitchen) and a well pump for water, but the restrooms were the old-fashioned kind, men's and women's joined, each the old two-holer variety. Sometime during the week of Vacation Bible School we could always count on a girl going into the outhouse, letting out a scream, and dashing outside. "There's a rattlesnake under there," she'd yell. "I heard it rattling."

When this happened the softball game (or classes, if they had begun) stopped cold and everyone rushed toward the outhouse. Dad kept the eager kids behind him, and we all slowed and walked gingerly when we got within a few yards. Then, we heard the sinister rattle and Dad would holler at one of the faster runners, "Go get Eddy!"

Eddy lived a few hundred yards down the road at the bottom of the hill. He did not regularly attend church or Vacation Bible School, but his star shone brightly once during each of these late-May assemblies when he was called upon to take care of the rattlesnake. Now it should be said that my father was extremely soft-hearted toward all creatures, that although he liked to eat the deer we brought home in the fall later, as teens, he had no desire to "harvest" them himself, that if he had seen a rattlesnake far from harm's way he would have said, "What a big fine fellow. No, put the rocks down, Boys, we'll let him go." But a rattlesnake under an outhouse used many times daily by his charges was a different matter. We boys did have a .22 caliber rifle of our own back home and had been taught to safely shoot it at tin cans, which Dad enjoyed along with us, but we were never allowed to bring it along during Bible School. Maybe Dad simply thought "Render unto Eddy things which are Eddy's . . . ."

Soon Eddy, clutching his pump rifle, would arrive with the boy who had been sent for him, neither breathing much harder than normal, though they had sprinted several hundred yards uphill. They were lean and strong boys, for the term "couch potato" and the behavior it describes had not yet been invented. Now the smallest children were kept back clustered around my mother, and the rest of us, boys and girls alike, approached the outhouse. The trick was to locate the rattlesnake by its sound, then judge which way to tip over the outhouse. We deliberately made enough noise to get the snake to rattle, went to the opposite side, quickly lined up, and with a tremendous heave, tipped over the building, jumping backward out of strike distance as soon as it passed the balance point. Eddy, every inch the white hunter, spotted the snake, juggled his position so that he was shooting in a safe direction, and dispatched it with one shot, usually rendering the snake headless. My parents' slide collection contains a memorable picture of this grinning boy, holding the snake by its tail, the rifle in his other hand and the rest of us clustered around. Sometimes, no doubt out of appreciation for the opportunity, Eddy would stay at Bible School the rest of the day. But he rarely returned the next.

It is time to restart the pickup and get home to enjoy my new-found daylight. I leave the church to its prairie silence. It is, thankfully, still kept up and used occasionally, mainly for weddings and funerals. Scenes from Hollywood pictures have also been filmed there. But there is no longer a choir or a Vacation Bible School. Eddy still lives at the base of the hill.

3

A decision about the stud colt · The story of the leg
A premature trip to the funeral home

He is three years old now. Although he is still slim in body and long in leg, the lithe hard muscles of a stallion are beginning to ripple under his sleek, sorrel hide. He will never have the massive musculature of the "bulldog" type of Quarter Horse, for his is a different mission. Instead of heavy, quick-twitch muscles for acceleration and speed in the short run, this colt will have what it takes for distance, for topping the passes of the Beartooths. His feet are dense with a thick hoof wall and plenty of size for his weight, the cannon bones in his legs are ample, and his back is short. There is great depth from his withers to his sternum, depth for the lungs he will need for Sundance Pass. He is an old-time traveling horse, the kind the old timers always said were "looking for the next town."

But what is between his ears? He learns quickly, is bored with any lesson that continues too long. There has been an aloofness about him since he was first foaled, when he single-footed, high-headed, blaze face in rhythmic nod, alongside his mother. He has been impeccable in every stage of ground training, but somehow between the two of us a kink has come, a short-circuit. He has discovered my leg.

A ship is most vulnerable when it drifts too close to the land, and an airplane most jeopardized when it, too, nears an alien element. When a human mounts a horse, makes that transition from two-legged animal to four-legged one, there is a moment of vulnerability. The stud colt has discovered this. Since my injury, I am still unable to mount without extreme clumsiness, still can't put more than a fraction of my weight on the left leg, and the colt has learned to try to buck at my weakest moment. He has not gotten rid of me. The problem has not become a full-blown bad habit. But it is a sour, discordant note in the song I want to sing with him, a fly on the future for which I've lived, as a horseman, my entire life.

So I finish currying the colt and slide the saddle onto him, reminding myself that the very first horse I trained, now an aged gelding, was more challenging than this one. I try not to hear the argument from the opposing attorney. "Yeah, but you were almost twenty years younger, strong as a bull, and you didn't have a screwed up leg." With his usual indifference, the colt eases through the corral gate behind me. Buddy, the dog, not yet used to the spring sun, retreats to the shade of the tack room, lies down, and watches. I take the slack out of the left rein to keep the colt turned toward me, face his rear (this is the easiest mounting method since I hurt the leg), twist the stirrup around to me, lock my left leg, insert my toe, and swing up. Part of me is still in the air, not quite seated, when he jerks up on me, but he has torqued toward me on the first jump, so I come down hard in the saddle, catch the right stirrup, then spin him twice. He stops dead. He's ready to work now, his window of opportunity gone. I call him a son of a bitch, and commence riding him.

He is now flawless. He is picking up leg cues. Already a spectator would have trouble seeing the nuances of rein and spur with which I guide him. I ride him for forty-five minutes. Sweat seeps through the hair on his neck. I should be triumphant, but I am not. During mounting something has happened, again, to my leg; a sharp pain has run through it. The saddle wants to list to the right, a sign I am babying the left leg by asserting less stirrup pressure on that side. When I come to dismount I slide my right leg back, dragging it on his rump so he knows it is there, grab the saddle horn, and gingerly lower myself gently to the ground. The colt stands like a rock. Yes, the leg bears weight, but the limp which has refused to recede in a year is not only there, but uglier. I turn the colt loose, go to the hayrack, and sit in the sun.

Elmer, my father-in-law, broke his leg in the line of duty, chasing horses out of a dryland hayfield. I broke mine on a six-inch pine tree, trying too hard to have fun. A year has passed since it happened, a year during which I was certain the leg would rebuild.

. . .

We had been planning, that April day, for a late-spring jaunt on cross-country skis. The snow was gone in the low country, but enough remained above Red Lodge to make possible one last trip around the seven-kilometer trail. Just a week earlier we had taken a group of students on the same trail. Since then, around the coffee pot in the teacher's lounge, my friends Roger and Tom and I had been plotting an early escape from school. My oldest son David, a junior in college, would be home on spring break and would meet us at the cross-country ski trailhead.

It so happens that on the very day of the jaunt I made what I like to think was an uncharacteristic boast. A student had arrived at school that morning, his newly broken arm in a cast. That fact had given rise at lunch time to a discussion of the various broken bones staff members had suffered. Though many of the teachers were younger than I, it surfaced that I was the only one in the lounge who had never broken a bone. Just a week earlier I had climbed to the top of tall load of hay on the back of my pickup truck, hay I'd bought. It sounds dreadfully dangerous and probably is, but the standard solo method of feeding cows with square bales off the back of a pickup truck is to put the transmission in its lowest ("granny") gear, tie a piece of bungee cord between the steering wheel and the gear shift lever to create a vehicle that is more or less self-steering, then release the clutch, get out, and climb onto the load.

So, with the pickup at slow speed I had walked along behind and loosened the ropes with which I'd tied the load for transport by highway. I had bought the hay from a farmer near my school, and it was already dark now after the long drive home. I would feed off half the load to the cows, reserving the rest for the next day. But it did not work as planned. Perched on the load, cutting the strings on the bales and feeding them off, I suddenly felt the load go out from under me. When the shock was over, I found myself on the ground half-buried in bales, cows standing over me, ecstatic at this wonderful bonanza of hay. Amazed that I was intact, I regained my feet and trotted to catch the pickup before it idled through the barbed wire fence at the edge of the pasture.

So on this April day I related this story to my audience of head-shaking friends. Several repeated their warning that if I kept up my crazy life, teaching and ranching, commuting 120 miles per day, feeding cows alone in the dark, I would sooner or later kill myself. And I, foolishly, capped the story with, "Well, I've survived Vietnam and several bad horse accidents without breaking anything. I'm not fast or flashy, but the old Norwegian bones are pretty durable."

Tom looked up at that and said, "Don't say such things on a day you're going skiing."

The skiing was fine. The pine smell was sharp on the mountainside, the sun warm, the company jovial. The only damper was the quality of the snow, for there was an ice crust on it. Even at this elevation the spring days were warm enough to melt the snow daily, but the nights were cold enough to freeze it again before morning. It was this change since skiing with students a week earlier that caused my miscalculation. David, ahead of me, had wiped out where the trail curved sharply down a steep drop. I had successfully rounded that curve a week earlier and now tried again, almost instantly finding myself in the trees, mowing down saplings, trying to find a way to stop, when suddenly a substantial pine rose up in front of me and took my legs out like a linebacker. I knew I was more than bruised. I was positive of it when I saw Tom's face after he looked at *my* face.

I was very lucky to be among good friends. Son David, with the leg strength that had once made *him* a first-rate linebacker, tried carrying me piggyback and was strong enough to do so, but I could not stand the pain in my dangling left leg. So David and Tom headed out for help, and Roger stayed with me. As the sun disappeared and the snowy north slope turned cold, Roger gave me his coat, an action I'm afraid caused him much discomfort during the several hours before the search-and-rescue man arrived by snowmobile. I was expertly but ignominiously inserted into a sleeping bag, placed on a sled, and propelled out. I felt foolish, particularly since I'm not fond of snowmobiles. I once ran a Malamute dog team, have winter camped with cross-country skis, taught winter survival in the Marine Reserves, and built my own snow shoes. I've always felt a snowmobile was no proper method of winter travel for anyone with two good legs. But then, I realized, I did not *have* two good legs.

At the trailhead they got me into David's car. "Follow us," Roger said. "I know where the emergency room is."

. . .

It was snowing very thickly now, the huge flakes of spring in the mountains. With foggy windows, darkness, and snow, even the small town of Red Lodge can be deceiving. We followed Roger's car around several blocks, miscues I assumed, then finally turned in by a lighted brick building onto a concrete driveway I took to be an ambulance ramp, and came to a stop. Only then did I read the neon sign. David rolled down his window and Roger did the same, his face exasperated and fatigued. The sign read, "Smith's Funeral Home." "Roger," I hollered, "don't you think this is just a tad bit premature?" Only then did the release come, only then did Roger's face change, and we all convulsed in laughter.

We found the emergency room, eventually, and I learned that the little bone in my leg was broken. My lucky streak was over. But it was only the little bone, I told myself, ignoring the look of concern the doctor had later when he cast the leg and said, "I'm just afraid you're going to have trouble with the ligaments in that knee. I think you bent it back when you hit the tree."

He gave me alternatives from which to choose, and I took the "see how it goes" one, the other being to "scope" the knee immediately. Gradually the leg strengthened.

I used a cane during my spring farming to help myself on and off tractor, finding that it made a pretty good tool for cleaning the mud out from between the disks on the implement. Soon I was riding, taking advantage of a gentle gelding's rock-steady stand when I mounted the right ("off") side laboriously. But the second undoing came while I was trying to sell a horse.

He was a very tall black gelding named Shadow, an honest 17 hands, that a true stick measurement, not a guesstimate. (Most people's 16-hand horses shrink nearly a hand—4 inches—when actually measured.) I've dealt primarily with very nice people in the horse business, so most of my horse-trading experiences have been pleasant ones. But the prospective customer in this case, who drove up in a mud-spattered four-wheel-drive Suburban, emerged clad head to toe in camouflage, face severe, long, dark hair tied back, looking for all the world as if she had just completed boot camp in the Montana Militia.

"Ride him," she said.

"No problem," I said. Really, it was a problem, since this was a gelding so tall I had wished for a step ladder to get on him even when I was in good condition. But I had learned I could mount properly on the left by tensing every muscle in the leg, holding it very stiffly while it briefly bore my weight. I did this successfully, although middle son Jonathan cast me a better-be-careful look. Then I put the gelding through his paces. I got off the same way, and the woman began attempting to find fault with the horse. Often the least-knowledgeable horse buyers are the most troublesome. Insecure, they have asked an "expert" friend what to look out for, and they harp on it without understanding. Someone had told this woman to make certain the horse wasn't stifled, but when expressing her worry she looked at the animal's front leg, not its rear one where the stifle muscle is located. She checked his feet by picking one up with an unnatural, clumsy motion. Oh well, the gelding was gentle enough to sell to a tyro if her money was good.

But after nearly an hour of bickering I felt annoyance creeping under my collar. If the horse was as horrible as she was saying, why was she still standing here?

Finally she said, imperiously, "I want to see him ridden again." I said nothing, walked quickly to the gelding, and started to mount. I forgot the leg, forgot to tense it. Halfway up there was a snap so loud that Jonathan, watching fifty feet away, winced. It was the sound of a nylon rope stretched to the limit, then snapping. I went down in a crumpled heap, Jon running over to offer help. The woman said, "I'll think about the horse and call if I decide I want him. You don't have to ride him again." Then she drove off. I was too preoccupied with my pain to throw a rock at the back of her car.

Well, that was the end of my anterior cruciate ligament, the infamous "ACL" whose loss has ended so many athletes' careers. Now, too late, I had the orthoscopic surgery, the specialist saying I had probably partially torn the ligament in the skiing accident, then finished it off by asking the leg to hold too much weight before the muscles had strengthened enough to adequately support it. "If you were younger, I'd suggest we try to rebuild the ligament, but I don't normally recommend it for guys our age. I lost mine skiing, too, and I still ski, play tennis, and run every day. Your knee seems quite stable, so I think you'll be okay."

Maybe. But riding the colt today has shown me how far I am from recovered, how fragile, yet, the leg is. I've been putting off the decision, but I know I must make it. The colt is at a critical period of learning. My trouble with him will be no more than a minor setback in the training of the horse of a lifetime if everything is done correctly from this point onward. But it could go the other way, and if it does, given the colt's intelligence, spirit, and ability, I could have an outlaw on my hands. He needs someone quick and agile to take him from here, to send him down the right trail. I *could* perhaps get the job done with much meticulous ground work. I *could* neglect spring planting and a host of other tasks that must be done in the few hours available on weekends and after school each day. But I know deep down that the best solution is to send the colt to my friend Tex, a good trainer, to let him seize this moment in the colt's development so that nothing is lost.

Why is it so hard for me? Tex has trained other horses for us, as have several other able people. But this very special stud colt is one of those few I would rather bring along completely myself, as I did old Rockytop, my first one. And, I suppose, I'm grappling with limitations I see in myself with which I would rather not cope.

In the early part of this century my grandfather learned to swim in northern Norway by being bodily thrown off the deck of a sailing ship by the older sailors. Swimming was not a recreational activity in that land of icy waters, could not at the time be learned in heated pools. When the time came, you were simply thrown unceremoniously into the fjord. Grandpa told me of this with a wistful smile on his face, with no resentment. "I had to learn," he said.

At age sixteen Emily's grandfather Magnus left everything and everyone he knew to come to America. In that day of slow ships, he certainly never expected to see his homeland again. He dedicated himself to making a new life, then did so. There was no quitting. I suppose I am linked very strongly to a tradition of self-reliance, of pushing on without thought of giving up. I do not think I am particularly brave. I became a Marine officer and went to Vietnam not because I believed it was a "good war," for I knew there was no such thing. But there was revulsion at the alternatives, at fleeing in the face of difficulty and danger when called upon to help, and it made no difference whether the battle was at Antietam, Guadalcanal, or Dong Ha.

When Macduff storms Macbeth's castle, he enlists the help of a grizzled warrior named Siward, an English general whose son dies in the attack. Siward wants to know just one thing, whether the young man died with his wounds on his front or on his back. He learns that his son has died facing his enemy and says he needs to know no more and will not mourn the boy, for he has died in the best possible way. Another father, one in the Montana story *A River Runs Through It*, asks the same question about his dead son when he inquires as to the condition of the young man's hands after he is beaten to death by thugs. When told the hands were wounded by the punches the boy had thrown at his enemies, the father is mollified. And when I made a study of the warriors of the Northern Cheyenne people I alternated between stunned admiration and the realization that I had come from a very similar cultural warrior tradition handed down since the Vikings, had been molded by it far more than I had realized.

So that is why it is so hard, this trivial matter made epic in stature. It is really no different than calling in a mechanic to fix a problem on a car with which I am having difficulty. But no matter how minor, the issue seems a battle that is mine alone to fight, the spoils mine alone to relish, and my feet drag as I pull myself into the house and dial the telephone. It is soon arranged.

I will keep the colt a short time more, long enough to breed a couple special mares of my own and one of an outfitter friend who likes fast-walking horses for the mountains. Then he will go to spend the summer with Tex. By the end of the summer, my leg will be better.

When the day comes, Tex puts his face next to the nostrils of the colt, something he always does when he first meets one. He believes that a colt's sniffing him is a first step in a bonding process that will mature as training progresses. I have watched him do this in the past with detached interest. Now, as he bends toward the stud colt, it is more to me as if he bends to kiss someone who is not his lover, but mine. Then the colt walks into the horse trailer and is gone.

4

Testosterone machines · *A spring ride*
Killer baby antelope · *Banks and noxious weeds*

*J*t is time to release the bulls. They have already broken one panel in the corral fence and now are sullenly restrained only by the electric fence wire I've added above the top pole around the perimeter of the corral. Their bawling is a constant bass cacophony as the four of them line up facing east toward the hills, where a mile away graze the cows and their newly branded calves. Like the bugles of elk, their calls sometimes begin low, then rise in pitch to a whistling crescendo. They may not know much, but they know their role. Pity anything that blocks their way.

The breeding of beef animals is the epitome of *vive la différence*. Replacement heifers, destined to become breeding mothers, are selected for feminine traits (yes, some cows do look more feminine than others) and for such things as milking ability and a pelvis of adequate size to predict ease of birthing. Bulls are bred for libido, birth weight of calves (calves born small which grow rapidly are most desirable), the quality of calves they are likely to sire and, of course, fertility. A complex set of statistics called "E.P.D.'s" are kept by the bull producer to be scrutinized by the buyer, statistics that are predictors of the bull's efficiency. One important measurement tabulated is the diameter of the bull's scrotum. After all, when you get down to it, these critters are simply breeding machines, and the testicles are their engines.

I find it easy to admire protective motherly cows, even though I cuss them when they are being contrary. Their single-minded attention to the needs of the calf cannot help but meet with our approval. Bulls, however, are another matter. A vehement feminist would find ammunition for even her most radical tendencies if she looked closely at bulls. They are big, dumb, muscle-bound testosterone machines. They will live peaceably together in the off season, buddies of the closest sort. Then it is breeding time. You open the corral gate and instinct to kill their rivals takes over. Violent enemies now, they turn on each other, head to head, the stronger shoving the weaker straight backwards, breaking corral poles and anything else (including you) that happens to be in their way. Our Angus bulls are hornless, thank God. (Breeders of horned bulls normally attach weights to the horns when the bulls are calves to make them grow downward, at a less lethal angle.) No matter. I'll have nothing to do with horns on bulls. They have enough tools with which to kill you as it is.

And so, on this fine spring day in May, I reach over from the saddle as I hold Major close to the gate, undo the latch, and back the horse up, pulling the gate open. Emily, mounted on Sugar, stays back to turn the bulls down the lane once we get them out the gate. I ride into the muddy corral, both Major and I cautious but throwing a good bluff. I yell at the bulls. They run out the gate, getting their licks on each other as they go. They hit the lane running, and Emily and I let our horses lope behind. This is just fine. The faster they go in the direction we want, the fewer the brawls, the more we like it. They continue to advance well, so we have a relatively easy time of it. Cows are grazing at the base of the hill, and they answer the bawls of the bulls. I see one cow mounting another, hormonally confused, telling us that the mounted female is in heat. The bulls will "get lucky" immediately.

I have heard that urban zoos now sponsor adult wine and cheese parties as fund raisers for their institutions. Couples come to the events, hear lectures about animal reproduction, then watch as animals "perform." I guess there is no harm in this, though the average ranch child, so used to witnessing the primary end of the reproductive cycle, would snicker at it. But I suspect that only the most easily titillated human couples would be aroused in the least by watching the antics of bulls and cows.

Cows "cycle," that is, go into estrus (heat) approximately every three weeks. Like most mammals, only during estrus, for just a couple days, are the cows receptive to the male. Bulls are not masters of seduction. Their "courtship" consists simply of sniffing the posterior end of the cow, raising and wrinkling their noses and then, if they do not detect what they want, moving on to the next one. The breeding itself is very quick, the equipment spear-like, the result, if successful, a calf in just over nine months.

Our four bulls will be more than adequate for the 85 cows we have turned into the hill pasture. This ratio startled a Minneapolis girl who came west with her minister husband in the early 1950s. My mom was standing beside Herman Hoines, looking over a fence after church at St. Olaf one Sunday. We had been invited to a ranch for Sunday dinner, a frequent thing. Both my parents were inquisitive, always wanting to know about the occupations of their parishioners, an interest not the least bit feigned. They would learn all they could, then relate it to us kids on the way home in the car.

Now this was a time when Victorian manners had not completely left the average Montana ranch. Cowboys and ranchers did not eat in restaurants with their Stetsons on, as they do today, and reproductive matters were not always discussed openly when women were present (though this was not universally true). When I was a fourteen-year-old working on my first ranch, a conversation at dinner about putting out the bulls abruptly stopped when I asked the gestation period of a cow, then resumed when two visiting town women took dishes out to the kitchen.

Herman Hoines, one of Dad's bass choir recruits, was a fun-loving cosmopolitan man, but he was only one generation away from the nineteenth century. That meant he tipped the brim of his hat to ladies, called them "ma'am," and treated the minister's wife like a queen. Mom was a pretty little woman in her early thirties.

Herman was enjoying her naive questions about ranching and her compliments on the appearance of his black, shiny heifers, even though he knew she would not have been able to distinguish a cull cow from a prize one. Seeing a particularly impressive animal close to the fence, Mom said, "Now that's a nice big cow."

Herman hesitated, but he could not in good conscience stay silent. "No, Mrs. Aadland, that one's a bull."

"How many of the others are bulls?"

"None of them. There are twenty-five heifers in the pasture and just the one bull."

Mom turned red. "One bull? Just one bull? That's bigamy!"

Herman turned red, too. "Well, yes, I guess it is." Then they both laughed. The story was repeated at dozens of potluck dinners in the church basement, and I can remember Mom telling it on herself, laughing until tears.

Emily and I have now moved the bulls to the barbed wire gate. I quickly dismount to open it, anxious to get the bulls through before they take matters upon themselves and tear down a section of fence. We herd them through. One heads left to a cow he has already spotted and checks her out, she being as coy as a cow is capable of being, moving away at his first two attempts to mount her. Then she stands to be bred.

Two other bulls find another cow in heat, make passes her way, then turn on each other and begin a violent fight. We get well out of the way. Dust flies and sagebrush shakes. The two bulls are too evenly matched to decide the issue quickly, and while they are engaged, the fourth bull quietly moves in on the cow and breeds her. "That one," Emily says, "has a higher I.Q."

Well, we have delivered the bulls, and the herd gradually lines out and heads up the gentler coulee to the north, the bulls in running battle, the little newborn calves staying out of the way. The next generation is commencing now, and next spring we'll be doing it all over again. There is, at this moment, a vast sense of relief in both Emily and me. Last week we branded; our small crew of five friends branding, vaccinating,

and castrating the bull calves. We do not rope and drag to the fire the old way, still revered by a few ranchers we know. Such occasions are exciting and give both ropers and their horses a good workout, and even more so, the ground crew that throws the calves and holds them down. Advocates of the old way say it is actually faster than using the modern calf tables that tilt sideways and hold the calf. They may be right, but I have always noticed that an awfully large crew is involved, half the people working, half holding video cameras and enjoying the show. We feel the calf table is a bit less stressful for the calf and faster if you have a small crew.

. . .

But all that is done now. The cattle will pretty much take care of themselves through the summer, our main job being to watch the fences, keep the salt trough full, and look occasionally for injuries or illness, for the calf with porcupine quills in its nose or the cow limping from "foot rot." We could turn our horses and go back to the house, but neither of us seems moved to do so. "Well," I say, "maybe we should ride the fence." There is really no need. On this range I can drive along much of the fence in my four-wheel-drive pickup and can eyeball it pretty well where it runs in coulees too steep to drive. Indeed, I have already been around the fence, pounding in a few steel posts and stretching loose wires. The fences are old, but they are in adequate shape. No matter. It is spring, and we get too few chances to ride together anymore.

So we ride to the mouth of Indian Coulee, the steep ravine in which Magnus found the tree burial when he first came to our ranch. We do not ride past the burial site, instead catching the trail which tops out on the tree-covered slope on the south side of the coulee. Very seldom do we ride up the bottom of the coulee on the cow trail past the burial tree. The tree is still there, but it is not standing anymore. It finally fell over in 1968, the year I was in Vietnam. It rests on the steep slope below the trail, its gnarled trunk and branches barkless and grey.

We are not mystics, but both of us have always claimed a certain feeling when we ride through the bottom of Indian Coulee, a feeling that does not always fit the day. With me it has gone farther, to a sense of the person buried there. I feel it was a woman, old and kind. When Nik, the artist of this book, looked at the site with me, he asked me why I thought that. I gave him the best answer I could. "I don't know," I said.

I do know some of the historical facts. The Crows suffered a terrible measles epidemic shortly before their agency was moved east, an epidemic that killed many. When the first homesteaders came to this valley, there were many tree burials in the coulees on the east side of the valley. I also know that the person buried in our coulee was an adult, not a child. Children, when buried in trees, were normally bundled and wedged into natural crotches in the branches. This burial was described by Magnus and Elmer as having a platform of poles, required for a larger body. Before the tree fell one pole remained.

We rest the horses halfway up. Major has suffered a bout with the "heaves" during the winter, and he is not completely over it. He occasionally coughs. I think of the lungs of the stud colt. Then Major hits his second wind, and we're over the top and onto the sagebrush-covered flat. We ride to the top of the knoll we know as the highest place on the ranch, turn our horses around, and just look at it. Everything is green. The barns and houses on the valley floor, ours and our neighbors', look like toys. Over the foothills toward the mountains there is not a single building to be seen, save our old homesteader's barn across the river on the west side of our ranch. We clearly see our broodmares, two miles away, grazing near the top of the far western ridge across the valley, see a little speck of an animal next to one of them and know we have a new foal, born a little ahead of schedule before we could get the mare home. Even at this distance, the appearance of a foal is exciting. We will drive over and check it out after our ride.

. . .

We turn around and begin a counterclockwise trip around the range, riding east along our south fence. We have not gone far before we spot, a half-mile east, two antelope does, their white rumps giving them away. We're excited to see antelope on our own ranch, a fairly recent development, for we are on the fringes of their range. But what really excites us is that each doe has a fawn by its side. We have seen many newborn deer fawns, both whitetails and mulies, but we've never gotten close to antelope fawns. We veer our horses to the left where the ground slopes off, taking them low enough that the gentle ridge breaks the line of sight, and hatch a plan for our "hunt." Emily says, "I've got to see those babies."

"If we stay low and just go parallel to them, we ought to be able to pop over the rise and see them at a hundred yards or so. That's as close to antelope as we're going to get."

So we ride quietly, holding the horses to a walk. I've picked out a juniper clump adjacent to where the antelope were at last sight. We'll ride to that, then veer right and quickly top the rise. It works according to plan, except that when we get high enough to see where the antelope have been, they are not there, but off to the left a ways, and then we only see the two does. They have spotted us and are beginning to move off, though by antelope standards they are still in low gear. But where are the fawns?

"I know they had little ones beside them," Emily says. She barely gets the words out. Then there is what I can only describe as a hiss and a crackle of sagebrush, and we look to our right and see two tiny missiles hurtling at fifty miles per hour straight toward us. It is unearthly how fast they come. With all the speed of their adult parents, in the blink of an eye, they are upon us, and the horses, too, have never seen anything like it. Both jump for the next county, both Emily and I spinning them to keep them from running off, both horses coming to a snorting stop as the baby bullets hurtle past. Mark Twain's statement in *Roughing It* comes to mind: "Why we couldn't even see them. We could only hear them whiz as they went by." And it's true!

We laugh. Both of us have managed to stay mounted on the suddenly spinning horses, and we feel foolish but happy. Both horses continue to stare in the direction the cruising critters went, both still snorting their indignation. "We were almost killed by baby antelope," Emily laughs. We can only guess that the doe antelope gave their fawns whatever signal means "Run for it," but did not specify the direction.

"Hey, I just read something about this," I say. While we ride the fence I tell Emily about an incident in Tom Leforge's book, *Memoirs of a White Crow Indian*. "Leforge would have died at the Custer battle with his friend Mitch Buoyer, the scout, if *he* hadn't been attacked by baby antelope. The very same thing happened. One ran straight toward him, his horse spooked and bucked, and he got thrown into some rocks and broke his collar bone. So he was out of action for a couple weeks. He was really disappointed he couldn't go along with Mitch Buoyer and Custer, but he lucked out." These two scouts from history, Mitch Buoyer, the part-Sioux, and Tom Leforge, the white man who married into the Crow tribe and had many children, some of them adopted in the Crow tradition, had much in common with us.

It is amazing to me how close is this past which features figures the likes of Mitch Buoyer, Tom Leforge, and General Custer. As a senior in high school I played my best football in a homecoming game against the town of Lodge Grass. (I was not a particularly good football player, but it all came together that day.) We avenged the previous year's loss to them. Early in the game their quarterback, a non-Indian, was put out on an injury. They placed a big Crow boy named Leforge in a tailback position and pounded him nearly every play to my side of the line. And nearly every play I brought him down. So I have grappled physically with a descendant of Tom Leforge.

But there is more to it than that. Twenty years before Custer and Mitch Buoyer died, the Crow agency was moved (the first time) from a location on Mission Creek near present Livingston, Montana, ninety miles west of us, to the location that drew Magnus to our ranch. The agency on Mission Creek was in the path of Livingston's famous, ferocious, south winds. So terrible was the location, there is a record of a visitor tying his horse in front of the agency on a winter day, going in to visit and eat, then discovering after several hours that his horse, tied in the path of the wind, was dead from exposure (hypothermia, in our modern vocabulary).

So when mining and white politics forced the first reduction in the Crow Reservation, those seeking a new agency site were given two criteria. First, they were to get some miles away from the Yellowstone River. That was the northern reservation boundary, and white whiskey traders were already set up where the town of Columbus is now located, ready to prey on the Crows. Second, they were told bluntly: "Get us out of this damn wind!"

The two men sent to scout out an agency site traveled up the Stillwater River and onto its tributary, the Rosebud, and they found the perfect place. These two men were Mitch Bouyer and Tom Leforge. So when visitors remark on the beauty of our ranch, when they remark that the wind doesn't seem to blow as hard here as in many places in Montana, I smugly say, "Well, the location was chosen by two of the best scouts in Montana history." And now, in the telescoping of time so commonly felt from the back of a horse, I've been nearly dumped in the rocks the way Tom Leforge was, and a century and two decades have become the blink of an eye (or the blitz of baby antelope).

.   .   .

We complete our cursory check of the east fence, then ride past the salt trough and along the remnants of the wagon road, the tracks of the old Bozeman Trail that runs through our ranch. In our lifetimes we have ridden many miles together. Our horses walk on the two wagon tracks in tandem, and so do our thoughts. If it could only be this, riding together on a spring day with no worries about details, about banks and mortgages, cattle prices, the endless tasks for which there will never be time, and the less satisfying things about our jobs off the ranch. If it could only be this, riding a good horse alongside someone you love in big open country with the spring sun on your back. But we are adults, so we know that everything has its warts. And as soon as I get to that part of my reverie, I see such a wart, a patch of mellow-yellow leafy spurge, one of the noxious weeds that has invaded the West, a foreign import like its partner in crime, spotted knapweed. I mentally mark it for future spraying, trying to think something profound about the noxious weeds of life.

We come to a place where the wagon road descends into a curving gentle hollow, a ridge to the west between us and the valley. We ride quietly, Emily leaning down to the side, studying the ground. She points out wildflowers, bluebells and shooting stars. A few crocuses yet survive. The sagebrush is light-green with silver tips. Under our horses' hooves we see a mosaic. We are startled when city friends describe these dryland foothills as barren because they are devoid of trees and buildings. A sister-in-law made nervous by all this openness once exclaimed, "I can see condos up here." I'm afraid we gave her withering looks, for her composure altered abruptly. "Over our dead bodies," we said.

We were riding through this hollow thirty years ago. We had made, very young, a commitment, then had been frightened by it and backed off. A terrible week ensued. At the end of the week we kept a previously arranged date, our most common kind, a horseback ride in the hills, and in this hollow, on this trail, the trouble ended when we reached out and joined our hands, our horses walking side by side, held hands as long as the rough terrain allowed. Today, middle-aged, managing to forget momentarily about mortgages and noxious weeds, our thoughts still in tandem, we each take the other's hand again and hold it until the trail turns down the steep coulee where we must go single file.

5

Stallions, mares, and foals · Centaurs and minotaurs

I am leading the mare, Gypsy. Her sorrel foal cruises by her side, sun glinting off its red coat, glides along in the running walk bred into our horses, head nodding with every stride. Gypsy is one of our most reliable broodmares. She never loses a foal, always breeds back, and now, at twenty years old, shows no sign of slipping in condition. She can also be a pain in the neck. In a small pasture she is always easy to catch, but out on range she sees us coming and not only runs away herself but takes the entire band, all the rest of them otherwise easy to catch, over the ridge.

We've finally learned to combat this, normally keeping her close. But when we saw the mare and foal across the valley from our vantage point on the hill, we suspected it was Gypsy and knew we'd better get her quickly before the foal had its legs completely under control. She still tried running when she saw the pickup and trailer, but the foal soon tired, and with a mind of its own flopped down in the sun and slept immediately, as babies will do. A slave to her motherhood, Gypsy had no choice but to stop, standing in protective posture over the little one while we slipped on her halter.

Since we have Gypsy home and close to the stallion we will try to breed her on the foal heat. I lead her to the stout corral fence. Piper, our stallion, trumpeting in anticipation, runs back and forth inside his pen. I bring her up to a strong post, quickly wrap her lead rope around it, then tie a quick-release knot. Piper thrusts his head over to her, singing his throaty, masculine combination of snort and whinny. She responds by squealing and striking with her front feet, anxiously twisting to make certain her foal is by her side and okay. I suspect she is bluffing. Some mares are extremely difficult to hand breed (the term for introducing the animals on lines, in a controlled situation). Some are so protective of their foals that they hide heat signs and can only be bred in a pasture situation where the stallion runs with his mares in closer similarity to natural, wild conditions. We have pasture bred in the past. It is extremely reliable, but a bit dangerous for a valuable stallion. Few veteran pasture-breeding stallions survive without at least some nicks and scratches and scars.

Piper cost, by our standards, a substantial sum of cash, so he is protected by a stall in the barn opening into a small corral and never allowed to run out. The testing for estrus we are doing now with Gypsy is called "teasing." Like cows, horses cycle approximately every twenty-one days. Unlike cows, most mares in northern climates shut down for the winter, begin to cycle again in spring with unreliable "transitional" heat periods, then reach full fertility as the longest days of the year arrive. The foal heat is sort of an extra estrus, coming about nine days after birth of the foal, shorter and somewhat less reliable than her regular twenty-one day cycles, but okay to use if the mare has recovered well from giving birth. Often the foal tells us when this early heat is occurring, for it will have a brief bout with diarrhea during that time, apparently caused by a chemical change in the mare's milk.

Gestation periods are longer for horses than for cows, a bit over eleven months rather than just over nine. Thus we breed the mares back either on foal heat or their first regular heat cycle, which occurs about thirty days after foaling. If unsuccessful on either of those attempts, the mare slips back a bit, foaling later, and if that progresses over several years, she might require a year off to get back on schedule again, for late foals have a tough time with Montana winters.

Piper puts his face next to Gypsy's, puts his nostrils next to hers, breathes her essence. She has not struck or squealed now for a several minutes, but has turned passive, though still nickering for the foal. And then, finally, she answers the stallion. She raises her tail and drops down at the rear. Under her tail her vagina twitches, the edges curling rhythmically back as if to turn inside out, this motion the mare's certain "yes" to survival of her species. She urinates thickly, the liquid dark yellow.

I lead her away, now with difficulty, for she resists. Piper licks her back and side as she passes down the corral fence, then turns wild as she walks around the corner of the barn out of sight. I tie her to the breeding chute, which is simply a hitching rail with a pole on each side, descending toward the rear to just above ground level. The chute's only purpose is to keep the mare from shifting side to side. There is no need for breeding hobbles on Gypsy. There are mares, however, that will tease to the stallion, let him mount erected and ready, and then kick viciously. We own no such mares, but occasionally a customer's mare falls into that category.

I wrap Gypsy's tail and wash her, then go into the barn and snap a long lead rope on Piper's halter. The lead rope is long enough to let him run safely ahead of me through the double barn doors, allowing control without too much jeopardy. Piper is an old pro. He approaches Gypsy from the side, stretching his neck out to nip and lick her, keeping his body out of kicking range. Ovulation normally happens late in the heat cycle, but on foal heats it is unpredictable. Gypsy must be very close to it because Piper cuts short other preparations and mounts. In spite of his libido, he's rather inept in aim, something common with stallions that have always been bred with the help of humans. I don't let him flounder around too long, for some mares become impatient and kick. After a few miscues, I reach down and grab his penis, holding and aiming, then as he penetrates, get out of the way. A jocular friend once watched me do this and commented that it probably would be illegal in Utah. "No," I laughed, "I've lived there, and it's not *that* straight-laced."

Piper finishes but stays mounted, his body draped over Gypsy's. He appears as if in a coma. I watch Gypsy carefully. She stays impassive, so I need not rush him away as I would with a mare more likely to kick. Then she shifts a little, and I pull Piper off and return him quickly to his stall.

Since we have put Gypsy's new foal in the little catch pen in front of the breeding chute where the mother can keep track of it during the process, we take this time for some early handling, "imprinting" as it is now called. (The term used to be used only for baby birds.) I catch the little filly with one arm around her chest, the other behind her rump, and pull it to me, restraining her body against mine. Soon she settles down. Then Emily halters her and arranges a soft cotton rope around the foal's rump so that there will be no pull on its neck. Before I release the filly, Emily picks up each foot and taps it in a mimic of later shoeing. She gently rubs its ears, face, and body. We talk to it continually. Then we release the little mare, leading her by halter and rump rope, using no more pressure than necessary. After a good lesson, we let her return to Gypsy's side.

In years past we would simply wait three weeks, then tease Gypsy back to the stallion. But we have gone high-tech. At fourteen days we will call the veterinarian, who will come and ultrasound the mare, telling us whether she is pregnant. If the test is positive, she can go back on pasture. If not, we can wait for the next cycle or even "short-cycle" her with medication, to make heat come on sooner. I have also learned to artificially inseminate, to collect Piper's semen when several mares are in heat at once and inseminate them, and also to ship chilled semen to other mare owners and receive it from other stallions.

We sometimes wonder what Magnus and Elmer would think of all this. The horses we raise we know they would love, for they are very close in appearance and gait to the favorite horses that have come down to us in photo albums, to Elmer's Silver, a horse he said "could do every gait in the book." With Silver, Elmer once yanked home a big steer on the end of his lariat rope, bringing it all the way from the east range. We think the modern breeding practices would also be pretty interesting to them, for horses were a huge part of their lives and breeding them well was a great concern. In the early 1900s Magnus teamed up with other neighbors in the valley to send all the way to France for a Percheron stallion. Before tractors arrived on the scene there was a tremendous need for good work stock in Montana. Magnus and the neighbors stood the stallion to every mare that walked—saddle mares, work mares, and Indian ponies—leading him from ranch to ranch behind a wagon pulled by a team. Until the early Fifties, when Elmer finally sold his work horses, the genes of that Percheron from France were still in both saddle and work stock in this area and probably, in a few cases, still are.

We watch Gypsy move into the pasture, her foal beside her. We will breed her again in two days if she is still in heat. Meanwhile, we have a half dozen mares yet to foal. Calving, because of a cow's shorter gestation period, is a distinctly different season from breeding time, but with horses the birth season and the breeding season overlap, the longer gestation period making it necessary to breed the mare back promptly. Thus we are breeding some mares back before others have foaled.

The birth of foals is exciting, quick, and usually missed entirely by the mare's owner. Mares still foal the way nature, intending to protect them from predators, programmed them, most often at night. The birth is extremely fast, the mare's contractions extremely powerful. In nature, preferably in early evening, the mare would give birth rapidly and the foal would, by morning, be strong enough to keep up with the herd. Rarely do mares have problems foaling, but when they do, because of the power of their contractions, the result is often disaster for the foal and sometimes for the mother as well.

It is also said that mares are the only domestic animals that can delay birth. Again, this is nature's programming, allowing her to wait until darkness or until a nearby predator goes away. Now domesticated, mares make use of this ability to foil doting owners who put their pregnant mares in stalls and watch them day and night. A typical scenario is the mare owner, watching to the point of exhaustion, sitting waiting in the barn, falling briefly to sleep, only to awaken to the disturbance made by a

foal rising to nurse. The first son of a famous race horse was lost even though it would have been worth a fortune at birth. People were hired to watch the mare day and night, but nature called to the watchman one evening, and when he returned the foal was born but dead, the birth sack over its head. Many people have raised horses their entire lives without seeing a colt being born. We have been much luckier, perhaps seeing a dozen or so.

When foals are born in confinement, we iodine their navels and watch closely to make certain they nurse and get their colostrum. Some mare owners worry too much and mess things up by rushing in quickly. It's desirable that the mare and foal stay connected by the umbilical cord for a while after birth, the mare pumping to the foal highly oxygenated blood. People sometimes intrude, causing the mare to stand and break the cord before necessary. And some worry so much the foal will not nurse that they do not let nature take its course. Usually the foal will untangle its impossibly long legs, stand, and nurse without help.

We do watch closely to see that the foal's plumbing works properly—many need enemas—and to make certain the mare sheds her placenta promptly, for that is more critical than it is with a cow, problems from a retained placenta occurring sooner. But we also let nature rule as much as possible, increasingly allowing our mares to foal out in a clean, natural environment. We do worry about the increasing incidence of foal losses to mountain lions in our area, however.

So now, in mid-May, we are heavily into it. It will be past the Fourth of July before all mares, ours and our customers', are bred back and certified in foal. Until then the stallion barn east of the house will be a busy reproductive headquarters, mares teased every morning, foals bounding by their mothers' sides. The kitchen counter will hold each day, after the breakfast dishes are cleared, the simple microscope I use for checking sperm motility along with various other tools of the trade. It will be a long haul, but a rewarding one, each foal a new life with personality and potential, each successful breeding another promise.

Working Gypsy's foal has been only a moderate exertion, and yet I realize sweat is pouring off my face and has dripped onto my glasses, blurring them. It is hot, really hot, for the first time since last summer. Our erratic Montana spring is gone. It has been a work-all-the-time season for us. I've remarked to Emily that it is a bit like

Dong Ha, when we worked from very early in the morning until midnight and beyond, keeping the trucks going, running the convoys on Highway 9. But through the frenzy of ranch work there is mixed the evidence of great reward as well, seen in the new life by the sides of cows and mares, the knowledge that the next generation is planted, and in the small amount of farming I do, the popping up of oat and alfalfa shoots.

. . .

Before going into the house for a cup of coffee (Norwegians drink coffee even in hot weather) I walk out to the highway and pluck The Billings Gazette from its special plastic mailbox. Inside, in the "state and local" section, I read a small story about a rancher losing two steer calves to one of the wolves the federal government has captured in Canada and released in Yellowstone National Park, a few miles over the mountains. This wolf, like many of the others, has not particularly liked the land of geysers and has quickly left, crossing the mountains north toward home, chowing down on some easy ranch prey en route. The article tells of an extensive helicopter chase lasting several days, sophisticated equipment on the aircraft homing in on the wolf's radio collar. She is eventually shot with a dart, tranquilized, scooped up by the helicopter as she was in Canada, and whisked back to Yellowstone in hope that tourists may be able to see her. The National Park officials are pleased as punch at their success in retrieving her. The rancher predicts she will return to kill again. (In subsequent weeks he is proven correct.)

Next to the article about the rancher is another related one, its headline considerably larger. This story tells of the efforts of a wildlife advocacy organization in compensating the rancher with money for the lost calves at current market prices. The exact amount, to the penny, is noted in the article. Apparently the rancher declined any opportunity to pose with the organization's representative while receiving the check, for he is not in the photo. The organization involved vigorously advocates various government programs to reintroduce large predators to ranching country, and its members feel that paying for losses (if they can be proven—not always easy) makes the programs more palatable. It is a well-meaning effort.

But why is it so hard to understand that more than money is involved? It is not that we do not like predators. I admire them, consider them beautiful, and am glad to have some around. I myself am a predator, an unabashed, unregenerate, unreformable meat eater like the Crow Indians who lived on this ranch a century ago, like the Zulu, the Inuit, and my own Viking forebears. I raise part of my meat, and when the aspens turn golden, hunt for some of it myself. I like my inherited, evolved position on the food chain, do not wish to move lower on it, and view my fellow predators with the same admiration that warriors hold for other good warriors. So I have no anger, resentment, or hatred toward the hungry creature that, displaced from her home range by the "superior" intentions of man, has headed homeward and has filled her belly the easy way while traveling.

But why can't these people understand that it is not just about money? Why can't they understand that it involves attacks on more than the pocketbook? Why can't they understand that the rancher in the newspaper has lost more than the dollars and cents the calves would be worth if sold at the stockyards that day? When you sit up with a heifer in a cold shed in the middle of the night and help her give birth, there is more than money involved. When you plan the breeding of a particular mare to a particular stallion, studying conformation, genetics, disposition, then manage the mating itself, the foal that results amounts to more than the money it would bring if sold. The collaboration of man and nature into the young born to our livestock makes the colts and calves part animal, part us. They are centaurs and minotaurs, even, if you will, our children. I suspect the rancher in the story would cheerfully refuse the money for his lost calves if he could have instead the understanding of every man, woman, and child in the country of that one simple point, and with that understanding, the legal right to defend what he has created.

I put down the newspaper, noticing for the first time the blinking of the little red light on our telephone answering machine. I punch the button. The voice is that of Tex, the trainer. "Did you know this stud colt could walk eight miles an hour for just as many miles you want to take him, and never draw a deep breath? [Yes, Tex, I knew.] Anyway, he's doing real good, and I'd like to breed him to the mare I call Get. [We know the mare, of course, for we sold her to him as a foal. Emily, best poetic sense intact, had named her Bonnie Bright Star, and has never quit harassing Tex for reducing her name to "Get."] She's starting to cycle now. If I don't hear from you I'll figure it's okay."

Yes, of course, it's okay. I test my left knee with a partial deep knee bend on just the one leg, but can't do it without pain. I think of the stud colt.

SUMMER

6

Pancho and Lefty · Running W's · The one-hoss shay ·
A bend in Butcher Creek

I am harrowing the meadow with Pancho and Lefty, our Belgian team. I sit on the spring seat of the otherwise springless forecart, looking over the backs of the two big sorrels, hearing behind me the dragging harrow I've constructed of old tire chains welded together. I should have done this earlier, for the timothy is growing rapidly. I have moved the broodmares to a different pasture. They had kept the field grazed to golf-green trim. But now it is time to let the field grow a crop of hay, and the manure droppings the mares have left behind are good fertilizer only if scattered, not if left in clumps. The harrow knocks them down and spreads them out. When I finish, I will give the field its first irrigation of the summer, then stand back and watch it grow.

Pancho and Lefty are new to this sort of work. Gentle, steady, and portly, Pancho shows little green-grass exuberance. Lefty, on the other hand, has let off a little steam on the first round, kicking up his heels with mock, controlled bucking, but staying within the traces as if running in place. Now he has settled down. The two were trained on Montana's high line, up north in the Bear Paw mountains where the wind blows and everyone is tough. (No one not matching that description has survived. Darwin could prove his thesis by studying ranchers on the high line of Montana.) A young man, one of two sons of a rancher who feeds many cattle exclusively with horses, trained the Belgians.

I once owned a Belgian stud and bred him for several years to the grade Belgian mares of a friend, each of us keeping half the colts. When I accumulated three and had started the oldest gelding under harness, I traded the Bear Paw ranchers the three colts for this trained, relatively young team. The rancher's son had trained Pancho and Lefty to a level too sedate to provide him with any more challenge, and he was ready for another project, a team with a little more fire. As I said, they're tough up there.

In the north country as a feeding team during winter, Pancho and Lefty had daily made a big circle, their wagon loaded several times in the course of the trip with big loads of hay bales which were fed to successive bunches of cows en route. Eventually, they completed their circle back at the home ranch. Thus, they do not understand today's routine, this circling around the nine-acre field, and after the first round they started to turn through the gate into the barnyard. They thought they were done for the day and must have believed it to have been an easy day indeed. They are catching on now, but each time we pass the gate they look hopefully in that direction and need a bit of right rein to stay on track.

It is a fine morning. Our nights, even later in hottest summer, cool to the point of chill, and mornings require some time to recover. As usual there is a heavy dew, the droplets on the timothy stems refracting the morning sun. I would not notice this were I dragging the harrow behind the tractor in a high gear or even faster behind the pickup. And therein lies the irony and the dilemma.

I have worked very hard the whole past week to free up one morning for this luxury of sitting low to the grass on a steel seat behind a team of horses. I have worked several evenings after supper, clearing the deck so that I can take the time to harrow the field in this relatively primitive fashion. The job could be done in an hour with the tractor. With my diesel pickup I could do the job in half an hour, humming along, the stereo playing Bach or Bluegrass. With Pancho and Lefty, the job will take all morning. So why do I do it?

I will be asked that question, I know, by some of the friends and neighbors busily traveling the highway on the west edge of the field. Several familiar pickups have slowed, their drivers waving, then sped away. Tourists slow too, one motor home stopping while a woman jumps out, camcorder in hand. I know I am now immortalized, that somewhere in a city I will be shown on a screen and called quaint or picturesque.

Well, maybe I am. The neighbors watching as I deliberately expand a small task to a large one seem to enjoy seeing the team but wonder why I have so much time on my hands. So I do not know just how I will answer the question. Yes, a team needs work, but do I need a team, when so much of my earnings go to pay interest and a little principal on an embarrassingly large equipment mortgage?

Ranchers in Montana don't often talk about the smell of dew on wet grass, or the scent of horse sweat, honest sweat generated from real, meaningful work. They don't often talk about the sound of a robin, or a magpie squawking, or the gurgle of the creek. Rarely do they mention horses as companions, personalities whose interaction livens up otherwise mundane tasks. But talk to those who occasionally work with a team and you do hear these things. You hear talk of getting work done accompanied by the creak of harness leather, the sound of the stream audible over the drag of the harrow. And you hear of a sense of satisfaction when the work is done that just is not there when it is performed with noisy machinery. And you hear also of touching the past, of renewing connection with that grandpa or uncle and his stories of working with teams of horses.

And are there ever stories! Talk to any rural grandmother seventy or older and she remembers work teams with a shine in her eye. She remembers the names of the horses. She remembers hearing of families traveling in snowstorms returned home through total white-out by the unerring sense of direction of their teams of horses. The sled or wagon stops suddenly, the team refusing to move. Father investigates what is wrong, groping along the flank of an icicle-covered workhorse, gets in front of the team, and finds they are parked at the yard fence of the homestead.

The power of workhorses is legend. Forget the three-horsepower label on your lawn mower engine when considering what a workhorse can do. According to the ormula for horsepower, a strong workhorse can generate up to thirty horsepower for short distances, and even that does not tell the tale, for we have here animals weighing up to a ton apiece with four hooves digging in to provide traction no tire can. My father tells of his car, buried in the ditch during a North Dakota blizzard, lifted in a way that looked effortless to him back onto the road by a single, black workhorse brought over by a farmer and hitched to the bumper.

Look around you, anywhere in America, at things a generation or two older than the interstate highway system and you are likely looking at something built with the sweat of workhorses and the men who drove them. The ditch, the canal, and the railroad grade were probably formed by slips of the same sort Magnus used to dig the first irrigation ditches on the ranch. A friend in his nineties explained to me that there was also a larger slip pulled by more horses and controlled by two men. The slip was the backhoe of its time. The basements of houses were dug with them.

Roads were graded in much the same way they are today, the grader really looking quite similar, but propelled by gang-teams of many horses. The timbers in that stately church were hauled to the building site by horses, and earlier, the logs that made them were skidded to the sawmill the same way. Our nation's infrastructure was built with teams of horses. In the cities, heavy commodities were moved by huge draft teams, larger horses than were practical on the farm, and the milkman and iceman both came to your home with panel wagons, short-coupled to turn sharply, pulled by single horses. Such delivery horses knew the route, knew at which houses to stop. The milkman could get out at one house, carry his bottles in, and the horse would move the wagon to the next house on its own. The horse was only befuddled when someone on the route moved or died.

Work with horses was not sedate or simple, however, nor always pastoral. It comes as a surprise to many who are good horsemen or horsewomen in the saddle sense, that in learning to drive they are entering an entirely new, potentially more dangerous, arena. The mechanisms for translating animal power to machine or wagon are complicated and require years of study. Some historians think civilization took a gigantic leap forward with the invention of the horse collar and hames, the setup that allows the horse to really apply power to the task without injuring itself. When tractors first appeared on the scene, the manufacturers of horse-drawn equipment refused to accept defeat, competing successfully for another generation by designing bigger and more complicated machines such as grain combines, pulled by hitches of many horses. Applying all that power evenly and effectively was the stuff of advanced physics.

. . .

The constant danger, however, was the runaway. Horses are flight animals, their first reaction to threat being to outrun it. All horse training centers on methods to channel horse behavior into acceptable directions, to overcome the tendency to run away. This is far simpler in saddle training than in training horses for harness. If a saddle horse has learned to yield to rein pressure on one side, the rider has a recourse if the animal tries to run. He or she can do what some Westerners call the "one-rein stop," can pull the horse around to the side, spin him if necessary. Horses cannot run if they're bent around, and for the most part, they cannot buck very successfully either.

Obviously, spinning an animal is not an option when driving the horse down a narrow country road, steep ditches (or worse) on either side. Thus training of harness horses emphasizes making them safe from their instinct to cut and run when something spooks them. In the late nineteenth century the United States government, alarmed at the frequency of serious accidents, issued training manuals showing severe techniques aimed at making horses completely compliant. While some of the methods would be considered abusive today, we must remember the absolute reliance these people had on their horses. The term "horse-and-buggy days" implies slow speed, which we tend to associate with safety. But speed is relative, and twenty miles per hour in a wooden conveyance with no protection around you can be speedy indeed. From what I can gather, there were many accidents, injuries, and fatalities on the highways of America long before automobiles, most caused by teams out of control.

In our area, many young draft horses were trained with a device called the "running W." This consisted of a line that ran from within reach of the teamster, through a ring on the side of the harness, down to a ring hobbled to one front foot, up to another ring on the chest, down then to the second front foot, and up to the opposite side of the horse, where it was secured. The line formed the letter W; thus the device's name. With this contraption the teamster had compound leverage, could yank both front legs out from under the colt with designs on stampeding to the next town. Good teamsters used it judiciously, however, to avoid hurting the animal. Commonly they would take the harnessed horse onto soft ground, a newly plowed field or one covered with deep snow, drive him until the inevitable spook, holler "whoa!" and pull the line. The colt would go to his knees. Smart horses needed only one or two treatments, after which they stopped in their tracks when "whoa" was softly spoken. Severe, yes. Effective, very.

My father-in-law Elmer preferred instead a similar setup he called "foot ropes." These could be rigged on just one front leg when the colt was easygoing and gentle. I had heard that Magnus had a strong reputation as a trainer of work teams as well as saddle horses, so I asked Elmer once which method his father preferred. He laughed, his blue eyes flashing. "Oh, he didn't believe in any of this stuff. He just hooked the bronc up beside a gentle horse and took off." Magnus "controlled" runaways by hooking to a fairly heavy implement, then simply letting the horses run around the pasture by the house until they grew weary and stopped.

Elmer's story meshes well with notes left us by his older sister. They tell us that Emily's grandmother, Kristine, fervently religious, sometimes called her children into the house. "Come inside, children," she would say, "For Papa is training a team and we must pray for him."

Seasonal ranch work often required many men and many teams. Since horses are a herd animal, liking nothing better than to run bucking and join a passing stampede, the existence of other teams working nearby presented problems. The job of mowing hay was often given to boys and could be dangerous, for the mowers were ground driven, that is, the steel wheels furnished the power to propel the sickle back and forth. Strict instructions were given to never get off the mower without taking it out of gear. But accidents could and did happen. The driver would forget, stop the team to unplug the sickle bar, and get off in front of the bar. If the team spooked at that point, there were sometimes horrible consequences.

A man who had mowed with horses as a boy told me he learned to watch the other teams working in the valley, even those a great distance away. So contagious among horses is the tendency to herd up and run away together that horses miles apart can spot the fun when others run off, then bolt themselves. This boy was told that at first sign of someone else's team running away he was to immediately stop, take the mower out of gear, get off and snap a lead rope to the dominant member of his team, then just wait until the altercation was over.

This same man, a retired rancher named Wayne, lived next to us for a stretch and took on the job of training a tall, black gelding to harness. The horse's owner wanted a classy buggy horse, but this particular gelding considered the harness to be pure abuse. He hated being driven, hated everything about it, and he tried his level best to convince his trainer that the job was futile. But a sixty-five-year-old man who has tangled in his life with every variation of ill-tempered equine is not easily shaken loose. The gelding was subjected to running W's, log dragging, and eventually, grudgingly, seemed to accept the inevitability of his fate.

The trainer had guts. Perhaps his supply of that commodity was excessive, for he constantly pushed the colt to successive stages faster than I would have dared. Soon he was making trips up and down the highway in an antique sulky with elegant curves, a beautiful piece of workmanship lent him by the horse's owner. The sulky, enameled in British racing green and pinstriped with yellow, was striking, and it made an impressive picture pulled by the big black horse with the proud man on the seat, his cowboy hat tilted at a rakish angle. But the conveyance was hardly rugged enough for this use as the training vehicle for a recalcitrant colt. And yet, all seemed under control, and the running W was removed.

We had gone to church that sunny Sunday morning. Knowing that our neighbor was planning to drive the gelding, we looked forward to seeing them on the way home. Two miles short of our house, lying in the middle of the highway where the gravel road named Lover's Lane meets the pavement, I saw a piece of leather strap. I remember nearly dismissing it as just another piece of highway litter but with the disconnected thought, in passing, that it looked like a bit of broken harness.

A half mile closer to home there was more strange litter—several broken sticks, painted. Perhaps someone had been taking trash to the dump and had spilled this junk off an over-filled pickup bed. We still did not worry, still did not connect. We drove another hundred yards. Now there were pieces of splintered wood by the centerline of the highway. Finally, slow on the uptake as we had been, the truth came crashing in. The paint job on the wooden pieces was a distinctive green, the green of sports cars, and we realized to our horror that we were witnessing evidence of the disintegration of a very fancy sulky. Then it got worse. A bent wheel, another shaft, part of a seat, and then it was there, the remains, twisted and abandoned, the once-proud sulky overturned in the ditch by the side of the road. The only levity mixed into this trauma was recollection of a poem by Oliver Wendell Holmes I'd recently taught describing the disintegration of another horse-drawn vehicle, the Deacon's one-hoss-shay: "All at once, and nothing first, just as bubbles do when they burst."

We fully expected to see driver and horse dead by the debris, but to our relief, neither was there. We sped the car the remaining half mile and slid into the driveway of our neighbor's house, piling out and running to the kitchen door. The wife waved us in. Sitting in an easy chair was the erstwhile trainer, tough old bird that he was, sipping lemonade, his eyeglasses gone and his face bruised but otherwise perfectly fine. We were quickly told that the horse, too, was okay and had been turned into the corral.

"Everything went fine clear to that corner," Wayne told us. "But when I turned him toward home he just started kicking, and those long old legs were reaching all the way back to me. My lines weren't long enough to both hold onto and stay out of the way. Both his hind feet were right at my nose—I'll never forget as long as I live how big those iron shoes looked that close up—and I couldn't lean back far enough to keep them missing me without letting go of the lines. When I did that he headed home like a goosed antelope. All I could do was just hold on—he was going too damn fast for me to jump off. The pavement would have made hamburger out of me. Well, I did pretty good until we hit that chuckhole—damn the county, anyway, for letting the road deteriorate so—and then, well, you could see for yourself, the sulky just started coming apart. I rode 'er as long as I could, just hoping there would be enough left of it to get me to the driveway and damn grateful we landed in a soft place of the barrow pit."

We took the pickup and retrieved the remains of the sulky. I was building a small boat at the time and had plenty of epoxy resin and fiberglass cloth on hand. With that and numerous bolts we did manage to patch the vehicle back together. It never regained its former splendor, but it became serviceable again. It looked okay from a distance.

. . .

To a degree it is always dangerous, no matter how gentle the horses, this business of harnessing the power of big bruisers like Pancho and Lefty. In saddling a horse there are perhaps a half dozen safety considerations to keep in mind. In harnessing and hooking up a team there are dozens. Always you hook up the neck yoke first and unhook it last, for nothing is more frightening than the thought of a runaway in which the front of the tongue (which steers the vehicle) skids along the ground ready to catch on something and cause the ultimate wreck. Always you are careful, avoiding any scenario that could trap or drag you.

But once you learn to drive a team, once you work out the complications and can operate safely, there are so many rewards I constantly wish I could do it more often. It is so quiet. You are applying all this power to a task, yet hear nothing except an occasional jingle or creak and the sound of the implement you are pulling. Farmers and ranchers have notorious hearing problems, particularly in their left ears. This is because most farm implements are to the right side of the tractor, and in constantly turning to watch the implement, farmers expose their left ears to the high-frequency cacophony of the engine. We've become unused to power applied quietly and are nearly startled by it, like one who is new to sailing, unaccustomed to feeling tons of boat move uncannily along with just the flap of the sails and the creak of the rigging.

And when you think of sailing rather than powering a boat, deliberately choosing a simpler, more primitive, yet more rewarding way to complete a task does not seem so very eccentric after all. Many of us paddle a canoe rather than power a motorboat. We have wilderness areas nearby where it is legal only to walk or to ride a horse. I heat my house with wood, grateful for the opportunity to use the ranch's cottonwood and aspen trees to substitute for oil or gas or electricity. The requirements of heating our home do not even touch the growth of our river bottom timber, so except for the wear on my back and the mortality of chain saws, the heat is free. My father-in-law Elmer, however, lived for the day he would never have to split another block of wood.

"It took twelve big cottonwood trees a couple feet in diameter per winter," he told me, "and we were always cutting one winter ahead, so this fall we'd be cutting for nearly a year and a half in the future. That way it had time to dry. We'd saw it into stove lengths with a two-man crosscut saw. That was a job! Then we'd stack it till it froze good and solid, like in January. Then we'd go out with mauls and wedges and split it and stack it again so it would be dry the next winter. That wet old cottonwood split a lot better when it was frozen, you see." When Elmer bought and installed a Ziegler oil heater in the front room of the ranch house he lit it, then as it warmed, held his hands toward this magical heat gotten without the push-pull of the saw, the muscles in his arms, the sweat on his brow, and he said, "Boy, that's keen."

And so our generation has an easier time of it, but we crave some of the older, simpler things. Thoreau's directive to simplify is not lost on us. Yet, most of us talk a better Thoreau than we actually act. We want the good things that go with simplicity, but we don't want to give up the extra car, the eating out, the computer, or the kids' college fund. And this, I suppose, is why I do not sell my tractor and other sophisticated equipment and do everything with Pancho and Lefty and a couple of additional teams. There are, of course, other reasons. When our ranch was in full swing as a horse-powered operation, a father and two sons did the work and were supplemented by a half-dozen more hands during haying and harvest. An extra woman was hired to help with cooking three huge meals per day. Such help would simply not be available today, and workers with draft horse skills are truly impossible to find, even if one could afford to pay the required wages along with the workman's compensation, medical insurance, and Social Security.

Yes, I could ranch solely with horses, but my operation would have to be much smaller, my lifestyle extremely Spartan by today's standards, and the need would still be there for an outside job. I am not ready to make those changes. So I content myself with this occasional sojourn back to a simpler and perhaps better time. I drive Pancho and Lefty on the last couple rounds in the meadow and look at the field with satisfaction. Instead of a flat green, pockmarked with horse manure piles, I see the velvet of the newly stimulated grass, know what the nitrogen in the horse droppings combining with rain from the sky and irrigation water from the ditch will do by mid-July. The timothy will be as high as the wheels on the tractor.

Pancho and Lefty are now truly tired. I drop the harrow from the forecart by pulling the pin on the drawbar. The two step off smartly, nearly lurch. It must feel to them as it does when you remove a heavy pack after a long hike and your body almost seems to rise above the trail of its own volition. I want one more thing from these faithful two, and now, pulling only the light forecart, they seem perfectly pleased to supply it. We drive down the lane and across the bridge over Butcher Creek, then left through a gate into a meadow we call the calf pasture, a name it was given two generations ago that has stuck, though none of us really understand anymore how it applied.

It is not just interaction with the past, I know, that makes me love driving these big, plodding horses. It is interaction with creatures of flesh and blood, with hearts that beat and with muscles that, like mine, grow tired at the end of a long day. They have memories, too. They are individuals whose eccentricities are remembered for generations. Tractors are rarely so honored.

. . .

I drive the ditch bank in the calf pasture to check the weed situation, then angle back along a suspect section of fence, assessing the number of posts I'll need to drive to straighten it up. Then I turn the horses toward the sharp bend in Butcher Creek. It is foolish, I know, to seek a spook, but I guess that is what I am doing, for I have been thinking not just of Elmer but of his wife Nora, my mother-in-law. She could not speak of this pasture without mentioning the sharp bend in the creek. They had a team, you see, that was one day pulling the wagon around this bend when, from below the steep cutbank, a noisy flock of ducks squawked their way into the air. The team jumped and tried to run, but was quickly controlled. Nora told us of it many times, always laughing. "Well, do you know that forever afterwards, as long as they lived on the ranch, those two could not go near that bend in the creek without snorting and rolling their eyes and, yes, even if there were no ducks at the bend, giving us a good spook when we went past it?"

So as Pancho and Lefty approach the bend I foolishly expect them to spook as a tribute to that past team, to know via some kind of racial memory that on this ranch this bend is the proper place to spook. They seem uninterested. Then suddenly, just as we come up to the edge, there is a great commotion, squawking, quacking, splashing, and a flock of ducks takes to the air. Pancho starts, but momentarily. Lefty puts on a good show, gives two little bucks, then a good snort. I hit the brake on the forecart, yell "Whoa!," then laugh so hard I nearly fall off the seat. All is well on the ranch.

7

A big head of water · Reedy River · Hunting fish ·
Dead end · Sweet Charlotte · Steeplechase

*J*t has turned dry. Not hot-wind dry or dust-blowing dry, but dry enough to cause concern. The early June rains have "made" the first crop of alfalfa, to be cut soon, so the worry now is more for the dryland grasses and the timothy hay. We've been through it before, so we know what to do, and good rain may yet come. Meanwhile, all up and down the valley, ranchers are sighing, dusting off irrigation boots not used since last summer, patching the holes poked by the top strand of barbed wire fences when in carelessness one's leg has dragged a little low in climbing over. The ditches have been filled where they divert from the river, filled without the cooperative gang-cleaning they used to get when I was a boy.

We have lost some of that, I'm afraid. Nonresident landlords own more of the ranches now, and those places are rarely as well cared for by their hired managers as ranches occupied by their owners. But also the hurry of the late twentieth century has caught up with ranching, and people don't take time for what needs to be done. When I first worked on ranches as a teenager, I was often hired to join the gangs of men that walked each irrigation ditch from diversion point down each spring. Father and son, boss and hired man, all carried shovels to pitch in and remove anything that would impede a flow of water. Most common were natural dams created by logjams of branches, then further sealed by dead leaves and grass. Beavers, too, had done their work. It is the beaver's solemn duty to dam any flow of running water he can find. In this respect he has a great deal in common with past officers of the Army Corps of Engineers.

But the beavers in our valley have plenty of natural streams to pick on, and they annoy us by including irrigation ditches in their flood plains. We must take out, at great labor, the abandoned dams they built the fall before, digging out by hand each stick so skillfully sealed with mud. Thus the game is played, beavers seeing profit in water that is dammed, their human rivals in water that can flow freely until it is turned onto the fields.

Backhoes have replaced gangs of men in maintaining the ditches. They can do far more and do it faster, but their hire is expensive. Because of the expense, we do not hire them for small jobs, and so, too often, the small jobs do not get done.

I will be irrigating across the river on the west side of the valley. We have a forty-acre hayfield there, not the best field we own, for its soil is rocky and sops water like a sponge. Keep it wet, however, and it grows a good crop of grass hay. I am working on the ditch above the field, knocking down a new willow patch that grows in the ditch, ready to choke off the flow when it comes. It is hard, over here, to keep water where it belongs. The ditch does not have enough "fall." That is, it was surveyed rather flat, without quite the drop in elevation it should have had, so the slightest blockage means the water can rise and spill over the bank in an unwanted area. Further, the rocky soil means that the ditch bank is easily washed out, and if a spill over the bank goes too long undetected it enlarges alarmingly, grows from a shovel job to a backhoe deal, expensive, so we watch it closely. To irrigate across the river is to hope daily that when you arrive in the morning to change your set, there will still be in the ditch a good head of water.

I make the initial set now, with ditch still dry. First I place a stout pole across the ditch and settle it into small notches I have cut with the shovel on each bank. In a ditch with great power I would drive a stake behind the pole on each end, to keep the pressure of the water from skidding the pole downstream. Here, the notches will more than suffice. Then I place a dozen boards angled from the bottom of the ditch, their ends about three feet in front of the pole, sloped back at about forty-five degrees to rest on the pole. Side by side they make a wall of boards across the ditch, angled back. Now I unroll my "canvas," called that by tradition, for orange plastic replaced canvas on our ranch many years ago. This I lay across the boards. The canvas is long enough to run up onto the banks and wide enough to lie on the bottom of the ditch well forward of the boards. On that part, I place several rocks. Now, when the water comes, it will press the canvas into the bottom, banks, and board dam and make a seal. I have done what the beaver does. My dam is no better than his, but it is more portable.

The water should be here soon, and I really do not have to wait for it. I know how this first set works, have opened the shovel-sized cuts in the bank so that the water can run out and spread itself over the upper end of the field after the dam backs it up. At the lower end of the field the excess water will run off and back into the river, as clean as it was before but now, in irrigation lingo, called waste water. What soaks into the ground will return to the river as well, eventually, for it is irrigation water that supplies the springs at the base of the field. It all works well. Like the beaver, the early ranchers have raised the water table through their system of dams and ditches. The valley is green, the production of feed for livestock, wildlife, and humans greatly enhanced, and the river stays clear for the trout.

· · ·

The water must be close now, not far up the ditch. Emily and I turned it in last night, riding to the head of the ditch on our favorite of all rides together. I've learned from past years that the water takes overnight to come down. It leaves the river and runs in an old creek bed around abandoned beaver ponds, then through a long ditch before it enters our ranch. It takes so long to run two miles because in many places it must fill old ponds and depressions until it rises high enough to proceed again.

For the ride we take together to turn on the ditch, the lovely ride along the edge of the timber threaded by the river, the ride through the tree-lined lane to the old homestead, for this favorite of our rides Emily and I have a name. We call it our "Reedy River Ride." The name belonged to a folk song sung by a group called the Limelighters. In it, Glen Yarborough solos, tells of a homestead by Reedy River where he and his young wife built a cabin and were happy. The song turns sad at the end, the narrator returning to his homestead after many years. There are no traces left of the cabin he built. "The many rains have leveled the furrows of my plow." And of course, there is near the ruins, the grave of the one who shared it with him.

Pretty sentimental stuff, true, but real as well, real for us every time we travel the trail to the head of the ditch. We rode last night on Major and Sugar, single-footing along, now and then letting the horses lope. Once as we loped a fox ran across in front of us, retreating to the woods, and both our horses spooked once, hard, and we laughed. The woods and river were to our left as we rode, the ridge to our right. The long June day was finally playing out, the trail a mix of late sun and shadow.

We passed the apple orchard. Its trees, the variety called transparent, one of the few kinds that survive our altitude, have run their course, lived their lives, though enough branches are leafed out to promise a green-apple treat for us when we turn the ditch off next fall. Then I will ride Major underneath a limb and pick one for each of us. Transparents must be eaten green before they turn mushy, at least *I* think so. I practically grew up on them. Oh, those summer days when we swam in the icy Stillwater River until our bodies turned blue. We would get back into our dry clothes and turn our bicycles toward town, the warm wind blowing through our wet hair. So strategically placed we thought it was intended just for us, was a big transparent apple tree by the gravel road. Neophyte kids swept under, stood on the pedals, and reached up for an apple. The pros let go of the handlebars, raised both hands, and got two. How fine was that tart taste, riding with one hand and eating with the other the rest of the ride home.

At the homestead the horses got "boogery," as they always do. All those falling-down sheds, the uninhabited house, the big woodchucks skittering for cover, all bathed in the tricky shadowy light of near-dusk, all these things are ample excuse to look for a spook. We haven't owned a horse yet that did not jump sideways at least once when ridden through here. But if there are any ghosts in the log house, any peeking from the shattered windows or out of the hole in the roof where the tree branch fell, there could be but one, and a very good-humored and friendly one at that.

·   ·   ·

His name was Bernard. He lived here with his young family on this ranch that was too small to fully support them, working out at various jobs, motoring down the highway in his extravagantly painted yellow-and-red Jeep. He was a master hunter of whitetail bucks and, although he probably did not know it, a master humorist as well. As a hunter he did not work particularly hard, but he understood his quarry thoroughly. Knowing that Elmer did not care to hunt but loved the meat, Bernard each year would unceremoniously drop a dressed-out buck on the front porch. At daybreak Elmer and Nora would hear the *put-put* of Bernard's Jeep, through the window catch a glimpse of him, buck wrapped around his neck and over his shoulders, then hear it thump on the porch. He was on his way to work and had no time to stop. The deer was his calling card.

This was a generous act, but one with complications. Though hunting season was in progress, Bernard was never particularly worried about the law, so the animal rarely bore the validated tag that made it legal quarry. Elmer, like most ranchers, was no stranger to butchering, but this buck, visible on his porch from the highway, called for immediate action. So out came Elmer's sharpening stone while Nora assembled the knives, and the work began.

It was something I found while fly fishing that confirmed my belief that Bernard's sense of humor was of a rare, fine, and subtle sort. I knew that I had never been able to talk to him without grinning, and I guess what I found by the river that day told me why. I love to fish, but do so rarely, the demands of summer ranch work letting slip by the delicious time when the river clears from its spring flood, drops in level, and lets the browns and rainbows and brookies see the grasshopper fly I land gently on the water. On the rare occasions I find time to fish, I feel no qualm about keeping a limit for Emily to fry golden brown, perfect protein, a king's meal.

On an early August evening still too hot for the trout to be terribly active, I found myself a couple fish short of a supper, thus continued working my way upriver. Fly fishing resembles hunting more than it does muddy-water bait fishing or trolling from a boat. Actually, there is more than a resemblance. Fly fishing *is* hunting. In working small, clear streams you stalk your quarry, watch for subtle signs of him in shady pools, for his rising and feeding, and you place your curling cast just so, wait an instant, then, if he takes it, set the hook.

I move upriver very rapidly when I fish. Soon, on this particular evening, I was well into Bernard's place, to waters I did not know well, for the river changes every year, and it had been much longer than that since I had fished this stretch. Finally, I could proceed only by wading up the stream, for the banks were choked with a jungle of willow and chokecherry bush. Also, it was only standing in the stream that gave me room for the backward part of my cast. As I fished, then ducked brush, then slipped and slid on the moss-covered rocks below the clear, swift water, I worked up a sweat and found myself getting frustrated. Then I entered a corridor formed by still another small branch of the stream, thickets on each side, every step up the cobble-stone bottom hard work. I paused to straighten up for a rest, and it was then that I saw it.

Nailed on a big cottonwood trunk, in a place where no one not standing in the river could ever see it, was a stolen highway sign. It read *Dead End*. I stood in the middle of the river and laughed long and hard. Bernard had died ten years earlier, taken by colon cancer at age forty. But he was there with me then with his throaty, hearty laugh, proving himself that rare type who could go to infinite trouble to create a joke that, on this rarely fished stretch, no one would ever be likely to see. But now I was in on it, and I wished there were some way he could know.

· · ·

And so, last night, while Emily and I rode our geldings to the head of the ditch, there was as usual much to talk about. But we were silent. Sometimes we are too full to talk. We rode past the place where Bernard put his haystack. Strategically placed to be shaded by a cottonwood from the afternoon sun, a mercy for the boy doing the stacking, the haystack has now been replaced by the big round baler of the rancher who leases Bernard's place. He hauls the hay out to his home place. But as we rode by I could see the stack as I built it and remember a day that was hay-stacker's heaven.

I was young and in good shape, used to stacking against two loaders, used to tightly cramming into its proper niche each of the bales brought me by one loader fast enough that I could sit down for a few seconds before the next one dumped another dozen bales. At Bernard's there was only his old Allis Chalmers tractor. That would have slowed the proceedings enough to cut my water intake by half from its usual gallon by noon, but there was also the man's disposition and the fact that we had in common, the night before, a Bette Davis movie at the Cub Theater in town. The movie was *Hush, Hush Sweet Charlotte*. Its haunting song was on my lips as I hooked the bales and stomped them into place, the Bette Davis eyes, big and sad in black and white, hovering still in my vision. Bernard was similarly haunted. He would bring me a load, which I easily stacked before he got his old tractor to the end of the field. Then I sat down to rest. But after the next load I would hear, as I bent to my task, the tractor's engine stop abruptly. I would finish, then walk to the edge of the stack and see Bernard sitting on the tractor looking up at me. He wanted to talk.

"How about that hand that's been cut off," he said, shaking his head. And then we would talk about the movie. Just when I was beginning to feel guilty about whatever wages he planned to pay me, he would fire up the old orange tractor and head out for a couple more loads. But I had to be happy he was paying me by the hour rather than by the bale, as the faster outfits did. There would have been little profit otherwise. He was the only rancher I ever knew (myself included) who would slow down during haying to talk about a movie, who would risk rain on the hay to get something off his mind. We had seen that morning the puffy clouds around the mountains that the old-timers called "scouts," clouds that mean thundershowers in late afternoon. But that did not keep him from giving *Hush, Hush Sweet Charlotte* a thorough wringing out.

"He was quite a guy," Emily said. She did not need to verify that we were thinking alike.

"He sure was."

"Remember the time you shot the buck on top of the hill and Daddy's Jeep quit?"

"Yeah. There was something about parking that Jeep on a steep hillside."

"So we walked down to the house and Bernard put us in *his* Jeep and we went up and gave Daddy's a pull."

"I was a little scared of that one-eyed dog at first."

"He *was* scary. And remember the time he brought the family down to visit when we lived in the little house right after we got married. And we played that new Chad Mitchell Trio record, and Bernard made us play 'The Marvelous Toy' over a couple times. He kept asking, 'But what *is* it?'—the toy, he meant. It drove him nuts that they never told exactly what the toy was."

"Yes," I said. I had thought I had run through my musings about Bernard, because in truth we did not see him that much or feel we knew him that awfully well. But everything Emily said brought back another scene.

She went on. "And remember we had Prince, the half Dalmatian and half Lab, and Bernard wasn't used to a shorthaired dog. And when Prince lay down and scratched himself, Bernard said, laughing that kind-of-dirty laugh he had, that Prince just looked naked to him."

At this point we arrived at the bend in the fence where several railroad ties are used as brace posts. We tied our horses to these solid posts, climbed the fence, and descended into the woods by the river. Our ditch setup here has been remodeled and now works pretty well. There is a small side channel out of which the ditch forks. Filling the ditch used to require standing in the river, throwing boulders into the water, renewing a little wing of rock that raised the level just enough to spill into the ditch. Now we are relatively modern. There is a steel headgate. The gate of steel plate at the head of a culvert is heavy, and last night I had to improvise a lever, using a pole and some fence wire to break it free. But when I did a gush of river entered the ditch. We could go home now. It was nice in this quite place, and we might have stayed a while, have in the past lingered there together, but the sun was completely down now, and it would soon be dark. Besides, we relished the ride back.

. . .

Our horses, too, have always relished the return. As usual, last night they would have galloped the entire way had we let them. The dark was setting in, so for safety's sake we only let them lope a little. Besides, a gaited horse is at its very best when it would really rather run but you do not let it, when you hold its head back in an arch, it tucks its hind end, and the feet go *rat-tat-tat,* the aspen trees along Bernard's lane flying by like a picket fence. We were soon back to our gate, then to the river, crossing its first branch in a cloud of spray. Between the rivers is a path I call my steeplechase, a path with twists and turns and logs to jump, and there I gave Major a few ounces less pressure on the reins. He responded by leaping into a lope. We flew around the curves and over the logs, Emily and Sugar just behind, Emily telling Sugar "Easy!" a couple times but still staying right on our tail.

Then we were to the second branch of the river, and we reined back. One splashing had been enough, and also it was now truly dark, so we eased the horses under overhanging branches, threading them the rest of the way through the brush, through the gate, across the highway, and home. It was a good ride, as always. It is a ride we relish, sometimes looking for excuses to do.

As we unsaddled in the dark Emily asked a question she has asked before. "We'll always be able to do that, won't we. I mean, if a rich Californian buys that ranch, we can still ride up there, can't we."

"Legally, yes. We have sole water rights on that ditch—it's named after your grandpa—and Montana law says that gives us an easement of so many feet on each side for maintenance purposes. On the other hand, it could get sticky if someone with bad intent had enough money. Remember that actor who bought the ranch up south of Livingston and promptly padlocked a gate into the Forest Service, a gate everyone in the area had used for fifty years, for hunting, fishing, hiking, whatever. Said he was 'protecting the critters.' Even ran the Forest Service off. He's legally wrong as hell, but he's got the money for lots of lawyer power, and its been in court a couple years and the gate's still locked." Emily shuddered, and I realized I had gone too far. "There's really not much to worry about, Hon. The extended family loves the place. I think they'll keep leasing it, not sell it; they'll keep it a ranch."

Now, early on the morning after, I remember Bernard again after setting my dam, and I follow his example. I need not wait for the water. My dam is set and ready. I have tasks to be done stacked a mile high back home. Yet, why do all this if it can't include once in a while a brief rest on the bank of the ditch, the morning still cool enough to make the warm sun seem pleasant, waiting for my head of water. I look at my watch, begin to get concerned, wonder if a trash dam above is spilling it all over the bank, and then I see in the bottom of the big ditch above me a trickle of water, dirty from its run over the dry ditch bottom, the vanguard water. I watch it bubble with air from cracks in the soil on the bottom of ditch, watch it the way a little kid would, surface tension holding the very edge of it back as it rises among twigs and blades of grass, then advances.

In fifteen minutes most of the head is here, rising in front of my dam, and in another fifteen it is high enough to run out of the cuts I've made in the bank. Rivulets begin to finger their way among the stalks of growing timothy, bubbling into the ground. I have what makes this valley green, what Magnus and others in his generation engineered to make this a productive place. I have a good head of water.

8

Dry times · A shovel for a shield

Two days after I begin irrigating across the river, we get a nice rain, nearly an inch, and I hear it with pleasure on the roof above the loft room where Emily and I sleep. She hears it too, snuggles, and repeats her dad's, "More rain, more rest." Then, "We don't really have to get up, do we?" During the school year we get up at 5 a.m. During summer we turn slovenly, sleeping an hour longer, knowing of course, that daylight saving time and the workload of a ranch, yeast-filled like sourdough starter, always expanding to fit more than the available time, will keep us working after supper until nine.

The rain will not affect my irrigating. It would take many inches of moisture before I would consider suspending it or postponing the twice-daily setting of the dam. But it takes the pressure off. I can imagine this rainy morning a collective sigh of relief all up and down the valley, other ranchers also staying in bed a little extra time under the luxury of rain on the roof. When it is dry, people turn testy. During an actual drought, *testy* is too light a word. *Nasty* would be better.

So this morning I enjoy myself thoroughly, even lingering in bed fifteen minutes after Emily has slipped downstairs, lie there until the smell of coffee brewing wafts up to me (for that fetches my Norwegian blood more readily than anything). And during that extra rest I recall a drought summer not too long ago, a summer when the grass crisped before the Fourth of July, when the cows suffered and we suffered and idiotic Billings weathermen described these conditions that were torturing every living thing except the grasshoppers as "nice, 100 degrees, no *threat* of showers."

The hay refused to grow well no matter how we irrigated, for grass hay especially seems to need something in real rain that irrigation water doesn't supply. The grasshoppers came down from the dryland and ate even the leaves off the chokecherry bushes along Butcher Creek ditch. It was during that summer that something happened between two old Norwegians named Nils and Helmar. I knew them both, for both attended my dad's church throughout my boyhood, and the sunny dispositions they exhibited there would not have hinted at certain other dimensions in their personalities.

Helmar was one of a large family of brothers, many of whom also ranch nearby. I knew him as good-humored, his lined face almost clownlike, his lips stained with an ever-present wad of chewing tobacco, referred to as "snoose" in these parts. Nils I knew considerably better, for he sang in my dad's choir in town and I, like my brothers, had been drafted into choir the instant my voice took a cracking downward turn. I liked Nils, talked to him a great deal, and heard many good stories. He told me of his arrival at Ellis Island with twenty-five silver dollars in his pocket. In a short time half were gone, he said, because everything in New York cost a dollar. A cup of coffee was a dollar, he said, or at least he never got change. This was early in the century, when a cup of coffee was five cents. Nils told me that another more savvy immigrant finally filled him in. "They're cheating you. You're supposed to get change."

"I felt pretty dumb," Nils confided, "but I'm glad the man told me that, 'cause my money was yust about gone." He told me too of being drafted for World War I, of the news of the armistice coming just as he was being loaded onto the troop ship, of a fight with a big sergeant who said afterwards, "That Norwegian's a strong son of a bitch." Nils, like Helmar, was already an old man during my boyhood, but I could see still the strength in his sloping shoulders, the knotted muscles in his arms, and the ease with which he carried his body. I have been told that when the local ski resort first opened up, he went there, strapped on skis for the first time in fifty years, and headed down the slope with complete aplomb.

I knew primarily Nils' sunny side, but I never had trouble imagining the other one. I'd heard tales of a terrible temper, and I saw plenty evidence of his stubbornness. But then, that was par for the course with the old Norwegians. They were tough people. They had left home, most at age sixteen, and set out for a new life in a place half a world away. Like most immigrants they had been at first abused and cheated, and if conditioning by the North Sea to be tough had not already been adequate, the frontier took care of the rest. And in this new world of the West to which they came, there was nothing more precious, nothing more essential, nothing for which they would be more willing to fight, than the water that ran in their irrigation ditches.

In this part of the West our culture, our industry, and our history as a people are intertwined with water. Even today in looking at a ranch to purchase, the buyer (if he or she is of our ranching mentality) looks first at its water, its springs and stream access for livestock to drink, and, on irrigated acreage, the legal standing of irrigation water referred to as "water rights." These are all-important, the earliest having precedence. On our ranch the filing of first water rights reveals how critical this issue was to the first generation. One of the squatters Magnus bought out, another Dane, had filed rights on his ditch not just with the local government but in Copenhagen, Denmark, as well! Perhaps wondering how long the upstart government of this wild territory would last, he sought some comfort from the seal of the government back home.

Well, take people who are strong and stubborn, throw in an inherited feud, let a summer turn dust-blowing dry, then think of the small creek that supplies both men's irrigation ditches as dropping day by day until it becomes a trickle. Mix this all together and you have a recipe for an explosion. This is the formula for the threat

I heard several times during my growing up, articulated in heavy Norwegian accent: "Well, I'll yust trow that sonofabitch in the ditch."

Only recently did I learn of the long-standing animosity between Nils and Helmar, for, as I said, they did not show it around my dad or the church. The most religious of the Norwegians considered church to be neutral ground and coexisted there even with bitter rivals. The Lutheran Church had been their state church in Norway, the pastors figures of authority on two counts, one religious, one civil. The people expected ministers to tell them what to do, and they behaved when the minister was around. There were those who would simply quit coming to church because it was frequented by an enemy, but neither Nils nor Helmar was in that category.

What happened on that dry day during that parched summer has been told to me by several friends, for it is now permanent folklore. All versions substantially agree, but I sought out that of a rancher friend who was actually there. He tells me that both Helmar and Nils had ditches running out of Antelope Creek, a small tributary that carries little water of its own in best of times and keeps running during dry summers primarily with waste water from irrigation projects upstream. This particular summer, as the drought intensified, there was no longer enough water to fill the ditches of both Nils and Helmar.

Helmar's ditch branched from the little stream a small distance above where Nils' turned out, so Helmar had an automatic advantage. The civilized way of handling the problem, of course, would have been to take turns. But it is hard to arrange schedules when you do not talk to your neighbors. Helmar had put a dam across the little creek, diverting water into his ditch, and this meant that down below there was not enough water for Nils to do likewise. So, muttering all the way, Nils had come upstream and yanked out Helmar's canvas dam.

The next morning Helmar popped the first chewing tobacco of the day into his mouth, donned his rubber boots, and headed out to the field, several acres of which he expected to find flooded with the irrigation water from his first set. But what had happened? Dry as it was, a night's irrigation should already show in the field. There should be a nice, green band of grass where the water had run, contrasting with the brown of the rest of the field. But there was no such thing!

Helmar found his ditch bone dry, traveled to its head, and discovered the heinous crime. Pulling out another man's dam is cause for war in this country. "Goddam," he said, "dat man's yust a goddam thief, yah, a thief." And he promptly resituated his boards and put back the canvas dam. Then he followed his water down the ditch to his other dam, the one that spilled the water onto the thirsty field, and watched with satisfaction as the water trickled through the cuts and down onto the parched ground.

That same morning, Nils did see a green band across his dry field, smiled with satisfaction, and went to his ditch to make his second set. But above his dam where water should have been backed up three feet deep there was nothing but mud already beginning to dry, flies buzzing around on it. A walk to the creek revealed why. He swore, swore loudly in both Norwegian and English, then positively fumed. He swung his shovel in an overhead arc, cracking it against a boulder so hard the handle snapped like a toothpick. Then he set off toward his house at a dead run.

．　．　．

Now, an hour went by before my friend and his father arrived on the scene, driving to check their cattle through the buildings of an old homestead near the ditches of Nils and Helmar. My friend got out to open a gate, caught a movement in the corner of his eye, then saw Helmar furtively walk toward them. He had recognized their pickup.

"What the hell are you doing?" my friend asked as Helmar slunk up to them.

Even today my witness can't tell me what Helmar said without nearly convulsive laughter. Helmar stuttered, especially when riled, and he said, "N-N-Nils has got a gun! B-B-B-But I held the sh-sh-sh-shovel over my heart so couldn't hit me there!" And as he said it he demonstrated, standing erect, his tall gangling figure at full

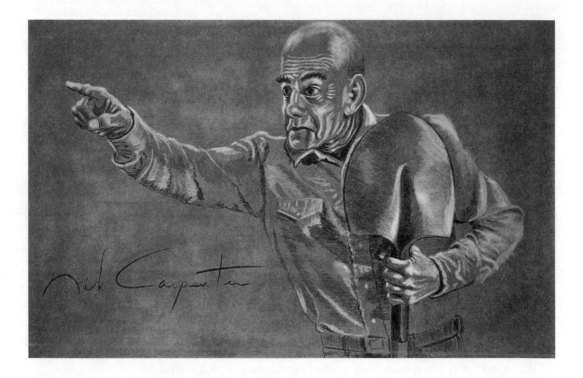

height, holding the long-handled shovel inverted with the tip of its blade just below his chin, the rounded blade with its shiny bottom turned out and catching the sun like Don Quixote's shield. His lined face was white with fear, his eyes big, his brown, tobacco-stained lips dribbling snoose juice from both corners.

It is not Helmar's fear that was laughed at that day or that we all laugh about every time we hear the story, for the man had a right to be afraid. We laugh because of the ridiculous situation. These were two old men, related by marriage, neighbors who had in common their religion, their ethnic background, their occupation, and even some of their relatives. One had survived immigration and a host of other vicissitudes, yet was ready to toss it all away by shooting his neighbor over a trickle of water. The other, equally foolish, really thought he was protecting himself with the thin blade of a shovel held over his heart.

Both men survived this and other conflicts and lived long. Both are gone now. We remember their stalwart qualities too, not just their foolishness. We understand how drought can drive a person wild. We had affection for them and miss them. And so, before I answer the call of perking coffee on a rainy morning I say a silent thanks for the rain on the roof, the rain that might keep us from going quite as crazy as two old Norwegians during a summer of drought.

9

White shorts and tennis shoes

*I*t has continued to rain. We appear to be getting a traditional set-in June storm, cold enough at our altitude to prompt a fire in the woodstove. Over several days three inches have come down, enough to keep things green well past the Fourth of July, so we take joy in that, even while edging toward cabin fever. Montanans do not do well when deprived for very long of their big sky. Also, relatives are visiting. It is nice to see them, but the rain makes it harder, for coming from territory totally paved, they haven't learned mud control. We do our best to train them in our nearly Oriental dedication to removing shoes in the "mud room," but this is difficult for them, and their shoes continually release squiggles of mud on the kitchen floor. It is a small thing, true, but I am stubborn and am certain I can train them. When they forget to remove their shoes I stare at their feet while I talk to them. Usually this works, but then I feel guilty. They are good people.

I have to get out of the house. Emily is not a very willing foul-weather rider, and I'm a lousy foul-weather host. She agrees that the cattle need checking (but she knows what I'm up to). I head out the door with apologies to the guests, my slicker under one arm, Tom Sawyer escaping from Sunday school. Major, too, is anxious to go. He is so wet that as I curry him I pull off sheets of water which splash down on my boots. But there is from time to time a brief lull in the rain, a thin spot in the clouds, a good omen.

Under the protection of the tack room roof, I take time to rag a coat of neats-foot oil onto my saddle. Then I throw it on Major and we "light out for the territory." Even in the rain I am liberated. I wonder what I would be psychologically without this space around me, shudder, and force myself to think happier thoughts.

We slog through the mud up the wagon road to the top of the hill. I have avoided the steep trail on the side of Indian Coulee, a concession to safety. Major has not yet been shod, and I'd rather not go skidding down a sidehill. The rain has all but stopped, the hole in the clouds enlarging. And then it hits, just as I top out, the stubborn sun finally born again, grudgingly at first, the sagebrush flat bathed in yellow halftone. Then the theater lights come fully on and the range in front of me is as green as Ireland. I'm quite smug about my timing.

The cattle check is routine, at least at first. I check the salt trough, find the supply waning, worry for an instant about getting up here with the pickup and a resupply, muddy as it is, then remember the two-year-old mare I need to start in training. Nothing more quickly trains a new young horse to accept weight on its back and to ignore strange touches and sounds than to pack a hundred pounds of salt up the hill. I can get her to that stage in a couple days, put a sawbuck pack saddle and panniers on her, and throw a fifty-pound salt sack in each side.

The next thing to check for is the presence of the bulls, errant critters who sometimes look to the other side of the fence not just for better grass but for hotter cows. (The guys always think the girls in the neighboring town are prettier.) I quickly see three of the four. Breeding is still going steadily, for the cows are in small bunches, a bull with each, not scattered randomly. Far to the south there is a large black critter that could be a bull, but he is too far away to tell for certain, and I've spared my binoculars a wetting by leaving them home. So Major and I ride half a mile until we can see that, yes, this is the fourth bull.

It turns out to be a fortunate detour. Along the way we find a black baldy cow whose calf moves strangely, it's head held just a bit to the side. We get up to the pair and I see what I feared—the calf has a nose full of porcupine quills. His face looks like a pincushion. From what I can see the steer calf has been spared the worst a porcupine can dish out, for his eyes look clear and I can see no quills through them. But he's a mess. Left unattended he will either starve or die from a quill working its way back into the brain. We worry about predators, but in some ways porcupines, rabies-spreading skunks, and marauding raccoons cause us more grief. All have their places in nature, I know, but I have little good right now to say about the critter that has caused my liberating ride to turn into actual work.

Oh, well. At least the rain has stopped. Before the work begins I shed my slicker and tie it behind the cantle. It is not yet all that warm, but by Montana standards the humidity is up there. Major's wet hide, heated up by the sun and his exertions, gives off clouds of steam. Were I a better cowboy and in condition to relish wrestling and tying this calf, I would rope it and pull out the quills with my Leatherman tool. But neither of those things is true, and the calf, born in February, already weighs about 300 pounds. Instead we'll cut out the pair and do our best to get them home to the corral. This will be touchy on such slippery footing, for the cow will have the edge on Major, who is barefoot and packing considerable weight.

It proves quite easy, however. The calf is enough affected by his condition to be rather subdued, and the cow is a good mother, sticking with him like glue. So the two line out down the wagon road. At the bottom of the hill we take them through a gate into the hayfield, down through a meadow, and soon have them trotting down the lane into the corral. In less than half an hour after discovering the calf, Major and I have brought them two miles in.

So now I need to get the calf into the alleyway which runs to the squeeze chute. This effort is hampered by what three inches of rain does to corrals—the mixture of mud and manure is a foot deep with the consistency of chocolate pudding. I feint this way and that, trying to get the cow and calf into the smaller pen, hear a sucking sound and realize I've left my overshoe-covered cowboy boot planted in the mud. I do a backward hop on my weak left leg and manage to insert my foot back into the boot. (None of the alternatives would be pretty.)

I know I should go to the house and get help, Emily and Steve, but I keep thinking I can get this done without the delay that would cause. So it's back and forth, slogging until the sweat runs down my face, flecks of mud and manure catapulted onto me by eight hooves every time I turn the cow and calf, my eyeglasses speckled with the stuff, my clothes covered, my disposition edging gradually in very violent directions, an involuntary stream of wretched language coming effortlessly from my mouth. And then I realize I'm being watched.

Visiting Relative is standing well back from the corral, where the gravel is good and there is no mud. He has been watching my frustration. He says, "Is there any way I can help?" He seems to mean it, and for a moment I'm encouraged, for one human standing in just the right place to keep the cow from running there would make this entire ordeal into a piece of cake. Then I look at him.

He is wearing a white knit shirt, white shorts, and white tennis shoes. He is spotless. No, he is more than spotless, he is squeaky clean. Alongside him Moby Dick would look small and dark. I swear I can smell his cologne. I look down at my decimated clothing, take off my glasses to wipe the droplets of brown manure into a translucent stain, and say back to Visiting Relative, "No, thanks a lot, but I'm certain I'll get it eventually."

And, of course, I do, and once the calf is in the chute pulling the quills is no big deal. And all along I think of just how right Thoreau was when he bragged about getting all the good things from his neighbors' farms without the work, the mortgage, and the worry. He can take walks across their fields, he says, for which the farmers can find no time. Visiting Relative will enjoy fishing in "my" river while he is here, something I will not have time to do, will take his family on several hikes, will kick back, drink beer, and relax. I will play catch-up on the work I missed during the rainy days. I do not begrudge him his fun, for this is his vacation and he works hard at his job. But standing in the mud and looking at him in white shorts and tennis shoes has been much like looking at a visitor from another planet. His offer to help, though sincere, is useless.

Those of us who stay on the land incur a social obligation, not just a business one. We are forever hosts to the extended family. At best, most ranches will only support a single family unit, so where do the brothers and sisters go? Los Angeles, Seattle, Cincinnati. And because a ranch is the ultimate home, it remains so to all, remains a place toward which part of the psyche of all who have known it inclines like the salmon to where it was spawned. This is understandable and good, for the ranch could be a lonely place without visitors.

But it brings wrinkles too. We have been fortunate, but I have heard many stories. At branding time on a neighboring ranch a new wife showed up with a Cleveland Amory book tucked under her arm. She criticized what she saw, was not taken seriously, then pouted in the house and refused to come out for lunch because meat was served. A city-dwelling brother was upset with the tearing down of a shed that was careening toward the creek, because he had good boyhood memories of it. It was his secret private place where he kept a clandestine pack of cigarettes, and it was hard for him to accept what thirty years does to an aged shed, that the building was beyond saving. A friend to whom I've explained the white shorts and tennis shoes syndrome tells me I was lucky in the incident described. "I've had similar things happen where the relative didn't offer to help, but stood there staying clean and told me how I ought to be doing the job, all the things I was doing wrong." The man who told me this operates a ranch in which other members of his family retain some financial interest, a common scenario. With today's divorce rate, such interests can soon be owned by strangers, strangers who, if they ever demand their shares be turned into liquid cash, can force sale of the ranch.

But that is the down side. I have been lucky and thus will not dwell on it. The magnetic field sent out by our ranch is primarily a good thing. It contains the grin on a child's face when I set the toddler up on Major, the reins firmly in my hand, the child wearing the cowboy hat his parents have bought him on the way to the ranch just for this occasion. And there are the rewards that come with seeing a skeptical urbanite gain respect for what we do here. A visiting lawyer, married to a cousin, tittered when we talked of breeding the mares, treated everything with a hint of condescension. When I showed him what we did, talked of timing the mare's ovulation for artificial insemination, explained the drug therapy we had used on the old mare to get her to cycle, he seemed puzzled at first. The scientific complexities of these things did not fit the stereotypes he held. Finally, the puzzled look changed to one of interest and finally, I think, even to admiration. He then began asking intelligent questions.

So after I get the quills pulled from the steer calf's nose I calm down, any anger I have had evaporating. I show Visiting Relative a place on clean footing he can stand and still be of help, for the cow and calf upon leaving the corral gate have to be initially turned the correct direction. With a glance at his blazing whiteness they not only turn the right way, they skitter off like scalded cats. I have them back to the hill gate in ten minutes. Then I go to the house and have lunch with the relatives.

10

Starting a filly

She is a pretty thing, bay, her coat edging toward red, with black mane and tail and a chiseled face. She is so well made we have called her China Doll. Her dam, Emily's favorite mare, was much like this daughter and, though spirited, was one of the easiest horses I ever started under saddle. I have found that intelligent, spirited horses are often the easiest to train. Perhaps this is because responsiveness is important in shaping a good horse.

She dances on the end of the longe line, circling around me in the round corral, trying in turn each of the three gaits with which she is most at home: flat walk, running walk, and canter. I will not do much of this. Our horses mature more slowly than Thoroughbreds or Quarter Horses, which have been selectively bred to compete at age two. Walkers often grow until they are five and seem also to be longer-lived. Work in a circle can be hard on their young legs and tendons, so I minimize this stage of training. I'm training impulsion. A canoe cannot be steered unless it is making headway, and it is much the same with horses. Going forward on command is elemental.

I will also begin to teach "whoa" on the line, train the filly to turn and face me and stop when she hears that command.

One can also do all this loose, without the line, using "whip training," a harsh-sounding name for a procedure that is actually benign and extremely useful. Whip training has nothing to do with whipping horses. The whip is a signal device. It's snap causes a zone of discomfort, while the trainer who manipulates it is within the zone of comfort. Colts that are quite wild and tough to catch often respond particularly well. Instead of roping and snubbing to a post in the center of the round corral (as illustrated in dozens of Grade B Western movies), the colt is simply kept moving round and round, with the whip casually snapped behind him to keep him moving. After a time he tires. He is allowed to stop only if he also turns toward the trainer, who facilitates this tendency by backing up and giving the colt space. The trainer turns tough only if the colt does the one thing that can't be forgiven or allowed, turning his back on the trainer. Remember, the back end is the loaded one. A colt's turning its back on the trainer is sometimes simply an attempt to escape. But at other times, when its ears are laid back, this action is as hostile as the growl of a German Shepherd dog.

Gradually, through a process psychologists call "shaping," the colt learns that standing and facing the trainer gets him out of all sorts of difficulties, and soon he learns that walking toward the trainer relieves him of yet more pressure. The process reminds me of the old story of the psychology class that decided to "shape" its professor. A plan was hatched one day before the professor arrived. It was simply this: The class gave a positive response to his lecture when he was located near the doorway. Since the professor was a natural pacer who used the whole front of the room in the course of a lecture, it was easy to sit up, nod in agreement, laugh at his jokes, and ask intelligent questions whenever he was in the vicinity of the door. When he moved away from the door, the students began to fidget. Their eyes glazed over. They quit asking questions, and their gazes strayed toward the windows. Supposedly,

by the end of the term the professor was delivering his entire lecture standing just inside the door.

A trainer skilled with this method and its tool, the whip, can often have a wild colt eating out of his hand in a very short time and with far less trauma or risk of injury than with that rope-and-snub approach. Each time the colt relapses by running away, the trainer simply keeps him going again, and soon the colt figures out it is easier to cooperate. After a bit the trainer can not only catch and halter the animal but rub it all over and pick up its feet. This method can be used to teach "whoa," an absolutely essential development, and a host of more sophisticated commands. On a higher plain the method becomes "free longeing," longeing without a line to the colt, the trainer using only body language and voice commands to start and stop the animal, to make it alter direction, and to make it change gaits.

I have done none of this with the filly, however. She was handled on her first day of life and has been several times since. Although she has not been haltered for many months, she merely circled the round corral a few times when I first entered, then allowed me to approach and touch her shoulder. At the first awareness of restraint, when the lead rope encircled her neck, she started back but did not pull hard. Then I haltered her and led her to the hitching rail. I rubbed gently on one of the places horses cannot resist, the spot just under each eye. With the other hand I scratched her withers. She accepted the curry warily, since it sneaked to previously untouched places such as the underside of her belly, but soon that, too, was okay.

So now I am teaching her the rudiments of longeing, not planning to accomplish too much on this first session. I'm simply establishing a relationship with her. Had she projected a different attitude when I first corralled her, I might have approached this project completely different. I guess I do not really have a "method" for starting colts, if that means a set of rigidly sequenced accomplishments. I know of and admire many of the modern equine gurus, John Lyons, Pat Parelli, Ray Hunt, and the several who claim to be the real "horse whisperer." I admire their work and concede that all have trained more horses some summers than I will in a lifetime. I am not a professional trainer (although I do occasionally start a colt for someone else), and my only claim to success is the fact that I've turned the colts I have started into good, useful, cooperative animals, that I have been pleased with the results.

But I'm *not* ready to concede that any one of these fine modern trainers has the last word or the only set of methods which work. Horse training is an area of life in which you learn something every day and every time you talk to another trainer. New horses teach you new things. You learn until the day you quit, and even then, you don't know everything. Too, horse training on a high level is a competitive, lucrative business. The famous trainers hold clinics that earn much money. They sell products tailor-made for their methods, along with videotapes and books. The implication that their methods are the best, even the *only* ones with which to approach training a horse, is understandable. Exclusivity makes for profit and success, and I have no argument with that.

I draw the line at stereotyping the horsemanship of earlier generations, however. So many times I have seen a television special about a trainer who does it a new way—the implication being that all past ways, particularly western ones, were cruel, crude, rough, and inhumane. Now wait a minute. Let's give some credit to several thousand years of horsemanship during which horses were not primarily objects of pleasure and amusement but tools so essential that you lost the battle to survive, to get your family safely moved, to get a crop in, to hold off an enemy, if they did not perform for you. And let's accept that you don't achieve the best performance by abusing or mistreating animals, and that intelligent horse trainers figured that out some centuries ago.

I told in the first section of this book about Magnus's traveling to the Crow Reservation in the 1890s, buying fifteen or twenty unbroke horses, picking one out for a crash course in being a saddle horse, and driving the rest 200 miles home with this new pupil. He would then saddle-train the others for sale. I'm certain he considered it all a pretty routine matter. Another man, now in his eighties and still driving teams, told me of a winter in the Thirties he spent training teams for spring farming. He had land to farm and no trained horses. So he bought a bunch of range horses between four and eight years old, most of which had never been touched by a rope. They were driven to his place in January. By April he had trained five four-horse teams and one three-horse team, twenty-three horses field-ready. Even though he hired a bunch of inexperienced boys to help him farm, he never had any problem with the teams. "I never had a single runaway," he said with pride.

"That was quite an accomplishment," I told him.

"Well, yes, I guess it was. But I never thought anything of it. I had to work through them and match them both in size and disposition. They were good teams when I got done." We'll never know whether modern trainers could equal the performance of these old-timers in a similar situation and whether, if they could, they would do so with the methods they currently espouse. Who knows, maybe they would do even better. And maybe they wouldn't.

There is a wonderful song once sung together by Willie Nelson and Waylon Jennings. The song deals with internal strife within a band, something with which both singers have great experience. If memory serves, its key line warns you not to cuss the fiddle player if you expect the fiddle to play in tune. That is a wonderful line about leadership, and it applies equally to the band, to the office, and to the corral. Leadership is not about abusing those under you, not if you expect them to perform.

. . .

Here is the "Aadland Theory" about horse training: "Training is the application of the very best principles of leadership to an unschooled animal, and schooling him while governed by those principles." Okay, so where does partnership fit in? We see a ninety-pound horsewoman exhibiting a 1,400-pound warmblood stallion in the dressage ring, and we are told that this represents the ultimate partnership between rider and horse. Sorry, but it does not, not if partnership means that the two are equal. They can now work as partners *only* because this little lady or someone like her early in the game applied leadership and made it absolutely clear who the leader was. But then, because the leadership was the good kind, the horse eagerly accepted its training.

There is nothing cruel about this. Most of us are leaders and most of us have leaders. The principle is simple enough. When I was a jumpy new second lieutenant in the Marine Corps a colonel walked to the podium and put us at ease. He said, "Sit down, Gentlemen. My name is Jones, but I'd like you to call me by my first name— Colonel." We laughed even while being reminded of our subordinate relationship to him. At a reception, one-on-one, this officer proved the most approachable one I had met, personable and kind.

My mention of the Marines is no accident, for in that organization I discovered the best leadership I have ever known, before or since. No, I am not talking about the highly publicized nose-in-your-face yelling with which drill instructors are stereotyped. I am talking about the leadership that causes men and women to do extremely brave things and to do them willingly. In the Marine Corps the officers eat last, after all the troops have been fed. They also do the things they expect their subordinates to do. The first time I rappelled out of a helicopter I went first of the thirty men aboard for one simple reason: I was the officer present. (It was my job to be an example, and I doubt whether anyone knew I was scared as hell. I stood with my heels on the edge of the chopper's tailgate, glanced over and down at the tops of the power poles below me and below them, eighty feet down, the pavement. Then I jumped backward into space.) And throughout their operations two principles of leadership are always made clear. First comes the mission. Second, and close behind, is the welfare of the people under you.

In horse training the objective may be to produce an animal to help harvest a crop, to herd cattle, to win a show, or to safely carry a handicapped person. The horse must be trained to do these things, for these are the mission. Close behind comes treating the animal well both for ethical reasons and so that it physically and psychologically becomes a willing team member in the effort.

So you don't cuss that fiddle. You find ways to make it play better. But you also aren't ashamed of your position as leader of the band. In the round corral it simply must be that way because you are dealing with a critter at least five times as big and strong as you are, an animal which, if it had its own way, would not be trained or controlled or ridden by you but would simply spend its life running in a herd of horses. All horses are strong enough to hurt you.

Assuming the role of good leader doesn't require (or allow) beating horses into submission. But you will not be accepted as leader without asserting your position as such. Hopefully you can do this by making it easier for the horse to do the right thing than the wrong thing. Then you can do little, subtle, harmless things that remind him your will is more important than his. (These are the equivalent of "call me by my first name—Colonel.") On your third ride the colt wants to turn left for no particular reason. So you turn him to the right. You do not let him stop for no reason. But if you want him to stop you make him stop, and that means stop and stand dead still until you say he can do otherwise.

·   ·   ·

Well, I've been working the filly longer than I intended. She is picking up on my body language, is now reversing easily. I had been moving to her front as I said "whoa," but she is stopping without that now. Sweat is appearing on her flanks and on my brow, so it's just about time to quit. Ralph, the farrier, will be arriving soon to shoe this filly and Major. Our training session will have taken the edge off the filly, making her more ready to accept another new experience. We've had a good start, but there are many repetitions of all these things ahead.

And I suppose that if I have a final objection to the impressions left by some modern training methods it is based on this thing of repetition. Training and teaching are not exactly the same thing. Ask a head nurse in an emergency ward, a football coach, or a leader of combat troops about training and each will usually say that training involves so many repetitions of doing the right thing that, under stress when there is no time to think, the right action is automatic. Sometimes people refer to this automatic response as "instinct," but that is incorrect, because instinct is completely unlearned. We are talking about learned responses, those learned by endless repetition.

At some horse training clinics spectacular things are done in a very short time. Perhaps participants ride their untrained colts without bridles. Or a previously untouched animal is caught, saddled, bridled, and successfully ridden by the clinician in just a couple hours. Perhaps the clinician emphasizes that this does not constitute a full training of the animal ("don't try this at home"), but his or her actions, not words, are likely to be remembered. Unfortunately the impression left is the one hungered for by a society craving instant gratification. And there is no instant gratification available to people who wish to master the violin or to train horses.

I lead the bay filly to the tack room hitching rail where Ralph will shoe her. We are off and running together now. Tomorrow I will gently rub her with a blanket and probably saddle her. In future lessons I will introduce her to a snaffle bit, teach her to yield right and left, then ground drive her with long lines just as I would a harness horse. At each stage I'll be feeling my way, trying to tell which things will work best with her. I will always end on a positive note, and if we have a setback, I will back up a lesson or two and start over. We will probably keep this filly as a broodmare, so there is no pressure. I can take my time. I sympathize with the professional trainer who must achieve a certain result in a certain time frame.

When the filly is completely used to the touch of ropes, cinches, and stirrups banging against her (packing salt to the hills will help); when she turns each direction with a light tug on that rein; when she stops dead and stays stopped; and, when she backs willingly, then I will probably step up on her. I'm looking forward to it.

Ralph is not here yet, so I will take time for a cup of coffee. I find myself wondering how the stud colt is doing. Perhaps I will give Tex a call.

II

Farrier tales

He drives up in a little red Toyota pickup with a white camper shell. On the back bumper is a sticker that says "Horse Shoer from Hell." He parks in front of the tack room, gets out, and ties on his leather apron. Then he unloads his toolbox and anvil and sits down on the tailgate of the pickup, cleaning a rasp. Although he is over fifty, there is the ease in his posture of the natural athlete. His arms are knotted with muscle. Like most farriers, he is not a large man.

We say our greetings as I walk up. He eyeballs the filly. "This the young horse you want done?"

"Yeah, and Major." Ralph touches the filly at the shoulder, stands there with his hand on her for a moment, then goes to work. He always shoes the young horse first. Major will stand with each of his big feet up in the air in turn, not moving until Ralph finishes and is ready to start on the next. He is one of Ralph's favorites. So it is better to get the filly done first, then have an easy time on Major. Even a gentle horse on its first shoeing is likely to give the farrier a workout.

Like most farriers, Ralph is an independent soul. He has been bitten and kicked by ill-tempered horses countless times. His hands and forearms are laced with scars, for horses often misbehave at the most inopportune time, those brief seconds between his driving a nail and twisting off its sharp protruding point—the horse moves and the nail point catches the shoer. He is partial not only to well-behaved, disciplined horses, but to those with decent feet, a pet peeve being the massively muscled, heavy stock horse with tiny feet. Those, he says, "with the feet bred out from under them" never last long. And he is partial to owners who have their horses ready for him and who help with any animal likely to pose a problem.

I guess we stack up pretty well in all this, for Ralph, like most shoers, simply won't show up at the ranches that have horses he does not like. He has an excellent reputation, plenty of work, and he sees no profit in taking abuse. He has been our farrier now for seventeen years. We had bought Mona, our first registered mare, heavy in foal with Rockytop. She gave birth to a big sorrel horse colt with a crooked blaze. I named him Rockytop Tennessee, inspired by the song and his ragged blaze. He was the first colt I ever raised from birth to saddle, the first I ever trained, and he was a handful. Had I known just how comparatively touchy he was I might have backed off and sought professional help, but maybe not, for we were cash-strapped and I was motivated in the strongest possible way. I needed a horse to run the ranch, and we'd dedicated Mona to raising foals. When a horse becomes your only one, it gets trained, that is if there is work to do, and Rockytop became a dandy. I kept thinking that when he was old I would not be so very young myself, and he is now in his late teens.

On a snowy day when Rockytop was six months old, Ralph came to the ranch, the first time I met him, and put size 2 shoes on Mona's front feet, nodding with approval at the size of her feet, big enough for her weight and frame. He was pleased also with the thickness of her hoof walls. As soon as he tacked on the shoes, I weaned the colt and headed for the mountains on an elk hunt. Rockytop complained with the usual colt whinnies when his mother left, but not for long. Mona never even looked back. She had already carried dudes and packed panniers for a decade as part of an outfitter's string, raised a mule colt for him (probably against her will), and never did really seem to care much about the motherhood role, though she took good care of the many colts she had for us. It's just that when you weaned the colt she made no fuss whatsoever. Like me, she was always anxious for the mountains. She died last winter.

So Ralph likes our horses a great deal and is a fine ambassador for them. I consider a first shoeing by Ralph to be an essential part of a colt's education. Ralph provides the right amount of discipline coupled with understanding that colts will be colts. And he has the athletic ability to bend rather than break, to hold a colt's foot up even if it hops halfway across the corral, staying right along with the colt in that impossibly awkward crouch farriers must assume, wearing the young horse down until it simply lets him have the foot.

The bay filly behaves quite well for her first shoeing. She experiments a few times with depriving Ralph of the foot, but she is never mean about it. When it comes time to set more tightly the driven nails, when Ralph hits each with a quick, hard, rap that sounds like the report of a .22 pistol, she flinches, surprised at the sound and the sensation. But she doesn't lose her head. Our horses are spirited but rarely if ever do they "blow up." Ralph likes that. He has had too many of the other kind, those that stand as if asleep and then, with no provocation you can identify, come unglued.

Ralph talks little while he shoes the filly, leaving most of the words to me while I hold her lead rope. It is only when he begins clinching the nails on her last foot, the right hind, that he can quit concentrating so intently. Then he says, "Well, I was up at Bert's the other day."

"So how is Bert doing?"

"Okay now. He's getting over it."

"Has he been sick?"

"No." He clinches the last nail on the hoof and lowers it to the ground, gives the filly a rump pat of appreciation. "She's gonna be a good one. You keeping her as a broodmare?"

"Yup, I think so."

"Good. That's the kind you keep." Another of Ralph's pet peeves is people who keep their most useless mare for raising foals. He knows we keep only our best for that purpose.

Ralph leads the filly over to the round corral while I bring Major and tie him to the hitching rail. He's going to make me ask, I guess.

"So what happened to Bert?"

"Damn near killed himself." Pause. "And I was right there when it happened."

"The hell." Now thoughts of Bert, the Indian over seventy years old who is married to an astronomy professor from an Ivy League university, the World War II vet, fly through my mind, and I try to guess: plane or motorcycle? Bert rides motorcycles barefoot, flies planes, alternates his life between Puerto Rico where his wife works at an observatory and a small ranch twenty miles from ours. He is a character. "Did he hail out his motorcycle?"

"No." Ralph picks up and cleans Major's left front foot. "I'd been trimming those horses of his and that great big young gelding, you know, the one he got by breeding the big old coldblood mare to your stud, well that colt was standing in sort of a low spot with his head down, grazing kind of facing away. I don't know what Bert was thinking of. The colt didn't even have a halter on. Anyway, Bert was standing there and got a little bored, I guess, so he walked over to the colt and just hopped on his back. Well, that colt's gentle, but he didn't even know Bert was there and I guess he thought a mountain lion had just jumped him. Anyway, it's not right to say he bucked Bert off. More like, he plain old hammered Bert into the ground, right on a pile of rocks. He landed square on his head, then flipped over on his back, and I was plumb certain he was deader than a wedge."

Ralph walks to the anvil, holding a number 2 shoe, spreads it slightly with the hammer, holds it up to the sky to examine it critically, then walks back to Major. "So naturally," he says, "I ran over there fast as I could, pretty sure I'd be calling the sheriff and he would be calling the coroner. But I could see Bert was quivering a little. Then his eyes came open."

"He looked at me and recognized me." At this point Ralph starts laughing. "I'll never forget the rest of my life what he said. He groaned and he said, 'I'm so damn stupid. I can't believe I did that. Don't call the ambulance. I don't deserve to live. Just let me die.' Then he closed his eyes and I thought for a minute he was really going to do it, but I was running to Bert's barn phone by that time, and I called the crew. We got him into the emergency room in Red Lodge. He's going to be sore a long time, but he's okay. I think he's just too tough to die."

Ralph may seem to be laughing at Bert, but his head-shaking is really respect. "'I don't deserve to live, just let me die.' I'll never forget it. They broke the mold after they made that guy."

"Yes, they did."

"You know, some of these guys who claim to be cowboys couldn't do half what he does. I showed up there one day and he was out riding that same colt bareback right down the centerline of the pavement on the highway. He, Bert I mean, was barefoot, wearing his Bermuda shorts and sunglasses and that little straw hat he likes. And he had that colt in that single-foot it got from your stud just straight as a die, and I'm thinking, this guy doesn't look the slightest bit like a cowboy and he doesn't claim to be one either, but he sure can handle that horse. Then I find out it's only about the third time that colt's ever been ridden."

Major is so laid-back while being shod that he practically goes to sleep. I sit in the pleasant shade still offered by the tack room, sit on the sill of the door. Behind me, smelling pleasantly of neatsfoot oil, are the saddles: Emily's, inherited from Elmer who bought it at age sixteen in 1919, and the other newer ones. Above the saddles are my new harnesses for Pancho and Lefty. After a year's use they could now use oiling, which I could tackle while Ralph is shoeing. But I'm not too motivated. I would rather talk.

Ralph moves down the valley. "Well, Willy's back on the booze again."

"He wasn't off it very long."

"No. They took his license away again, but he drove the pickup into town and the judge finally told him he had no choice but to lock him up for a weekend. He figured it would teach him a lesson. Well, he let Willy choose the weekend, but Willy hadn't had too much variety in his life for a while, so he was eager to try out the jail and he wanted to go right away. His wife delivered him on Friday night, and she was all enthusiastic, too, hoping this would accomplish something. She bought him three new books to read, every single one of them having something to do with prison.

"Anyway, it didn't work because he enjoyed himself too much. The highway patrol came to visit him—he hunts on Willy's ranch and wanted to stay in good with him. All the deputies came to pay their respects, too. Hell, they didn't even keep him in his cell, just let him have the run of the place. He's a smart man, you know, so he wanted to learn all about the radios and the computers.

"Well, since the weekend in jail didn't reform him, the judge sent him to drunk school once a week. Hell, that was the best recreation he'd had in years. He made his wife drive him in to it early, he took notes, he added all sorts of wit and wisdom to every point the instructor made. He was damn disappointed when the course came to an end."

"He used to be quite a horseman."

"The best. Probably still could stick on one better than just about anyone I know, providing he wasn't too far into a fifth." Son Steve walks up, having emerged from the steel shed covered with grease, frustration on his face. He has been working on Elmer's old Jeep, trying to discover what is making brake fluid drain away. He notices for the first time Ralph's "Horse Shoer from Hell" bumper sticker and a smile cracks through the grease. A wheel is too frozen with rust to remove with any tools we own, so I point Steve toward a different project. He is a huge help to me, this last of my three-son work force. I'm awfully glad to still have him working summers. He is a good mechanic, too, though a much better musician, with a trumpet that soars and a singing voice much like my father's.

Ralph finishes Major's last foot, dressing the hoof with his rasp, then leads Major down the gravel driveway, watching him walk, finally tying him next to the filly. "Damn shame, that big ranch of Willie's almost gone now to booze. House is the same as it's been since I was a kid, except it's got more old cars in front of it. When one plays out they just park it in line like it was some kind of ornament."

I lift Ralph's anvil into the pickup bed while he picks up the tools. "I'll go in and get you a check."

"You said you'd be needing the other two geldings done in a couple weeks. I'll just catch you for it then." He gets into his pickup and takes off. I walk to the filly, untie her, and lead her into the round corral. She has already had all the learning she needs for the day, but I free-longe her a couple of circles just to see how she adjusts to the shoes. She walks well. Tomorrow I will see how she likes the saddle.

12

First ride · A lady vet · Horse trading · Bicycles for bracelets

A week has gone by. We are getting ready to cut hay, so Steve, my resident mechanic, has been working to ready the "haybine," a machine you pull with the tractor and which both cuts the hay and puts it in windrows. Thus it replaces both mower and rake. I have progressed with the filly, have ground driven her, then introduced her to a sawbuck pack saddle. At each stage she has been spirited, aware, and cautious, but proud, too, and quick to learn. She is the image in temperament of her mother. I have long subscribed to the theory that while we brag about our stallions, it is the broodmares that contribute most to the foals.

When the filly was thoroughly used to the straps and cinches of the pack saddle, to the strange feel of the breeching over her rump and under her tail, I hung blaze-orange nylon panniers on each side. When those were no longer intimidating, I dropped a fifty-pound sack of salt in each. She humped a little, skittered around me in a circle, then figured it out. Next was to pony her behind Major up the still-muddy wagon road to the salt troughs. All that went well.

Ground driven she now yields well in each direction, stops on a dime, and backs. She is used to being touched everywhere, is no longer goosey about anything. So I think it is time to climb on. I know a certified Pat Parelli instructor who is a little horrified by how quickly I ride colts, and I agree with him in a way. Certainly much teaching on the ground should be the prerequisite for a first ride, and many things are more easily taught during ground work than while mounted. Unfortunately, I have the Westerner's itch to get in the saddle, to get it done. Our horses do very little work in any arena. A few rides in the round corral and they are out in the sagebrush. Even though I can't claim genetic connection to Magnus, Emily's grandfather, I can claim a cultural connection. There is work to be done on that horse, and the best way to teach him is to just go do it.

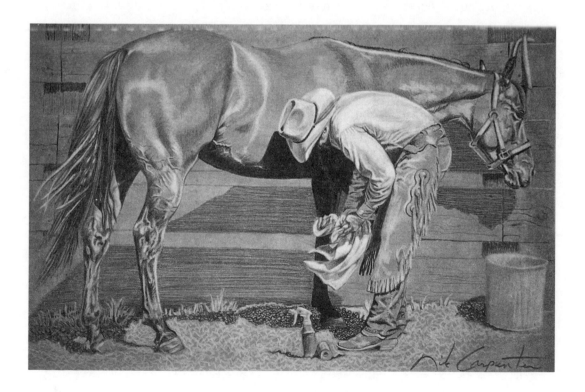

I have switched saddles on the filly a couple sessions back, retired the pack saddle for an old and shabby stock saddle which can get knocked around without worry, and today have switched again, this time to my own saddle. (If the filly could only know, having *my* saddle placed on her back would be a sure sign to her that something new was about to happen.) I have done the usual slapping of stirrup leathers against the filly's flank, have stepped into one stirrup just part way up to accustom her to the strange sensation of weight on one side. I guess I'm getting old, for I reserve first rides for a time when someone else can watch, don't usually do them if I am the only one home. But Steve is in sight working on the machine and Emily has been alerted, is watching out the window and will come out for moral support. This is overkill, really, for the filly is gentle. It is extremely rare for any of our colts to attempt to buck. Nine times out of ten the first ride on our stock is completely uneventful. But there is that tenth time . . . .

And so, after many tests of the stirrup on each side, much stepping up halfway, I put my left foot in the stirrup and simply swing up on her, first having taken slack out of the left rein so that I can quickly pull her around if need be. She stands stock still for an instant, surprised at a weight more than twice that of the salt she packed, then does get scared and shows it not by trying to buck but by a sideways scurry as quick and smooth as the leap of a cat. I keep the left rein just taut enough to steer her left in the round corral, and we go smartly around it, her body by the second revolution starting to relax under me, her gait as smooth as her mother's. My slightly sick stomach sensation drifts away. I know I am grinning. Emily walks up to the corral, gingerly, because when colts first have a rider aboard they often spook at something that would never normally bother them. "Well, I guess I missed the show. Will she be like her mother, Red? You rode her just four times and then handed the reins to me and said, 'Here, she's broke.'"

I keep the filly going as I talk. "Well, you have to admit it was true. In another four rides you had a neck rein on her." It really did happen that way, but one should not brag about shortcuts, for even though it worked it was not the right thing to do.

I will not ride the filly long, for she is small for the weight she carries and young. I have very limited goals for the first ride. If I can go first one, then the other direction around the corral, stop the young horse relatively well (this may mean turning it toward the fence), and get it over any initial surprise, that is good enough. The filly does all this extremely well, but I still stay on edge, never completely relax, for strange things can happen on green horses.

Many years ago when Rockytop was turning two and was already nearly 16-hands tall, we had designs on keeping him a stallion. That was a foolish idea, but a common one among horse owners, barn-blind it is called, the state of thinking a horse you have is such special stuff that the entire realm of equine genetics would be sorely cheated if your colt never sired any babies. The truth is that the best geldings are colts you really think were stud material, and the best stallions are even better yet. Too many people keep stallions, few are really qualified to handle them, and many inferior genes are passed on.

·   ·   ·

When Rockytop became nearly unmanageable, we got the message. There were two considerations. First, I needed a using horse to do the ranch work. Rockytop was a big, beautiful animal. I could not afford to buy another horse, and, besides, I wanted *him* in that role. As a stallion, he wasn't going to be tractable enough to do the job. Secondly, hard as he was to handle as a stud colt, would it be intelligent to choose him as a breeding stallion? "No," was the obvious answer. So we called Diana, our lady vet.

Diana was the first woman veterinarian to come to our area. A prophet could not have picked a better one for that role. Big, strong, and no-nonsense Diana arrived about as prissy as General Patton, yet pretty when you saw her dressed up at the Grizzly Bar on Saturday night. During her first year she spent a hellish few weeks pregnancy-testing hundreds of cows. Something happened that showed her she had been accepted, but it was an incident that might have made a weaker person head for the shelter of a small-animal clinic in the middle of a city.

Cows are pregnancy-tested in the fall, "open" (not pregnant) ones normally being sold, for it is not economical to feed them through the winter and yet another year before they produce a calf. The cows are corralled, then run down to a squeeze chute. A head catch and squeezing panel restrain the cow, and the vet slips in behind, rapidly giving a "yes" or "no" to pregnancy and also telling whether the cow will calve on time, for the owner might want to sell an animal that will be calving late. This is all done extremely rapidly, a vet sometimes pregnancy-testing several hundred animals in a day.

Cows are pregnancy-tested rectally, not vaginally. The vet inserts his or her glove-covered arm up into the intestinal tract and feels the fetus through the intestinal wall. It's a tough, physical, messy job, often performed under frosty and muddy conditions. Diana, after weeks of this, was exhausted. And so, on still another day, she was in the middle of a band of cows—the knot of men around the squeeze chute hanging on her every word to get the verdict she announced for each cow—and also doing the other "doctoring" jobs performed in the fall, vaccinating, worming, and pouring the lice-killer on each animal. Virtually in a stupor, Diana inserted her arm into the rear of still another animal, felt around, and said, "Well, I'm afraid this one's open."

None of the men moved. Normally the boss would have waved off the others, for there is no sense wasting medications on an animal "going to town." Another of the men would have chalk-marked the animal with a line across the rear of its back, a signal to the stockyards that the cow was open. But no one moved. Then they cracked. First it was a ripple. Then, they convulsed with laughter. All the men laughed so hard they looked for a place to roll around on the ground and hold their stomachs, but were forced to stay on their feet, given the sea of corral mud around them. As they laughed Diana, in her stupor, took her first good look at the rear end of the animal she had just examined. There was no vagina. The men had slipped a steer into the chute among the cows.

A lesser lady might have broken under this, trying hard as she was to establish herself in a male world. She might have turned icy, coldly completed the rest of the day's work. The men would have turned quietly formal. They would have felt guilty and embarrassed, and probably sought a different vet next time. She could have gone home to pout and circulate her resume. Not Diana. She knew she had been accepted. She knew that these men would not tease a woman they did not like, not play a joke on someone they considered incompetent. And so, exhausted, Diana instead slumped on the side of the chute and started laughing with them, laughed until tears, then finished testing the cows, secure among her new friends. "You bastards," she said.

When Diana castrated Rockytop she laid him on his side with drugs first, the common practice today. While he was out cold I deftly touched his left shoulder with the brand we inherited from Elmer and Nora, a reverse E lazy J, like this: ⊐ (Elmer had left me three irons, the largest for grown cows or bulls, a smaller one for calves, and a smaller yet for horses.) Then Diana cut the colt, and I felt an instant of loss. She waited around until he regained his feet, for she never leaves when an animal is still down. As he groggily stood up she said, "Well, he'll be fine now. He'll be just a little bit sore for a week or so. Spirited as he is, getting on him for the first ride while he's still a little sore might not be a bad idea."

It was a good idea. A couple days later I rode him with much the same result I've just had with the filly, although he and I were both more tense. He felt like a loaded cannon underneath me but he never went off, and he became our old-reliable, though never a horse for a beginner. On that first ride we had just one big spook. We were in a pen next to a boxcar used as a granary, and the afternoon sun cast our shadowed silhouette on the boxcar each time we passed. About the third time around the corral Rockytop noticed the shadow and gave a big hop and spook at this strange intruder he saw chasing him down the side of the boxcar. But he settled down quickly. He and

I have since been many miles together, have crossed many passes. It is hard to see him get old.

· · ·

I am putting the filly away when a small car drives in from the highway and parks by the tack room. In it are a young couple interested in looking at the horses. They are Quarter Horse people, but anxious to learn about gaited breeds. The young man had been on an elk hunt the previous fall and had admired the new walking horse of a friend, a true "ground-covering fool" as he calls it. So we lean on the corral fence and talk horses. They are nice people, the woman a bit more knowledgeable than the man, a common scenario today. We don't get to the point of bargaining for any particular horse, though they see when we walk to the calf pasture a yearling they like. They promise to return. I like them well enough to promise to saddle Major for a demonstration when they visit again.

Most of our horse business consists of just this, visiting with people both in person and on the telephone, not having any idea whether we will see them again. You learn to be careful about prejudging the people who stop by. When we first had colts to sell, a man and his mother showed up to look at what we had. The mom was tough-talking, and both were in clothes that had patches on patches. The Western phrase for how they looked is "rode hard and put away wet." They liked two of our colts, heard our prices impassively (we thought them high at that time), and said they would return. We decided not to hold our breaths. But in a few days they rolled in, a horse trailer behind their rusty pickup, and counted out hundred-dollar bills for the total we had asked.

Conversely, we have had people pull in with matching pickup/trailer combinations worth more than some people's houses, yet haggle over the last five-dollar bill. Mostly, our horse trading has been pleasant. The most knowledgeable people are the easiest to deal with; those to whom horses are mysterious are likely to be more

suspicious. Then there are those innocent souls who really want a horse but, truthfully, have no business owning one. Some are so overweight they lack the leg strength to mount, others so timid that a wise horse might quickly take advantage of them. And there is still, hanging over this entire business of horse trading, an unsavory aura, a reputation that dates from when horse traders were the used-car salesmen of their day. Actually, they were considerably craftier, with wisdom gleaned from years of training in making a bad horse look good and fooling a knowledgeable customer.

The truth is, of course, that a horse-breeding operation like ours is the same as any small business. Reputation is everything. The dissatisfied customer will tell many others, while the satisfied one will return for another horse. The horse as a piece of "merchandise," however, presents some problems. It is a complex creature of flesh and blood, easy to ruin and harder to fix than a mechanical device. Elmer used to say that it takes seven or eight years to make a horse that is really broke (he meant trained in its highest sense), but that "any fool can wreck one in five minutes." Thus, many sellers are reluctant to send horses home on a trial basis. To send a horse, particularly a young and impressionable one, home to be experimented upon by God knows who, then be expected to take it back, is a bit much. The five minutes of idiocy which could occur may have ruined the horse forever or at least require many moons of training to correct. It has worked well for us to let prospective customers try the horse all they want here on the ranch, tell them exactly what the animal is, and guarantee that it will be as we represented it.

Of course, since horses are living creatures, subject to vagaries of behavior, you hope the animal you are trying to sell will be on its best behavior when the prospective customer drives in.

As with your child at church, that isn't likely to be so, although it can happen either way. Sometimes that last emphasis you have put on the training of a young animal because someone is interested in it has really been effective, and your subject is an angel on the trading day. But it can certainly work the other way.

· · ·

Each of our three sons owned a broodmare to help him through college. When we first started that idea, we were looking for a suitable mare for David, our oldest. We found her, we thought; a stately palomino owned by a young lady whose husband had insisted she sell her. That should have been a clue. But her story was plausible, and the mare had a good set of registration papers. We bought her for a modest price out of a suburban backyard, had some difficulty loading her, then brought her home. She seemed well trained, neck reined well, had magic-carpet gaits, and seemed, all in all, a decent acquisition. But the second time I mounted her she began backing up, rapidly, and did not stop doing so until her rear end hit the corral fence. Then she shot forward. Well, this was strange. Emily and I both rode her, both with the same results. She did not buck, try to run away, do anything particularly antisocial, she simply went backward about half the time you got on her, and boy, could she back. She could—honestly—do a running walk backward.

We suspected a training quirk, not a genetic aberration, so it might have been okay to keep the mare as David's broodmare. But he wanted something he could ride. So we worked on her hard, trying things that seemed plausible remedies. We gradually made progress. We discovered that you didn't sit around on this mare. She was a tremendous goer. Your best chance of success in riding her was to mount and immediately head off, not expecting her to stand still for any length of time. Now I told all this to the stout young man who called me after we had decided to list the mare for sale. We had come close to fixing the mare's problems, but it would have been both foolish and unethical to say nothing about her quirk.

These things did not seem to bother him. He was a confident guy, whether justifiably I could not tell. (He looked a little too much like a "weekend cowboy" to me.) I saddled the mare, demonstrated her, then dismounted, intending to adjust the stirrups for him, since he was a short and stocky man. Before I could do so he hopped deftly on her back. "Could you shorten these stirrups a little for me?" he asked, sliding his left leg forward so I could reach the quick-adjust stirrup leathers.

I knew that in keeping the mare stationary we were on borrowed time, but the mare was standing well, so I quickly went to work. "How much should I take them up? You think about two notches will do?" And those were the last words I got out, for that weird, hidden aberration in the mare's mind took over, and she started to back up. This might not have been so bad had we been in the corral, but we were out in the open in front of some old sheds I have since torn down. One of these sheds was a chicken house. Early ranchers figured out solar heat, so they often built chicken houses with expanses of glass facing south to help warm the interior during winter when the sun was low. This old chicken house and it's ten-foot-long panel of small glass panes became the target for the mare's rear end. She backed squarely into it with the sound of a motorcycle crashing through a plate-glass window.

Actually, the sound was worse than that, more like a case of china hitting a sidewalk, and it was enough stimulus to make the mare kick her gearbox into forward. But her direction was not good. David and Jon had parked their bicycles on kick stands a couple feet apart on the side of the driveway, and the mare bulled right over them. That wasn't all. She managed to put both her front feet right through the spoked wheels, one bicycle on each side, and, so help me, she just kept trucking along. The bicycles were just big bracelets to her. She tucked her rear end and hit the kind of "big lick" gait that would make one of those trainers of padded-up walkers down in Tennessee completely proud, a bicycle colorfully flapping on each front foot.

Then, finally, the young man, still aboard, got her stopped. I walked up to the pair. The mare had shed the bicycles, and there was nothing more than a superficial scratch or two on her front pasterns. Her rear end was similarly unscathed. I, on the other hand, fully expected to be sued. Instead, the young man simply moved his leg forward again and answered the question I had asked before the explosion. "Yeah," he said, "a couple notches will be fine." He was the most singularly cool customer I've ever met in my life!

So, hands shaking, I got his stirrups adjusted on both sides. He headed off into our fields, and I wished sorely that Diana were around to shoot me up with some kind of tranquilizer. When the young man got back he announced to his wife that he liked the mare and would buy her. And that was that. I have never sold a horse with better conscience, for this man had seen the very worst the mare could dish out and considered it mere child's play. But I spent a day helping David and Jon fix their bicycles.

13

A big expensive bucket of bolts · Overshot stackers ·
Sergeant Fleming · "A time to sow, a time to reap"

The Fourth of July has come and gone. The summer is getting tired, the hill grasses now seeded out and brown, the thermometer on many days too high for my Scandinavian genes. We have cut, baled, and stacked the alfalfa under Butcher Creek ditch. That forty-acre strip is our most fertile field, with deep soil that holds moisture so well that we irrigate it only once each year, between the two alfalfa cuttings. More irrigation simply kills that alfalfa, for the roots need oxygen. We are halfway through irrigating it now, Steve covering the morning set while I do other jobs. I catch the evening set after supper.

When you cut alfalfa a dry stubble field is left behind. If the submoisture is good, tiny new green leaves quickly appear at the bottoms of the coarse dry stems, a regeneration. Usually, in Montana, we must irrigate to affect this. Our dryland alfalfa fields above the ditches give us just one cutting, the alfalfa going dormant, sometimes tweaking back into life when late-summer rains come. The irrigated alfalfa waits for our efforts, the transformation happening several days after each set when the water has had time to soak to the deep roots, come back up, and kick things into life again.

There is great satisfaction in irrigating dry alfalfa. The ground bubbles mightily, the water diving into the fissures that have opened up in the baked soil. Almost immediately there is a distinctive sweet smell. Emily thinks that dry alfalfa drinking water smells like beer, but that comparison doesn't quite work for me. It smells much better.

Grass hay matures later. The field by the house, the one I harrowed at the beginning of the summer with Pancho and Lefty, produced a good crop of timothy hay which Steve swathed into king-sized windrows. Then we played the usual cat-and-mouse games with the weather, with the late-afternoon thunderheads that drop just enough rain to set the haying back but not enough to relieve the dry hills. Anyone believing in the veracity of five-day forecasts as dished out by modern weather bureaus need only try to cut hay on the strength of such forecasts to be quickly disillusioned. On Sunday night the weatherman shows a graphic of the next five days, each with a smiling sun on it, predicted temperature in the nineties. Great. You can cut hay on Monday and Tuesday, bale it on Wednesday and Thursday, stack on Friday and Saturday. The windrows you bale on Wednesday will be the ones you have cut Monday, for with our low humidity and those hot temperatures, the two days' curing time should be adequate.

So you swathe on Monday. That evening there is a slight equivocation on the part of the weatherman. He shows a few clouds around the edges for later that week, but the pattern should still be hot and dry. So, now more uneasy, you swathe again on Tuesday. That night you know you're in trouble, and it doesn't take the weatherman to tell you, for thunderheads have built up by supper time, and although they've missed you, you can see a pattern developing. That night the weatherman grins and shakes his head. Those fronts from Seattle are awfully hard to predict, he says, some making it over the mountains, some not. He still thinks the pattern will be dry with just, perhaps, a twenty percent chance of rain.

By four p.m. on Wednesday you're pushing more hay into the front end of your baler than it was ever built to handle, and it complains by frequently breaking a string, bales sometimes dropping out the back end and then bursting stringless as they hit the ground. There is nothing that can make a righteous man curse the entire creation more than a malfunctioning baler when the lightning starts popping on top of the Beartooths and you're racing to get every possible bale made before the windrows get drenched. And so, by four-thirty, the weatherman's twenty percent showers descend like the hoards of Genghis Khan, and you run from your cableless tractor, fearing the lightning that pops in the tops of the cottonwood trees, getting quickly away from that big hunk of wet iron that might draw it to you. Inside, your wife goes through the routine of unplugging appliances to prevent their being fried when lightning causes surges in the electric lines. And then, almost as quickly as it started, it is over again, the sun out, the dry hayfield smelling musty with its brief wetting, the haying delayed, the ultimate quality of the hay hurt.

We dodged this scenario fairly well with the all-important alfalfa. Grass hay is more tolerant, so the brief wettings this field suffered have not been too serious, though Steve did have to hook to the old side-delivery rake and turn the windrows over once before we could get them dry enough to bale. I am now entering the field with the larger tractor. I am pulling a big, complicated machine called a bale wagon. To give this monster so innocuous a name as "bale wagon" is like calling King Kong a good-sized primate. Bristling with sprockets, pulleys, and hydraulic cylinders, this mechanical marvel picks bales up off the ground (assuming the bales are on edge and you drive just so), puts them on a small table which, when full, trips and rotates them up onto a second table. When that larger table is full, it too rotates, placing the bales vertically into what will become a tier of a stack. When this has happened seven times and you have one hundred four bales on the wagon, you back up to where you will stack, and again, if all goes perfectly well, hydraulically stand up the whole affair. If you are good at it the stack stands, and you continue to add additional increments. It took much heartache, cussing, and restacking before I became even remotely good at it.

As this monster churns and grinds behind me, as I watch the bale pickup with eagle eye, knowing I'll soon have a crick in my neck, I ask myself, "Why?" The answer is, of course, labor help, which becomes increasingly difficult to find. With the machinery I now have I could put up the entire hay crop myself. Magnus and Elmer, doing it with horses, needed a half-dozen good hands. They could afford the help more easily than I can afford this machinery. But seasonal help of the sort they routinely hired is not available at all now, so what does a guy do? Typically he buys more and more expensive machinery, and then, to finance it, takes on more and more work. It is not a sensible circle, but it's also like a very rapid carousel, not at all easy to get off.

And so, earplugs in place with hopes that I'll retain some semblance of hearing by summer's end, I tackle the day's work. (The hearing is handy when fall comes and choir practice resumes at church, for I am the director, a job I inherited from my father.) The contrast with that earlier stint on this same field, Pancho and Lefty quietly stepping out, nags me. Emerson and his friend Thoreau had many wise things to say about this dilemma (but were less wise at finding ways out of it). "We do not ride upon the railroad; it rides upon us." The farm machinery is supposed to help us, make life easier, but we work harder because we have to pay for it and do more work with less help.

It is true, however, that I did not pay all that much for this machine. A new one would have been out of the question. This one came to me used, well used, a veteran of many hay wars. Before we bought it we stacked the old way, David on the stack, I running the loader on the tractor. With just one machine that was a slow way to go. David, a good stacker and strong as a bull, could have easily kept up with a second machine.

I like to visualize this valley when it was all done with horses. That is easy for me to do because I can look from my tractor seat straight east and see at the base of the alfalfa field two surviving overshot stackers. They are gradually deteriorating now, of course, but they stand as relics right by the same hay corral I now use, facing the machine-made stack I put up two weeks ago.

Then, as now, it started with mowing. A team pulled a ground-driven mower, its driver perched on a steel seat. (A friend, a teamster, tells me that mowing hay behind a team of horses was, simply, the best job in the entire world.) In this area the sickle bar was normally only five feet long, so that was the width you mowed. But if two mowers and teams were going, and the teams were good, fast walkers, a decent amount of hay could be knocked down in a day. This fallen hay lay in the sun for a day, then was raked with a dump rake. The dump rake was dragged along behind the team, crossways to their direction. When it accumulated all the hay it could drag, the driver tripped it upward, leaving the hay behind. The driver kept going across the field, dumping at intervals. On his return pass, he dumped hay next to his previous piles, so that he was gradually building big windrows perpendicular to his line of travel. The end result was a windrowed field much like those our swathers create today but with windrows more widely spaced and larger.

· · ·

The next step was stacking. Hay was accumulated with a buckrake, an affair that actually was pushed along ahead of the horses, its toothed hayhead looking much like the loader head on a modern tractor. The driver would proceed down a windrow until his hayhead was full, pull out of the windrow, and push his load to the site of the haystack, depositing it on the similar hayhead of the stacker. On an overshot stacker, a horse pulled a cable which raised the load of hay higher and higher, then over backward in an arc that dumped the hay onto the stack. (In later years Nora pulled the stacker cable with Elmer's Jeep.) On the stack two men, if available, put their pitchforks to work, for loose hay stacks were built as meticulously as those with bales, great skill and strength being required. Emily remembers admiration expressed for the man who could stack alone against the equipment.

One such was a big man named Gabe, a favorite hand. Elmer told me that Gabe could work his fork through the loose hay, moving it this way and that, until fully a hundred pounds accumulated on its tines. Then he would raise his load, slowly, the handle of the fork bent in a tight arc under the weight. Finally Gabe would deposit the hay to lie just so, eventually building a pretty stack, a stack with a top almost as good as a thatched roof at resisting the invasion of moisture. Of course, when winter came these stacks were dismantled the very same way, with pitchfork, the horses pulling flatbed wagons called hayracks up close to the stack to be loaded for the cattle.

Sometimes the modern can be combined with older methods, a happy medium resulting. A few ranchers put hay up loose but with modern equipment, a tractor with loader to stack (though not as prettily as when done by hand), then feed in winter with a hydraulic grapple fork on the head of the loader. The tractor can bite into the stack and pull out hundreds of pounds of hay in one shot, which is shaken off to the cattle. The rancher willing to work this way need not own a baler, a savings of many thousands of dollars.

But the system I covet more is the big round baler. Producing bales weighing over a thousand pounds, this system eliminates the bucket of bolts I drag behind me today, for the bales can be stacked by tractor, each the equivalent of twenty or more square bales. Then, in winter, they can be fed with attachments on a tractor or pickup that either spin the bales or allow them to roll out on the ground. With a welder and some ingenuity, systems can be built that allow feeding the bales with a team of horses. If Pancho and Lefty could know my musings they might see a whole new future chapter in their lives. And I, for the first time since age fourteen (save my college and military years) might get totally out of using my back to stack and unstack every year ten thousand bales of hay.

But I can't muse too much, for stacking with the bale wagon requires concentration. Sometimes the first table fails to trip or trips too soon. I then go through a ritual of taking the tractor out of gear, putting on the parking break, and stopping the power takeoff, which makes all those sprockets, chains, and cylinders on the bale wagon stop dead. Only then do I dare touch the thing, much less climb on it. I can think of few less desirable fates than being on the second table of the bale wagon when a lever trips and the thing powers up into vertical position, sandwiching a man between two tiers of bales and likely crushing or smothering him. All you could hope for would be someone spotting a foot or an arm sticking out from between the bales, then being savvy enough to know what to do.

Today, however, it goes fairly well, for this field is level and smooth. Soon a haystack has formed in the barnyard of the old house, the one lived in by Magnus and Kristine and Elmer and Nora and in which Emily grew up. I close the gate to the field behind me, which is now cropped short and clean of hay, and feel some satisfaction. Since it is a grass field, a nice lawnlike green is left behind rather than stubble. After I park the tractor I remove my earplugs, again hearing the chatter of grasshoppers and the water in the creek. There will be time after lunch to work with the filly and get irrigation water right out onto the field I've just stacked. Grass hay won't make a second crop, but the timothy will grow back into lush pasture for late-summer feed.

Noon hour is the customary time for ranchers to make telephone calls, since it is only then during these long, busy summer days that the party you are calling is likely to be in the house. After eating, I call a neighbor living above me to see whether he's using the water from the ditch with which I irrigate the field I've just stacked. He still has hay down, so the water is available. Then I get a call from Tex. He'll be bringing the stud colt next week after he returns from a quick trip to see relatives. The colt has done well at every turn, always did, and he can see no benefit in keeping him longer.

It is hot, really hot, by the time I go back out. The filly is swatting flies with her tail while standing under the tall cottonwoods that line the lane. I waive off riding her.

Hot as it is, there is no sense putting her (or me) through any unnecessary exertion. I have ridden her seven or eight times, have progressed from round corral to the bigger arena. She is very smart. She stops well, turns with gentle direct rein on the snaffle, and is beginning to pick up leg cues. I am riding her with a loop rein, the way I prefer to start colts. In turning her left I give gentle pressure on the left side of the bit, but also press the rein into the right side of her neck and cue her with my right heel at the cinch line. The first of these signals is the one she knows from ground driving. The other two she will come to associate with the first, and she already is doing so, is already picking up the idea of a neck rein. I find myself riding her more often now with just one hand, able to give both the inside pressure and the neck pressure with the rein that way, helped by her growing understanding that she should turn away from my heel. In earlier days I would have had her in the hills by now, but age and some lumps have kicked in more caution. As it is, though, the next ride will probably be out to check the cattle alongside Emily and Sugar.

In the evening after supper, after the summer sun dips and makes the shadows grow, delaying deliberately until the evening cool begins to cut the August air, I go up to Butcher Creek ditch to make a set. Steve has progressed with the water to the point where Indian Coulee drops down and mouths out above the ditch. I scan the timber above me, see several mulie does and one nice buck, his horns velvet, beginning to venture from the shadows, their stubby tails twitching against the flies. Buddy, the dog, zigzags through the alfalfa field, helping me irrigate without knowing it, for his splashing feet tell me how far the water has reached.

I change the dam, close the cuts Steve has made for his set above me, then open those to let the water out on the new set. There is a small lateral ditch below in the alfalfa, just shovel-sized, that must be cleaned for twenty yards to divert water toward a high spot that would otherwise be missed. Elmer was a master at irrigating this field, balancing the water on all the high spots so it would evenly distribute. I must wait for a few minutes before I can clean the lateral, wait until the water arrives there to soak the baked surface.

I am high enough to see much of the valley as shadows settle in. I can see the meadow I stacked today, its green already brightening under the water I sent to it this afternoon. The new stack by the old house looks neat from this distance. Across the valley on our west range I can see several of the mares, mares bred back and verified in foal and thus turned out, their foals of this year mere dots alongside at such a distance.

. . .

Waiting for the water to reach the lateral, I go below the dam and sit on the bank of the ditch, boots dangling into the scant water that remains there. The now-ebbing afternoon heat and my position on the ditch bank facing west toward a sun about to run out bring back another ditch, another time. I am sitting on the edge of a sharp trench perhaps six feet deep. A red sun is setting through the dust kicked up by men and machines. To my left is a six-pack of beer, spilled open, and left of that a large strong man with sergeant's chevrons on his sleeve. His name is Dave Fleming. He is my platoon sergeant, I the platoon commander, and we are having a party of two the night before he rotates back to "the world."

In one of those rare, fortunate coincidences, this man had been my platoon sergeant on Okinawa, then had shown up in dusty Dong Ha with a half-smile on his face, reported into our company, told the C.O. he had worked for me in the past, and was promptly assigned to my platoon for the two months that remained on his tour. A natural leader, physically impressive, with a talent for delivering an unpopular directive in a way that made the Marines want to cooperate, Fleming's arrival was like a blood transfusion for me. I don't believe I ever heard him raise his voice, yet everything in the platoon began to run more smoothly the very day he arrived.

Our company was charged with organizing and running a "rough-rider" convoy of several hundred vehicles each day up dangerous "Highway 9," really just a dirt track. The platoon commanders in our company alternated, so Fleming and I were in charge every fourth day. I rode in the third truck back (we'd abandoned the control jeep as too obviously that of the leader, and equipped instead a truck with the necessary radio). Fleming brought up the rear in a radio-equipped wrecker. If incoming came, the doctrine was to keep going as fast as you could, because a stopped convoy is a dead duck. We were luckier than some of the other teams that ran the convoy, never having a serious attack and never losing anyone, although a sniper's bullet did once hiss over my head when I stepped out of the vehicle at our destination.

Fleming and I were as close friends as we could be and still be sergeant and his commander. This paradox is easier than it sounds, well understood and accepted in the military, although civilians within a "chain of command" seem to have all sorts of problems with it. You both have two personas. The second one, that of simply "friend," would just have to be postponed. We had no difficulty with that. But we had made reference to it once, when we did a rather foolish thing. A new colonel had demanded an inventory of all equipment in the battalion, suspecting that some had been appropriated by other units (which invariably happens in combat). To steal from another Marine unit was considered borrowing. To steal from the Army was considered admirable. The Crows who once lived on this ranch were allies of the Shoshonis, but each tribe would still gladly steal from the other. It was a game and also a necessity. We Marines were much the same.

But the colonel wanted his stuff back. A private had seen a water trailer (called a "water buffalo") with our unit markings up north at Con Tien, right on the Demilitarized Zone. Most of our troops were on the convoy, so Fleming and I, both suffering from cabin fever and wanting out of our dreary compound, hopped into a 2-1/2 ton truck, armed ourselves well, put on flak jackets, and headed up after the phantom water buffalo. The terrain was open and deserted, the road lonely. We kept a sharp eye out.

Con Tien, when we got there, was a village of sandbags and bunkers with no above-ground buildings whatsoever. It seemed nearly deserted, but was not, of course. Most of its inhabitants were underground. That got our attention. The place lived up to its reputation. Perched on the D.M.Z., Con Tien was often bombarded by the accurate Russian-built 130mm artillery pieces twenty miles north. These guns would fire sporadic bursts, then be quickly covered with camouflage again, since our planes would immediately head their way to retaliate. Later, an American president, attempting to help get his buddy elected, would call a halt to this retaliatory bombing, the result being that the guns could fire with complete impunity. And boy, did they, blowing hell out of everything. But that is another story.

Fleming and I found the water buffalo and backed up to it. We were a little sorry to take a piece of equipment from fellow Marines, but we grew less so when we saw the plentiful number of water trailers around. This unit obviously had an excellent "scrounger," very successful at collecting them.

There was an eerie silence as we hooked onto the trailer, just the hot wind flapping the flags on the headquarters bunker nearby. The people in the compound were ready for incoming; we were naked above ground. To make matters worse, we hit a mud hole as we pulled out, sticking the truck fast. A lance corporal in a three-quarter-ton pulled up. He was one of the few moving creatures we had seen on this anthill, and he was kind enough to latch onto us with a winch. He didn't waste a single moment, just gave us respectful greetings, pulled us out, unhooked, then spun gravel with his truck. We saw him park it and run to a bunker. We knew what they expected, could almost hear the terrifying airy whistle of incoming artillery, familiar to us down Dong Ha way. The guns reached us there, too, though less frequently. Sergeant Fleming gunned the truck. Neither of us spoke for some minutes. Finally, heading southeast toward "home," our truck and trailer kicking up a rooster-tail of dust, we eased back in our seats. "Someday," I said, "I'll look you up in Minneapolis and we'll have a drink and a good laugh over this." He agreed, and we both laughed, naughty boys who had just gotten away with something.

So that last evening he was there, having already checked out of the unit and thus no longer one of my troopers, Fleming brought up a six-pack and we walked over to the trench by the chapel. Every building had a trench or bunker with canvas panels on the bottoms of the walls so you could roll out during incoming, then in a couple more rolls, drop into a trench. We sat and drank the beer and talked of both military and nonmilitary things. He warned me of the condition of some of the trucks and had suggestions. I learned he was a bricklayer by trade, a partial explanation for his powerful arms and shoulders. Then he left, a friend now and soon to be a civilian. We promised to look each other up someday. But we have not done so.

Just why I think of this brief friendship and of a place I knew so long ago, now, on a summer evening irrigating in Montana, I have no clue. Perhaps the late yellow sun settling down among the peaks to the west recalls sunsets in Vietnam. The northern part I experienced was, in spite of the war, a beautiful place. There were green mysterious mountains that beckoned to a Montana Marine, in appearance Shangri-Las, but holding danger and death. There was a beautiful grove of hardwood trees with green underneath to contrast with the powdery red dust thrown up by our truck tires on Highway 9, a peaceful-looking place I wanted to go, but knew I should not.

Even more chiseled than my memories of people in my life are my memories for place, for terrain. At night in bed and even during busy daytime hours a field or a tree or a stream that I saw just once, many years before, will flash into my consciousness with the detail of a Rembrandt. There is no pattern to these memories. Some come from happy times, some from stressful, but often the memory is of a scene I experienced only once, very briefly, and which had no particular meaning to me. Maybe it is love for the land that causes this, and maybe that is why I am a rancher.

·　·　·

The water now has bubbled its way to the lateral ditch that needs cleaning. I work my way down the depression, peeling a layer of wet soil with my shovel, flipping the blade so that the earth removed forms a small dike on the lower side of the lateral. Thus I divert part of the flow, string it out toward the piece of relatively high ground, the part that would be ducked by the water if left to itself. All the ground is lower in elevation than the ditch, of course—I can't make water run uphill. But the water would run down where the grade was steepest—I modify that with these lateral ditches that keep moving it out of the "valleys."

It is nearly dark when I finish. The air is still very warm. As I walk toward home, though, away from the high ground where the warm air resides, I feel stirrings of cool, almost cold air intermixed, threaded through the August warmth, marbling it with hints of September. I realize that I am now a little tired of summer. It is a season you wait for all year. But it is a season of long workdays, of growing things to get you through the times that lie ahead. It is a season of preparing for things to come. Maybe the Marine Corps recollections have caused my thinking this way, for fighting men are always most ill at ease while they wait, then are settled, resolute, and happier when the battle call is sounded. The first frost for me is a call to arms, a call to the fall in which I am most alive, the winter that follows being my necessary payment for the glory of fall.

I walk home, the shovel over my shoulder. Walking downhill in irrigation boots I still limp a little, but my leg is better. The stud colt will come home next week.

FALL

14

A dusting on the mountains · New neighbor ·
A nice Lutheran girl · Return of the stud colt

It is on Labor Day that I first see it. It has rained during the night, then cleared. I turn off the alarm clock, pull on my jeans, and look south toward the mountains out the window of our loft. In the dawn light, pillowy clouds hug the bases of the mountains, and above them, just catching the dawn, are peaks newly white with what for us, down below, was merely rain. I stand for a minute and watch while this dusting of new snow gets its first pink sun.

I have awakened thinking of a Labor Day years ago, when the boys were tiny and we lived in Bridger. We hadn't yet made the decision to move here, fearing the long commute it would cause for me, and instead bundled up our whole family nearly every weekend and aimed the old GMC pickup toward the ranch. Nora was still alive then, living alone in the white ranch house. In addition to seeing her we needed to check on our fledgling livestock, mostly Holstein calves we had bought at dairies and raised on the bucket during the summer.

Our house then was but a one-bedroom cottage, built by Emily's uncle Art and his musical wife Dorothy, a teacher. The whole house, complete with custom cupboards and cabinets, was built in 1930 for a total of $5,000. The couple apparently never planned children because they built the house without room for any. When we decided it would be easier for me to commute than to dislocate the family not only in summers but nearly every weekend, we hired a carpenter to convert the attic to three small bedrooms with dormers. Then, a year later, I doubled the size of the house by building a south addition, a big living room with this sleeping loft and window designed expressly so that on dramatic mornings when the mountains caught their first snow we could look out the window and see it. (Art and Dorothy, liking their privacy, had ringed the yard with lilacs, producing a hedge to which Emily is more attached than I, so a higher perspective is needed to see the mountains.)

I had never built anything before, but the addition turned out well, post-and-beam construction with masonry Trombe walls inside south glass, free heat from the sun in winter. On the Labor Day I'm recalling, this addition had not yet been built, of course, and where I am standing would have been in midair, south of the house, hovering over the little enclosure that protected the well and pump. We had come over on Friday night, unpacked things, primed the pump, then held our breaths until the water system pressurized and the pump turned off. (That meant I would not have to crawl under the house with my soldering torch to fix leaks, a common occurrence.)

We were no sooner settled than a car pulled in. Our neighbor and his eighty-year-old mother got out and walked to the back door. I knew, then, how I would spend the weekend. When my neighbor brought Kate so soon after our arrival it was not just for coffee but because she still handled much of the ranch business, including any requests for help, and I'd seen alfalfa fields thickly covered with second-cutting hay bales at their place on our way in. After a few pleasantries she asked if I would come and stack for them. This was not an era in which it would have occurred to any of us that I had an option to say "no," that the projects I had planned for the weekend, that even time with the family, might have taken precedence over helping a neighbor. So I said "yes." They would pay me fairly, the money would be useful, and what choice was there when Kate asked me to help? So I stacked Saturday, Sunday, and Monday, finished bone-weary, then packed everybody up and returned to Bridger that evening.

I do not recall this Labor Day "holiday" with feelings of regret or of having been put-upon. But that memory has come simultaneously with another, quite different one, an experience Emily had last winter. She received a call at school. Our cows were out on the highway. Securing permission from her principal, she drove quickly to the scene. A gate had been rubbed open, and, yes, the whole bunch of cows was grazing contentedly along the highway, working their way toward town, already having progressed a mile or more. Emily parked the car with flashers on and began doing her best to turn the group back toward home.

Soon a well-dressed rancher parked a flashy pickup behind the car and got out to help. The two turned the cows and began pushing them south. Between yells at the cattle the man turned to Emily and said, "Thanks for stopping to help get my cows back in."

"Thank *you* for helping *me*—they're our cows!" Emily replied, whereupon the man turned on his heels, walked smartly to his pickup, and left her there alone. She was stunned. Luckily, the cows had turned, others stopped to help, and soon the naughty creatures were back where they belonged, the gate tied securely. We learned later that the man was a neighbor we have never met, a man who came here with much money, bought a ranch, hired a manager, and built a mansion by the river. He raises registered Angus cattle, which made his confusion preposterous—our cows are mixed black Angus, red Angus, and black baldies that look nothing like his. Perhaps he was embarrassed. No matter. I've wracked my brain ever since the event trying to think of one rancher I've known, one rancher's spouse, one rancher's child who would fail to help a woman with a herd of cattle out exposed to vehicular traffic, who would not stick with her until the situation was under control. I cannot think of a single one who would leave her there alone. And so, this morning, I think of the unquestioning help neighbors have given to me and I to them, and I hope the rancher down the road is not a portent of things to come.

.   .   .

But the unsettling feelings that come with this contrast are easy to shake off this morning. There is frost on the roof of the chicken house Elmer and Nora built during their brief flirtation with large-scale chicken raising. (They soon abandoned the idea. Elmer's lungs, damaged by cigarettes and hay dust, could no longer stand the cleaning of chicken coops.) The sun now fully lights the mountaintops with neon white. The air after the rain will be fresh and crisp, and the stud colt is in the arena. By shifting to the east window I can see him, his red coat glossy as he makes passes up and down the board fence in a proud running walk.

Emily and I start slowly this morning, for we are in a holiday mode. We have both returned to school. Summer will not seem truly over until the second cutting of alfalfa is put up. I'll have to mow next weekend, weather permitting, then bale and stack evenings after school. It will take all week even if the weather is good, because my helper, Steve, is also back in school, and second-cutting alfalfa takes longer to cure. I can envision it and smell it, lush, dark green, packed with protein, stubborn about drying, because the September sun has already subtly slipped south and gives itself to us an hour or two less each day than when the first cutting was down.

At breakfast we critique the weekend. "Well, we proved our ranch horses could stand a parade," Emily says.

That was on Saturday. "Except for the Shriner's Oriental Band," I say, and Emily laughs. That band was too much for even gentle Major. The black, Arab garments and the strange instruments of this exotic group kept the whites of Major's eyes showing, kept him snorting with a sound like that of a mad cat spitting. We had been assigned a position just behind the Shriners, but before the parade was half over I could see

Major wouldn't put on much of a show for the reviewing stand unless something could be done. So once when the band stopped to play we eased around them, Emily and Sugar on one side, Major and I on the other, Major doing a beautiful sidepass all the way around the noisy crew, refusing to take his eyes off these bearded humanoids. Then, once around, this massive spook behind them, our horses reined back into a pretty running walk just in time for the announcer, who adjusted to the altered order and said, "And here are Dan and Emily Aadland on their beautiful Tennessee Walking Horses." So it worked out just fine. I was even hoping people saw the sidepass and thought I was making Major do it deliberately!

After the Shriner band nothing was worthy of spooking Major, not the fire engine that periodically tested its whistle, not the steel-wheeled wagon pulled by a friend's Belgians, not the myriad little kids running out onto the pavement to retrieve the candy thrown by the jaunty clown. So our ranch horses got an initiation and we, after some jitters, had fun.

That night there was a street dance, fueled by a band that didn't know whether it was rock or country, and so did some of both. The street was crowded, most people lubricated by the free flow of spirits out the doors of the two bars. We cruised the sidewalk, running into half a dozen old classmates we had not seen for a while. There had been a rodeo, and some of the performing cowboys were there, mild celebrities, taking ribbings for rides that hadn't lasted eight seconds. Mixed with the cowboys and ranchers and western girls, with big hair cascading from under their Stetsons down their backs to leather belts with their names tooled in them, were tourists in shorts, town people, and miners, muscular from holding jackhammers to the ceilings in the shafts of the palladium mine near here.

We ran into a ranch hand named Sam, who had recently started working for a very unpopular man. I asked him how he liked his job. He took a sip from the Coors can he carried, threw his head back and squinted, warming up for something profound. "It ain't as bad as I thought it would be. The only thing I really hate is that when I'm driving one of the boss's outfits, no one will wave at me." He took another sip. "Boss's nephew came out from back East to help for two weeks. First thing, we go out to stretch barbed wire and he strips off his shirt. We were next to the highway so I suspect he wanted to flex for any tourists comin' by. He'd been eyeing the cars through his mirror sunglasses. I said, 'What did you do that for?' He says, 'Well, I got to think of my tan.' 'Tan, hell,' I said, 'You're gonna look like you had a bad fight with a pissed-off cat by the time we get done.' And he sure as hell did." Sam went for another sip, shook his empty can with disgust, took his bearings, leaned toward the door of the bar and said, 'See yuh, Dan.'

. . .

The Saturday night on main street was pretty much as these occasions always were, even back when I was a boy, the minister's kid cruising town with my friends on foot, glad for the excitement. The band was better then. Led by the town electrician, a good fiddler, that band in the Fifties had cranked out Bluegrass and country hits, Marty Robbins gunfighter songs, a good, driving rendition of "Orange Blossom Special," and one more that sticks in my mind: I can still hear their rendition of "Does Your Chewing Gum Lose Its Flavor on the Bedpost Overnight?" That song ran through my mind for a whole day, the day after one of these bashes, when I stacked bales in the heat while nursing a jaw so sore I could not imagine chewing anything, much less stomach the thought of used chewing gum.

I'd had a "fun" fight with my friend Dicky Peterson, a fight in which we never got mad but just the same in which we beat each other with mighty left hooks, knocked each other down in turn in a kid version of a John Wayne, haymaker-throwing, barroom brawl. None of it seemed to hurt that much, which makes me suspect in retrospect that we must have gotten hold of some beer that night. When one of us landed an especially good punch the other congratulated him. This took place long after the streets had cleared and the bars had closed. Once Dick knocked me down and I lay on the pavement laughing, for the black tar was still warm with the sun of the day, and I was enjoying every minute of this madness. Then I got up and knocked Dick down.

The next day, however, neither of us was quite so chipper. Our faces were bruised, our arms and chests sore, and our jaws dysfunctional. Dick worked for the same rancher, ran the loader that brought me the hay. At noon, at the table, after trying to chew a piece of cube steak, he asked me under his breath, "Why the hell did we do that?"

All I could say was, "I guess we thought we were having fun." And Fred, the rancher, just tilted his head back and gave a hearty laugh. He'd been watching us all morning and was veteran of enough western partying to know exactly what was going on.

But on this Saturday night, thirty years after my brawl with my friend, Emily and I headed home before any fights started. The next day I got a critique of further events from a rancher who stopped by to tell me he was missing a bull. "Well, you left before things really got rolling last night."

"I'm getting old."

"Kathy Evenson won the wet T-shirt contest," he said in a confidential tone, as if I'd really missed something.

"Thank goodness the honor went to a nice Lutheran girl," I told him. I relay this conversation to Emily now at the breakfast table and she merely says, "I'm not surprised. She's well-equipped for it." Then we laugh and refill our coffee cups. It has been a fun weekend, and we do not want it to end, do not want to head back to the grind of our double lives tomorrow. Yes, it has been good to go back to school, good in the sense that school means friendly "hellos" from students who have jumped a big notch in their trip to adulthood just over the summer, students genuinely glad to see me. It has been good to walk into the teacher's lounge and trade outrageous stories with the crew of good friends there. But this is all colored, too, by the tough times I know lie ahead, the struggle with short winter days and darkness that I think of with an odd mixture of relish and dread.

. . .

I stand to look again out the kitchen window toward the arena. Emily says, "He really is pretty. He's grown since we sent him up there."

Tex brought him back toward the end of last week. I watched the stud colt back out of the trailer, a good friend coming home after a temporary estrangement. His muscles looked lean and hard; his big eyes missed nothing. He trumpeted to our breeding stallion and to any mares within earshot.

Tex described their experiences together. "You'd put it all there already, all he needed was ridin'. Never had any trouble. Boy, can he cruise."

Major was tied to the tack shed hitching rail, ready for Tex, who pulled his saddle from the tack compartment on the trailer. I got mine from the tack shed. We curried the horses and saddled up. I felt no apprehension when I turned the stud colt's stirrup and climbed aboard. My ease was not because my leg was better or because I knew Tex had done a good job, as he always does. It was because I knew that this test ride, this ride Tex wanted for showing his workmanship on the horse, was irrelevant. There would be no problems. And there weren't. We took a nice two-mile turn up to the top of the hill, and the colt was wonderful, just as I expected, Tex having refined all the cues I had started earlier and introduced some new things, too. He had the colt neck-reining and sidepassing. He could open and close gates from his back and could drag a rope behind. I complimented Tex on his first-rate job, but I knew, too, that all was not square yet between the colt and me. This ride was not the last word, was not the end of it. The colt would try me, would test my leg and my quickness and my resolve when Tex was out of sight and it was just he and I.

And so, on my third cup of coffee, stalling, I turn quiet, and Emily knows what I am thinking and what I plan to do. "I guess I'll ride the colt."

"You sure? It must have rained half an inch. It'll be muddy."

"He's got good caulked shoes," I say, and look her in the eyes, and she knows, too, that it is time. So I pull on my boots and go outside. After doing a few chores I catch the stud colt, tie him by the tack shed, curry him and check his feet. He is tense under the shiny coat, not yet readjusted to my touch. He has always been extraordinarily thin-skinned, not goosey exactly, just ultrasensitive. I saddle him and turn him around several times. There is a slight hump in his back, so I elect the round corral and move him around me several times in each direction in an abbreviated longe.

Emily's estimate of last night's rain is, if anything, short, for the round corral is ankle-deep in mud. I put the stud colt against the rail, take the slack out of the reins, and turn the stirrup. I know what will happen. There is a watchfulness about him, a seriousness, and I know exactly what he will do. What transpires is not because of any fine planning on my part, but still, it is simply perfect. I touch my foot to the stirrup and start to quickly swing on, but before I am half mounted he gives a giant bucking leap. He has miscalculated. My right foot has not yet begun its arc over his back, so I simply drop it back to the ground and pull my left out of the stirrup as he shoots upward. So I am standing holding the reins while he pays the penalty, for he has lost all footing with the force of his upward leap, his feet slipping from under him in the mud, and he comes down hard on his side making a mighty "whoosh" of breath being knocked out of his body. Mud splatters into the fence and onto my legs. He lies there a second, surprised, unhurt, foolish. Then he pulls his front feet under him and begins to rise. As the stirrup comes up off the ground I step into it and rise with him. I back him two steps, say "whoa," and sit there on his back while the shakes go out of his body. Finally, he heaves a giant, sighing breath and relaxes.

I take a few quick turns around the round corral, first to the left, then to the right. Then I get off, say "whoa," and get back on. I do this several times on both sides. Each time he stands stock still as if with utmost respect until my opposite foot catches the stirrup and I tighten my legs to tell him he can move forward. It is the lessons we humans teach ourselves through our own trials, our own miscues, that have the most power. It must be the same for horses. The stud colt has taught himself well, has given himself a lesson better than any given him by either Tex or me. He has mis-behaved while I mounted and has taken a humiliating, frightening fall because of it.

So we ride. We take a couple more turns around the corral before I lean over and pull back the piston latch on the gate to let us out. Then it's down the lane and across the bridge over Butcher Creek, through the meadows and across the blooming alfalfa. We go over the hill on the trail up Indian Coulee, across the flat, then start to drop down into the next drainage, Beaver Creek. There are many gates to open and close. Each time, when I get back on, I vary my manner, deliberately being clumsy, giving him every chance to take advantage. But he does not do so.

·   ·   ·

My father-in-law Elmer was a gentle man. He knew the necessity of discipline, but he so disliked controversy that what for most was a mild discussion with slight dis-agreement was to him an argument or even a fight. He believed in commanding absolute respect from horses, but his preferred way of getting that, whenever possible, was for the horse to discover the limits for himself. And so, if a horse had an obnox-ious tendency to swing its head into him hard, to use him as its rubbing post, Elmer met the swing toward him with a sharp jab into the horse's neck with an elbow. But he did this without letting his body or his voice hint that the jab came from him. He was an expert at this. It took an extremely perceptive observer to see the jab at all, and the horse had no idea it came from Elmer, for the man's body language and soft monologue did not change. He murmured affectionate syllables into the horse's ear the entire time.

Once while I watched him, Elmer turned to me and said, "I can't let him get away with that, but I don't want him mad at me. So this way he thinks he's doing it to himself." Now as the stud colt flies over the sagebrush toward Beaver Creek, Elmer's face and voice and manner come to me, and the scene in the round corral is reenacted, but with him standing leaning on the gate and watching. He is wearing his brown felt cowboy hat, his jeans are turned up once at the cuff (the style of his youth and to which he adhered), and he watches intently with those blue eyes that miss nothing. The colt makes his jump into the air as I start to mount, comes down with a splat of mud Elmer would liken to the result of a great big cow crapping on a flat rock. As the colt comes down the intent look on Elmer's face changes to one of concern, then resumes its shine when he sees that I am all right and that the colt, landing on a mattress of mud, is fine too. And then he says, "That's lacking nothing. It's perfect. Nothing a horse hates and fears more than falling down. You could have done it, you could have pulled him over, but you wouldn't have wanted to, and besides, it wouldn't have been the same."

We hit the county road that peters out into a hard dirt track, this being its upper reaches where it merges into the private ranch road of the Millers, our neighbors to the east. The stud colt flies up the packed dirt, his hooves in perfect four-beat cadence, the fence posts flying by. A startled crow lifts from a gnarled cedar post, cawing his surprise, and in the creek below a steep bank, a heron extends it delicate, balsa wings and strokes itself into the air. We reach the Miller corrals, pause a moment at another gate, then fly up the fence line onto still another neighbor's land. At the foundation of the old homestead in the coulee, alongside the skeleton of what once was a grand old touring car, the stud colt shies sideways, dodging the spooks that lie hidden in the junk pile of the place, then takes the spring creek in the coulee bottom with an effortless leap and heads up the steep south side. If he has yet drawn a deep breath, I have not detected it.

On top again I play games with the sagebrush, reining zigzag around clumps of my choice, helping with leg cues so light they are actually just twitches of my calf muscles. So thin-skinned and subtle is he that these mere kisses at his side are signal enough to make him respond with a sharp turn. We will reach it, the two of us, and it is not far away, the ambiance so subtle that as rider I will be aware of giving no cue at all, as if my very volition is read by him and interpreted in the way I want.

Just once, on top, I let him briefly gallop, but with taut rein, for at this stage of training the edge of control feels very close. We hit the crest of the hill and drop back into our own valley on my neighbor's Jeep road, the stud colt going faster on this steep downgrade than I have ever allowed a horse to go. But I don't feel foolish or reckless. The colt inspires confidence. His balance is perfect on the steep slope, his gait now a sliding, rhythmic pace, both legs sliding down on one side, then the other, the back-and-forth motion that of a dance. In a flash we are home.

At the tack room, I look at my watch. The colt has taken me five or six miles over rough terrain, has been allowed to lope for only one brief stretch, the rest of the time held to a walk or running walk, and scarcely forty minutes have passed. He has worked up a nice sheen of sweat, but there is no lather on him. I rub him under each eye. Then, standing in front of him, I drop my forehead to his bony face just below the eyes with a thump harder than intended, hard enough it hurts me a little, though he does not flinch. Resting it there I say to him, "Howdy, Pard."

15

Roundup · Elsie's pets

There are four of us. During this dawning of the "empty nest" portion or our lives, Emily and I sometimes have nice surprises, and this is one of them, a gap in work and school that allows Jonathan, our middle son, to join us on the weekend we move cattle down from our east pasture.

My grown boys often tease me about having horses saddled or tractors idling at their moment of return in readiness to take advantage of their help. I go along with the exaggerations and make them worse: irrigation boots in their sizes lined up and ready, pairs of gloves with their names on them, a list on the refrigerator of jobs saved up for their services.

But if the job happens to be moving cattle I get few complaints. The work we call "cowboying," working cattle on horses, represents a very small percentage of most ranchers' actual time. Little time is spent sitting in the saddle compared to that spent sitting on the driver's seat of a pickup truck or tractor. Most of us wish it were the other way around. It's just such a fine job, mounting a good horse, teaming with it in mutual effort, riding hard when necessary. The world is different from the back of a horse. You are taller, thus see better. The creature under you is the original "all-terrain vehicle," capable of going places no wheels could dare, yet is flesh and blood, interacting with your environment. Sometimes that means a sudden spook when a mule deer flushes from the shady spot under a juniper bush at the head of Indian Coulee, where you almost always find one.

We have started early. Even in cool September, we move cattle early, for when the sun warms, they take to the shade in the coulees, trying to fight flies. So we arose in the dark, Emily fixing breakfast while I slipped out to saddle the horses. I could have hollered at the boys, but Jon, after all, is on vacation, and Steve, back at school, deserves to sleep until sunup on a Saturday. Besides, I like going out in the cool dawn, tying four good geldings to the tack room rail, currying them down, and saddling them one by one.

Good old Rockytop, in his late teens but still much horse, is for Steve. He is the biggest of the lot. Sugar, high-headed, a blaze that broadens on his forehead and circles a patch of sorrel, is next. An old friend once referred to the top of the blaze as a target and for several years called periodically trying to buy "that gelding that had the target on his forehead." Sugar is Emily's, though, and has never been for sale. I lifted Elmer's Connolly Brothers high-cantled saddle aboard. Elmer bought the saddle new, for his sixteenth birthday, in 1919. We have his journal entry. The price was $75, a high price in those days. The saddle is narrow in the tree, right for Sugar but reflecting the narrower, higher-withered horses they rode in those pre-Quarter Horse days. It is very heavy with its long skirts and built-in saddle bags. It is also the only saddle Emily will use. I often accuse her of choosing a large husband and keeping him around all these years only so that she has someone to throw her dad's saddle on her horse.

I then saddled Monte, the young gelding Jon will ride, and finally Major, for me. The stud colt watched the proceedings from the arena, nickered, seeming to want in on things. But I am not yet ready to introduce him to cattle. This fall we will continue to build what is developing between us. If I *needed* him for work, we could do the job now. But since I have good ranch geldings I would rather continue to bring the colt along under circumstances I dictate and can fully control. It is not merely a relationship I am building with him, but a marriage. I will lay the groundwork as perfectly as I know how, hoping that it will last a long, long time.

After saddling I went back into the house. The sun would not be up for some time, but the clouds hanging over the east hills were taking on a hint of rose, and to the south I could see the mountains. As I filled my coffee cup I asked, "Boys stirring yet?"

"Yeah. I did have to call them a couple times. Jon's in the shower, and Steve has been there."

"I'd think they would shower *after* we move the cattle."

"Oh, they will then, too," Emily said, laughing.

Soon the boys came into the kitchen, grabbed coffee cups, and did the compulsory grumbling. "Do we really need to move cattle in the middle of the night?" Jon asked.

"Actually, we're already behind schedule," I told him. "Just pretend it's hunting season, and you know a massive whitetail buck is easing his way along that willow patch by the ditch in the calf pasture. And you have to be there to greet him."

"Sorry, but that doesn't work. Cattle just don't motivate me as much as whitetail bucks."

And now we are in the saddle, in the lane, four of us, with sixteen hooves striking gravel and giving off enough of the aura of a Wild Bunch to make it fun. We could be a posse headed out to do its work, a cavalry unit on patrol, or some of the pilgrims headed toward Canterbury. The sun has not yet crested the east hill—it will peep out just to the right of Indian Coulee this time of year—but it is close, telegraphing its intent with a bulge of bright above the ridge. The breeze is still chilly. Even I, the warmblooded one of the family, have retained a down vest, and the rest wear jackets they can tie to the saddle strings later on.

The four horses, two tandem pairs, rumble across the boards of the bridge over Butcher Creek. We discuss strategy. When we enter the range, Steve and I will go left, beginning a clockwise circle of the range. Emily and Jon will go right, counterclockwise. We will make two half circles and meet. It is very important to stick to the perimeter of the range, kicking cattle inward, not leaving any of the coulees unchecked.

We go through the gate to the hills, say "see ya," and part. Steve and I will most likely ride a mile or more before seeing cattle, for I'm certain they are all on top. But it is a ride that must be made, because there are two prominent coulees north of the one we named after the tree burial. We will ride past the base of each, look up it, then continue to the north fence. The first coulee is almost too wide to be called that; some would call it a small valley. (The term "coulee" is a pretty broad one in Montana, however. In the north of our county there is a huge depression several miles across named Big Coulee. But to me the term means a draw or gulch or arroyo that feeds into a larger valley below.)

Through this broader coulee on our range runs a Jeep road we haven't used for years, erosion over time having made it too dangerous. It never was very safe. Elmer would drive the Jeep up to take salt or fix fence, engine rumbling in the lowest gear, seeming to ignore a sideways slant that made you hope there was glue on the tires. Going up, the passenger was on the uphill side of the Jeep. Nora would tolerate that, just barely. Going down was the opposite, so she would make Elmer stop on top and let her out to walk down.

We see no cows so we continue along the base of the hill, then turn up through the pine-studded coulee on the north edge of our range. This one used to be "chuck coulee" but is now "elk coulee." There were always many rock chucks here, the gaping holes of their dens to be watched when horseback. But then one day after Jon and I had ridden freezing on a fruitless elk hunt in the mountains, Jon and Steve sauntered up on our own range looking for deer and saw in this coulee two magnificent bull elk. They were not legal game here, but it was a thrill to see them, for none have occupied this ranch in anyone's memory. Since then, after a big early snowfall, a large band of cows and calves bedded two nights on our ranch. Elk are a great success story for those who manage wildlife. Big, challenging to hunt, and wonderful to eat, elk have grown steadily in number, herds having filtered into the lower ranges they once called home, occupying no longer only the mountains. After seeing these two wonderful apparitions, Jon and Steve promptly renamed this draw "elk coulee."

We top out, Major and Rockytop both blowing a bit now, and near the fence that marks our north boundary, in a tiny draw, we find half a dozen cow/calf pairs. Now the work begins. The animals eye us sleepily, trying to make us out, for the new sun is now behind us. Then they respond to our hoots, bawl for their calves, and work their way to the sage flat on top of the ridge and onto the wagon road, heading south toward Emily and Jon. This is what we want. We continue our circle, finding more scattered pairs, starting them toward the center.

This time of the year the independence of calves can cause problems. Weighing 400 to 500 pounds, the calves now only nurse two or three times a day, the rest of the time considering their mothers rather useless and freely roaming the range on their own. The potential for missing a calf and leaving it behind is the main reason we do this little drive in two stages. We will round up the cows and their calves, bring them to the home corrals, sort off the bulls (whose services are no longer needed), then hold the cows and calves overnight in a small pasture near the house. If all is quiet during the night we can be pretty certain we have not inadvertently separated a pair. Then we merely jump the herd across the highway in the morning to let them graze their way through the cottonwood bottom and across the river to the west range we have saved for them as fall feed. If, however, a particular cow bawls all night, we know we have missed her calf. Either she will take matters into her own hands, jumping a fence and heading for the hills to find her calf, or we will help her out in the morning, turning her loose to be retrieved when she and her calf are paired up.

Now Steve and I work our way downhill again, on the east part of our range that slopes toward Beaver Creek. We haven't yet seen Jon and Emily again, but we do see evidence of their work, twenty cows and their calves coming toward those we have found, but from the opposite end of the range. There is a magnet in all herd animals, a cohesion that helps in gathering tasks. The bawling of the cows signals "get-up-and-go," so that even cows not yet pushed by humans on horseback begin to find their way toward those already herding up.

Now to my left, however, a smart and contrary red cow decides she will have none of it and takes off in a lope east, the wrong direction, toward the old Dickinson homestead. She is an excuse for rough riding. I rein Major left, kick him into a lope. Steve reins hard on Rockytop, enforcing on him their duty of staying on the flank while I run down the renegade, for the big gelding would much like to stampede after us. We go through a low swale, jump the spring in the bottom, and overtake the cow halfway up the other side. She turns, caught red-handed, and heads toward the main bunch, picking up her bawling calf on the way.

As I work toward the top of a small ridge after turning the cow, I look south, and over still another ridge see Emily and Jon, just the tops of their hats first, then their torsos, and finally their horses. They are pushing another small bunch of pairs in front of them. By the time we meet up we have what looks to be the entire bunch in a loose herd, scattered over five acres or so. We stop to compare notes. "Did you check the forty that juts east?"

"That's where we found these," Emily assures me.

Quite certain that we have them all, we can now push the herd into the valley. Some of the cows have already gone. Cows have good memories. The older ones in this bunch know that better feed and a welcome change lie ahead. We will not attempt to keep the bunch together heading down the hill. Each side of each coulee dropping into the valley holds at least one cow trail, and the herd will finger out, taking their trails of choice. We spread out, each descending on a different route, pushing the cows ahead of us. At the bottom we soon have them bunched near the gate, and when we're satisfied that we have them all, I open it and we push them through. Then, for a quarter mile, we work very hard. The alfalfa, since its second mowing, has grown eight inches tall. It is lush and potent, no frost so far having been sharp enough to wilt it. The mouthfuls the cows grab as we push them through aren't enough to pose risk of bloat, but the stuff must taste awfully fine, for every cow turns leaden, and it takes many whoops and hollers and gallops left and right to keep the bunch together moving down.

There is always a great deal of noise when you work cattle, a cacophony of bawling. The uninitiated observer might think the animals are uncomfortable or abused, that they are bawling their protest. What is actually happening is simply communication between cow and calf. A mother cow might be content to let her calf graze a half mile away, but move into her space and her first thoughts are of her maternal duties. She has but one way to keep contact with her calf, and that is to "moo" for it. Once herded up, the bunch is like shifting sand, and the cow keeps constant tab with her bawls and the calf's replies. When all members of our little eighty-five-cow herd do this, the din is considerable.

Each cow knows the sound of her calf (and each calf that of its mother) and can separate it with complete precision from the similar sounds of all the others. But I suppose there is nothing so surprising about that, for animals of other species and humans, too, have that ability. My mother once picked out the cry of my baby brother from the pandemonium on a crowded beach, recognized it through the din of many children crying and playing and went straight to the lost child. Perhaps those who know little of cows are surprised at their ability to interpret sounds that, to people, sound so unvaried.

. . .

We get the cows through the gate at the bottom of the alfalfa field, and into the grass meadow. Now it is an easy shot, the critters bunched up, a moving mass in front of me. It will not happen on this short drive, but that moving mass of animals in front of you can be nearly hypnotic if you stare at it all day. I remember nights in bed when

I could not close my eyes without seeing a mobile mass of squirming sheep, like white worms in my mind's eye, this after two long days spent helping Jake move his band to summer pasture.

Jake and Elsie, his wife, were family friends and members of my dad's church. Even before I was old enough to work on ranches full time in the summer, I started helping Jake when he needed an extra hand. Jake could work beside you all morning and say scarcely two sentences, a fact that made some find him odd and cold. But I soon decided they simply did not know him. He had a subtle sense of humor and occasionally said something totally outrageous but with a look of complete solemnity on his face. Elsie was a huge woman, absolutely the best cook in the valley as far as I was concerned. As a minister's son I had sampled the fare of just about every ranch in the valley, never tasted ranch food I didn't like, but none came up to Elsie's.

During shearing Jake would hire me to pen, the lowest of the shearing jobs, but I was just a boy, unskilled, not thinking to covet the glory of the shearers themselves. Those men were Herculean, biceps bulging under their long-sleeved shirts, as they bent over all day, held by a sling around their torsos, clippers flashing and smelling of hot oil, the best of the men shearing up to 200 sheep in a day, a task I found astounding. Next down on the pecking order (and pay scale) was the sacker, usually an older, athletic boy. Wool sacks are burlap affairs about eight feet long, and they are packed with fleeces until tight as a drum. This is accomplished by hanging them vertically from a special frame with open end on top protruding through a circular hole in a wooden platform. The sacker throws fleeces into the sack, then jumps in feet-first, jumps up and down to pack them, crawls out and adds more fleeces thrown up to him by the kid doing the tying, and then packs some more. From my boyhood vantage point, the boy who tied the fleeces was another step down on the scale. His job was to fold each fleece neatly in on itself and tie the bundle with a particular quick-release knot, then toss it up to the sacker.

Finally there was the penner (me), charged with keeping several sheep instantly available to each shearer. These were held in little individual pens, one for each shearer, with an opening toward the man, covered only with a canvas curtain. Through the curtain the shearer thrust his hand, grabbed a sheep, pulled it out, then held it in a belly-up position that looked comical to me. In a few minutes the sheep was turned loose, devoid of its woolly coat, looking skinny and naked compared with its appearance moments earlier. Penning was hard work, though, involving much pushing and shoving on the bodies of the woolly creatures. Soon my jeans would be wet and shiny with lanolin, the smell of it tolerable but persistent. As penner it was also my duty to brand the sheep after they were sheared, using an iron not dipped in fire but in a special paint.

Elsie would fix three banquets per day: breakfast, dinner, and supper for the small army of shearers and helpers who would descend on her kitchen. We would go into the mud room and wash up, one at a time, at the utility sink out there, the shearers washing first, of course, each man doing a thorough job, soaping up to the elbows under his turned-up sleeves, and when hands were clean, soaking his face too with a double handful of hot water. This did not disperse all the smell of lanolin, but Elsie's cooking did. There were gallons of mashed potatoes and gravy, ham or turkey or roast beef, corn, and the best hot rolls I had ever tasted, then pie and ice cream for dessert. There was not a single fat man on the crew. They could eat this way three times each day because their output of energy was prodigious. They were plenty hungry for Elsie's supper at six o'clock.

In June, when the lambs were larger and the hill grass ready, Jake would trail his 1500 ewes and their lambs from his home place on Butcher Creek, down the country road and onto the highway, through town, and finally to his summer pasture on a creek we call Jackstone.

He would come to get me to help him, normally without notice, for his generation of ranch men still did not believe in doing business by telephone. The telephone was for the women and their chatting on party lines, listened in on by ranch wives up and down the creek. So Jake would show up and visit with my dad while I got a few things together. Then I would ride to Jake's ranch in his Willys Jeep pickup.

Trailing the sheep on the road meant a long walk but easy work. Ahead of the column were Jake and Elsie in the pickup pulling the sheep wagon in which their herder would live for the summer. They warned traffic and closed gates to the pastures on either side of the road and to the lanes of other ranch houses. Behind the column I walked with the herder and his dog, pushing the ewes along, occasionally helping a lamb out of a jam or over an obstacle. It was far more pleasant than helping old Ramsland, the crippled, Bible-quoting prophet, with his cows, as my brother and I had done. We walked that little bunch twenty miles over county roads, the good but severe old man driving his ancient Plymouth, brother and I thinking we would die of thirst, lunch consisting of dry biscuits and a pull on Ramsland's water jug. When you helped Jake and Elsie there was always plenty to eat and drink and little yelling or stress, for they were thoroughly professional sheep people. No one knew the business better.

. . .

At the end of the first day we camped just over Johnson bridge (named after a different Johnson family, not Emily's) in a nice cottonwood grove, where two county roads met. From the site I could see our swimming hole in the Stillwater River, but I did not long for it, because the water was still far too cold for swimming. It was easy to hold the sheep overnight in this shady grove. To mark the edge of the camp and to guard against the sheep moving east, I held my end by setting up an army cot squarely in the middle of the county road and sleeping on it. There was little traffic, and if a car happened along it would surely see me and the sleeping sheep straddling the road. I marvel at this today, for the river along this road is now lined with cabins, the road clouded with dust in summer from heavy use.

The last time I camped with Jake's sheep by Johnson bridge, ground had been broken for the very first of the cabins in this immediate vicinity. A concrete slab had been poured. The workmen had left, so we did not know that the concrete was still soft. Before we realized it, several ewes and lambs had walked across a corner of the slab leaving inch-deep tracks. Jake was afraid the people would be mad, but I thought it was rather neat. It's just a nice signature, I told him, same as when you scratch your name in a new wet sidewalk. So, in an instance of a kid contributing to the delinquency of an adult, I persuaded him to scratch the year next to the tracks of his sheep—1958.

. . .

In more recent times the Aadland family has had a little ritual on some summer evenings. We go into the Dew Drop Inn and buy a soft ice cream cone, then take a brief ride around "the horn," a loop along the Stillwater River that passes the place where we camped sheep. It has become a game. I start telling the story. "Boys, did I ever tell you about the time I was camped with Jake's sheep . . ."

I rarely get that far. "Yes, Dad," they groan, "and the sheep made tracks in the new concrete slab under that cabin right over there, and if it ever burns down or is moved you could go over there and see them fresh as the day the sheep made them."

"Well, yes, that's about right." But I nearly always can find something else to add to the story, something true that they have never heard before. "But did I tell you that just before we arrived at that campsite that day we had a sudden, hard shower? And the boards of the bridge were shiny and slick and the sheep would not cross. We pressed them in every way we knew, but the front ones braced their legs at the edge of the bridge and flatly refused to move. So finally Elsie got out of the pickup. She waddled right into the middle of the white mass of sheep, calling 'come lambs, come lambs,' and walked steadily to the middle of the pack. And in the middle of that huge flock of sheep, all of them looking identical to me, she found what she was looking for, one of her 'pets,' meaning a ewe she had raised as a bum lamb on the bottle. And when she found the ewe it sniffed her and followed her, right behind her on the path she made through the rest of the sheep, then followed her carefully out onto the bridge and across. And, of course, the rest followed." While I told them this the boys quit licking their ice cream cones, so I counted the story a success.

· · ·

"Dad, what are you thinking about, that stupid red cow is going to get back on us." Steve says this as he spins Rockytop and kicks him into a gallop. He retrieves the stubborn cow, gets her back in the bunch, and grins with pride.

"Sorry. I was thinking about sheep."

"That the best you can do?" he laughs.

And now the cattle are in the lane. Soon we have them corralled. Then we cut out the bulls and turn the cows and calves loose into the pasture by the old house. All go immediately to grazing. We do not think any calves have been left behind, so we unsaddle and grain the horses and walk to the house for lunch.

16

"Some people prefer dogs" ·
On eating your friends: Napoleon and Squealer

During the late 1970's and early Eighties, Emily and I were eager participants in the new "homesteading" movement. Although we had mentally never strayed far from the land, we had been for nearly a decade far from the home ranch, living on both coasts while I was in the Marine Corps, then in Salt Lake City while I chased the degrees necessary for the profession of most appeal, that of teaching college English. Things changed. The magnetic pull of the ranch intensified, and Emily's parents aged and needed help. Eventually we became the full proprietors of this ranch, but first there was a transition period when most of the land was leased to another rancher, when we had just our small house and a little acreage. During that time we strove to come as close to the live-off-the-land ideal as possible, raising much of our food. There was a huge garden, a Brown Swiss milk cow, even for a short time, milk goats. We built an addition to our house heated by wood and the sun. I taught at a high school, leaving Emily "free" to can beans, pick chokecherries, milk cows, and raise our little boys.

The intent was noble enough and we did enjoy much of the result—crock-pot meals of fresh potatoes and other vegetables we had grown, simmered all day with a lean round steak of grass-fed beef we had raised, about as organic and "natural" food as exists on the planet. Emily made cottage cheese from the bounty of Swiss Miss, the cow. On our pancakes we poured chokecherry syrup, gleaned from the shrubs surrounding us. There was rhubarb pie, the source the same patch by Butcher Creek frequented by Emily's mother and grandmother before her, sunny-looking halves of squash, and corn on the cob. Even today we haven't completely given up on this; every couple of years I *must* have a garden, plant one, neglect it, still manage some good meals even though I am in the hayfield and Emily back at school when harvest time comes, the raccoons being the greatest benefactors of the effort.

But it is fall, now, and I find myself constantly reflecting on this "time to reap," this miracle of harvest and meat-making that has come this time of year to mankind in temperate climates for thousands of years. The harvest falls this time of year, because the plants have matured. The grains turn golden. In the little enclosure we call the "acre," the place fenced by Magnus for the first church building and later used for gardening, there is, festooned with chokecherry bushes that grow up through every gap in its iron, a horse-drawn grain binder. I look at it often. I see waving fields of golden grain, then bundles neatly tied in rows behind this machine and its team and operator, and behind that, a team and wagon with a man walking on each side, pitchfork in hand, pitching the bundles into the wagon. The bundles will be taken to a central location, to a noisy, steam-driven monster called a threshing machine.

Meat-making fell this time of year as well, but for different reasons. Before refrigeration, people could not preserve meat in the heat of the summer. Thus fall, when the nights turned sharp and cold, was the time to butcher, for a skinned animal could be hung to chill thoroughly, as much of the meat as possible eaten fresh, the rest smoked or dried or cured. The early mountain men were astounded at how well meat kept in the Rocky Mountains. Hailing mostly from the southern states, these men considered this some sort of miracle, sometimes referring to the region as a land where meat did not spoil. But the answer, of course, was simply cool nighttime temperatures that chilled the meat. The Indian tribes, although they harvested hundreds of plant and root and berry species to eat, still counted on red meat as ninety percent of their diet. An Indian village dried, literally, tons of the stuff to get them through the winter.

Farmers butchered their hogs during fall and made hams that hung in cool cellars until eaten. Farm wives butchered the fryers that had grown through summer and sometimes canned them, one whole chicken to each large jar. And in the late 1970's the Aadland family tasted the result of the first fruits of their efforts at raising cattle for beef.

We started in a way that I would be reluctant to recommend, buying baby calves from dairy farms and raising them on the bucket. The modern dairy is an incredibly productive food factory, but it produces one by-product that is not particularly valuable, baby bull calves. Milk cows must have a calf every year to "freshen" them, to start them producing milk again. The heifer calves are valuable as replacements, the milk cows of the future. The bull calves have little value. Dairy animal breeding is almost all by artificial insemination, only a very few males of extraordinary quality being kept as bulls. There is nothing wrong with Holstein steers as beef animals—they get blocky and absolutely huge eventually—but to feed them to the point where they will satisfy the American palate takes much longer than for a steer of a beef breed, not an economical proposition for cattle feeders. Because of their low cost, baby bull dairy calves have long been the entry animals for people wanting to raise a calf or two for beef.

Susceptible to the "if a little is good, more is better" philosophy, we reasoned that raising milk calves in a fairly big way would pay for our own beef and raise a little cash besides, so we soon had a Holstein nursery with as many as fifteen to twenty calves in it at any particular time. Alas, our success was mediocre. Dairy animals are bred for milk production, not for the survival traits of their beef brethren. We were always assured by the dairymen that the calves had either nursed or been fed colostrum, that crucial first milk, packed with the mother's antibodies. But sometimes we wondered.

The couple near Bridger we trusted implicitly—they knew all their cows by name and babied every creature they had—but the big factory farms sometimes had helpers who seemed a little abrupt and impatient with us. Whatever the reason, all too often a calf would get scours and no matter what we did, sink lower and lower, finally into a coma, and die.

It was Swiss Miss who bailed us out. She was already well up in years, probably in her early teens, and I knew her well, for our neighbors owned her. Kate, at eighty, was tired of milking and consented to give up the gentle Brown Swiss. Her son, wishing to properly disclose any defects in the cow before taking our money, said, "There's something I have to tell you about the cow. She's a three-titter, you know." I did not know that she had injured a "quarter," had put it out of commission many years earlier, but I wasn't worried. Many times, while on the way to the hayfield, I'd watched the gentle matriarch lying chewing her cud. Her bag was huge. Two summers during high school I milked for dairy farms, once having sole responsibility for a fifty-cow herd, so I knew enough to be confident that even producing at just three-fourths capacity, the cow would make a good account of herself.

We had been feeding our baby Holsteins "calf milk replacer," a sophisticated powdered milk for the purpose, scientifically formulated to supply a calf with all conceivable vitamins and minerals and all nutritional needs, along with a medicinal formula to prevent scouring. Yet, if you fed a tad too much of the stuff the calves would scour. The trick was to walk a tightrope between malnutrition and scours, keeping the calf hungry and eager but well.

The instant the calves tasted the foamy, hot stuff directly from the bag of Swiss Miss they came as close to smiling as calves are capable. Their condition and color improved immediately, and this was with rations that were only half from the cow, half from the nutritional laboratory. So we quickly followed the investment in Swiss Miss with the purchase of another cow, this one a young, horned Swiss we promptly named Chocolate Cow. Now we were milking two cows twice a day, but the calves were considerably healthier. (So today, I am not surprised to hear the frequent reports on the news of additional discoveries documenting the superiority of mother's milk in humans to the best substitute stuff scientists can turn out.)

Purchasing our calves from the dairy farms created a transportation problem. We had no horse trailer, and even if we had, dragging it along to retrieve a couple baby calves weighing eighty pounds each would have seemed a waste. We had at the time a Ford Fairmont station wagon. We soon developed this technique: we would line the rear of the wagon with a tarp, folding down the back seat if necessary for additional space. Then, we would tie the calf's four feet together and lay it in on the tarp. The calf could lie comfortably with its feet tied—the idea was to keep it from standing up and possibly landing in the front seat if I had to slam on the brakes.

Mostly we bought these calves from large farms north of Billings, Montana, sixty miles away. This city was also our supply center, and our small boys coveted trips there. Absarokee, our town, had no fast-food restaurants, no shopping mall, so the boys were always frantic to go to Billings whenever we could, hungry for a drive-in stop almost the moment we left, even if Emily had seen to their intake of a hearty breakfast only moments earlier. We would go to Billings, make all our necessary stops, then, last thing, go to the dairy farm to pick up the calves.

At first this seemed to work well. The boys were still too young for that adolescent mortification at being seen with their parents, although David, the oldest, was beginning to show tendencies. (I had noticed that when passing back through our town with calves in the car he tended to sink lower in his seat, sometimes dropping his face down onto his hand and turning his head inward from his window seat, that he particularly did this if there were kids hanging out on the street corners.) On one trip to Billings we were returning on the freeway with two calves on their tarp behind the back seat. The calves were extremely docile and content, rarely trying to stand up, instead lying side by side seeming to enjoy their view out the back window of the station wagon.

I had noticed in my side mirror that the car behind us was loaded with happy teenagers, jamming, no doubt, to a deafening stereo. Suddenly the driver's eyes riveted onto the back of our car, he alerted the whole crew, and they pointed at the rear of the station wagon, laughing and elbowing each other. What they were seeing were two very cute calves with identical faces, black with large white diamonds on their foreheads, staring out the window at them. Wanting a closer look, the car pulled up tightly behind us, then moved into the left lane and drew abreast of us. I couldn't resist. It was hot, so all the windows were down, and when they got even with us I hollered over, loading my last syllable with disdain, "Some people prefer *dogs!*" At that the teenage laughter turned to shrieks, they waved happily, and sped away. Only then did I notice that David had disappeared completely, retreated virtually to the floor of the car.

Forever after, during our baby-calf years, a certain scenario would unwind on Saturday mornings when a Billings trip was planned. Mom would say to one of our sons, "We're going to Billings today. Want to come?"

Son would reply, "Well, uh, maybe, though I've got some stuff to do. Uh, were you going to pick up calves?" If Mom said "Yes," Son said, "Well, I'd really better hit the homework and fix my bike today." If she said "No," Son would eagerly enlist.

But the calf operation at large was an activity from which our sons learned much. They learned the responsibility that fell on their shoulders in keeping domestic animals. The animals give us food, but we must provide their care, their food and water and other needs. No good livestock person can be comfortable eating a good meal if his or her animals are hungry. The boys were involved with feeding the calves and doing their best for those that got sick.

Nor was the ultimate destiny of these calves ever hidden from our children. Farm kids are not raised with Walt Disney illusions about nature. Even as a preschool child, David repeated to me that ultimate truth about nature he had learned from "Sesame Street": "Big fish eat little fish."

Think back. Until Jane Goodall and other hard-headed scientists influenced the production of nature films, we never saw predator eat prey. In those days we saw the coyote-buffoon attempt to catch the rabbit, but he was always foiled. The narrator would say, "Well, Mr. Coyote will just have to wait. He's not going to make this rabbit into a meal." Later, we were told by those manning the cameras that they were instructed to distract the predatory animal at the last moment so viewers would not see death occur.

We have raised in this country children increasingly divorced from the simple principles of nature, the simple truth of "big fish eat little fish." These children are now adults. Food comes from supermarkets. Nature is a place where everybody is happy. But farm children never were given such rose-colored glasses. The beef they ate at the table was the calf they raised in the corral. The carrots they ate were pulled from the ground, the rest of the plant that produced them thrown aside to wither and die.

Children seem quite accepting of these truths of nature if exposed to them early, if never allowed to grow into adults without learning that death is as integral to nature as birth, that animals live because others die. Farm children learn that although the ultimate destiny of an animal is death, that is no excuse to treat it badly when it's alive. The death of an animal is a fact of nature. The life of a domestic animal, however, is one that the child can influence. He can give it a straw bed when it is cold, food when it is hungry, and extend these kindnesses while accepting what the animal is, not pretending it is a human in disguise.

. . .

So the boys learned the facts of existence from our attempts to be self-sufficient, but we wondered if the case of Napoleon and Squealer might not push the envelope. Napoleon and Squealer were pigs. David named them, for he had just read *Animal Farm*. I acquired these weaner pigs in a trade with a friend that involved a service to our first stallion and a little cash. From the beginning, Napoleon was twice as large as his partner, and Squealer, well, yes, squealed all the time.

In a grain bin in Nora's chicken house was a ton or so of wheat. It had been there for thirty years, but knowing that wheat found in the Egyptian pyramids actually grew when planted, I was certain the stuff would be as potent as ever. Wheat is too "hot" for horses, so I'd been puzzling what to do with it. But now we had milk cows. Everyone knows that baby pigs will thrive on a "slop" mixture of milk and grain. So at milking time we'd pour some excess milk into a half bucket of grain, let it sit and soften the grain and begin to ferment until the next chore time, then feed it to Napoleon and Squealer. It was filet mignon to them. They attacked it with extreme vigor. And boy, did they grow. They seemed to double in size every month, though always Squealer was considerably smaller.

We had the usual problems of containment, since pigs are smart animals and can enlarge tiny holes in fences into pig-sized tunnels. Napoleon and Squealer were often irritating, but yet were the court jesters of the ranch, always entertaining. Soon October came. Swiss Miss and Chocolate were drying up, the calves were weaned, the nights cold, and the meat supply in the freezer, not yet augmented by venison, had ebbed. It was time to convert Napoleon and Squealer into bacon, pork chops, and hams.

The boys were at ball practices after school one evening. With considerable difficulty and some chicanery, I got the two hogs loaded into a home-built horse trailer we had just purchased and hauled them to the butcher's shop at the edge of town. A twinge of regret passed over me as I unloaded the two, but I combated that with thoughts of a ham sandwich on Emily's rye bread, toasted, with mustard. Later, I told the boys where the two pigs had gone. There was no major reaction—they had expected it. In case they were hiding emotions like those I had felt, I used the same tactic that worked on me, whetting their appetites for pork chops, a favorite meal of theirs.

Two weeks later, when the pigs came back in neat, white frozen packages, with four real whole hams, two huge ones from Napoleon and two moderate ones from Squealer, we loaded the freezer. Emily kept back some packages of pork chops to thaw, and as supper neared the aroma of her cooking filled the house with pleasant anticipation. David brought home his friend Jimmy, a boy as lethargic as David was industrious. Jimmy had visited before and rarely said more than a sentence or two during supper.

After we said grace, Jonathan eagerly grabbed a pork chop and passed the plate on. For an instant he looked critically at the chop he had chosen, then cut off a big chunk and plunged it into his mouth. His white-blond face lit up, and he exclaimed, "Good! Boy, Squealer is really delicious."

David, meanwhile, had taken a somewhat larger chop. He too bit into his first piece and said, "Yeah, this is good. But I can't believe this is Squealer. I'm positive this must be Napoleon." Then the argument started, David pointing out in his older-brother wisdom that he had helped cut up deer before, that he knew pork chops come from the loin, that there was no way that puny wretch Squealer could have pork chops so large. Jon countered that the pork chop he was eating was extremely tender, that big old ugly Napoleon would be tough. While the two were arguing I happened to glance at Jimmy. He had taken a big bite of his own chop (Jimmy was shy, but not about eating), and chewed a couple of times. Now he stopped dead, his mouth full, his eyes converted to the quick ones of a cat as they darted between David and Jon. He seemed to turn a little pale.

Emily intervened to stop the argument. "You're both being silly," she said. "I knew you guys would be hungry, so I cooked two packages. There was probably a package from each of the pigs." That mollified the boys. I looked at Jimmy. Slowly his eyes returned to normal size, and his color came back. Then, in a few moments, he tentatively began to chew again. I made a mental note to lecture the boys about being a little more sensitive when they had company. Finally, Jimmy resumed eating with his usual vigor, and I guessed everything had turned out okay. Before we were done, Jimmy took seconds.

17

Moose

He yaf nat of that text a pulled hen
... That seith that hunters been nat hooly men;

CHAUCER ON HIS MONK, THE HUNTER

Fishermen, hunters, woodchoppers, and others, spending their lives in the
fields and woods, in a peculiar sense a part of Nature themselves, are
often in a more favorable mood for observing her ... than philosophers
or poets, even ... She is not afraid to exhibit herself to them ... science
reports what those men already know.
... perhaps the hunter is the greatest friend of the animals hunted, not
excepting the Humane Society. ... We cannot but pity the boy who has
never fired a gun; he is no more humane, while his education has been
sadly neglected.

HENRY DAVID THOREAU

Major's shod hooves, slipping on the wet rocks, make metallic scraping sounds. To my left, down twenty yards from the ledge trail, the river froths and rumbles and tumbles its way down the mountain, its roar deafening. The rope to the lead pack horse turns just once over the horn of my saddle, then snakes under my knee where I can release it instantly by a lift of my leg. The pack horses, Sugar in front, the tall black named Marauder, then the young black mare called Rodeo, are connected to each other by breakaway loops of twine. The thought of one animal going over the edge and pulling the rest with it is frightening beyond belief, so any possibility must be prevented.

Although they are nervous, the horses are handling this better than I am. The sound of the river along this steep, narrow trail is like a heavy curtain that shuts out all else for them, so they methodically step exactly where Major steps, quietly following. They do not have my worries, one of which is meeting another pack string on this treacherous stretch. Finally, we advance to that single pine tree at the right of the trail, that crazy solitary pine that somehow grows out of a crevice no larger than a dinner plate in the granite cliff, that pine I have kept fixed in my sight for the last two hundred yards and which marks the place where the trail breaks out of this corridor into which it is squeezed with the river. Then we are free. The river widens to a pastoral trout stream, the trail now soft soil and pine needles under the horses' hooves, the woods to my right dark and quiet.

I have won the lottery and am now just beginning to revel in it. No, I did not win the Montana Power Ball nor, for that matter, the Publisher's Clearing House contest. But after many years of applying, many summers of hoping, my number was drawn for a moose permit in the Stillwater drainage in south-central Montana. Each year just five such permits are granted, the biologists having determined the moose population of the drainage can be best kept healthy with that number culled each year. Apparently they are right. This is a drainage heavily used by backpackers and fisherman in summer, its first lake accessible enough that people less physically capable easily reach it on Sunday afternoon day hikes, and almost everyone enjoys seeing moose. That does not mean converting one to winter meat is automatic, however. I have heard too many frustrating tales of someone drawing a permit, seeing moose everywhere during summer, then having them strangely disappear when hunting season came.

The only down side of my good fortune has been a dearth of companions to come with me. My sons are grown or in school. My friends are all tied down by work, those who are teaching not anxious to blow their precious few days of personal leave so early in the school year. I am fortunate enough to have three days available, enough to give me the mountains from Wednesday, the season opener, through the weekend. Emily has no such privileges. But she has been involved, nonetheless, for she helped me over the weekend pack in the heavy items of my camp to a special, prechosen place in a meadow near the river eight miles up the drainage. We set up the wall tent, left

the woodstove and two plywood boxes of heavier supplies, but no food, lest it draw bears. Then we fixed a good meal and spent the night. It was a nice interlude in the best of all seasons when the aspen are golden and the woodstove cuts the chill in the tent. The ground was white with frost the next morning. We rode rapidly out, our packhorses unladen.

So today I arrived at the trailhead in an early morning rain with four horses in the trailer but with no human company. There was a flutter in my stomach. Undertaking a solo pack trip and hunt is no small thing. True, I have confidence in skills learned during years of packing our family into the wilderness on many recreational trips, but much can go wrong with a group of young horses and no helping hand. Soon I had the packs on and adjusted. Major looked upwind into the canyon, the wind ruffling his foretops. His demeanor was that of a good, confident war horse, and by the time I tied my saddle bags on behind the cantle, I too was ready.

For a Westerner there is little left in life that can match the feeling of sliding a good rifle into a saddle scabbard, swinging aboard a first-rate saddle horse, and grasping the rope of the lead horse in a packstring that contains everything needed to go anywhere in the back country. In an instant you are one with the Plains Indians who ascended these canyons to cut lodgepole pine and pick berries in the fall, with Lewis and Clark, with the beaver-trapping mountain men. You are using the same skills, the same transportation. Things look and smell and taste the same. You are able to temporarily forget that so little of our country is still like this, that so much is now paved and lined with endless shopping malls and fast-food restaurants and streets with stoplights, choked with traffic.

Very soon the wilderness absorbs me. I relinquish all else, just as I have in the past when I've nudged my canoe into the swift current of the Yellowstone River. Now, in fall, the Nike tracks on the trail have disappeared, recreational hiking having gone with the fair weather. This time of year the use of this trail drops to a trickle: a few die-hard fishermen, lucky people like me with special hunting permits, and packers taking the long way into Slough Creek for the early elk bugling season.

On the entire trip to my camp I see humans only twice. First I overtake a tall, dark woman carrying a pack over which is slung a hunting rifle. In spite of the season she is wearing shorts; in every other way she looks fit and prepared. Nearly simultaneously I see her husband up the trail twenty paces. I stop briefly to visit while they rest and drink from their water bottles. I learn they are from Kentucky, that they have bighorn sheep permits and will soon turn out of the main valley up a steep, feeder creek into a rocky drainage they scouted last summer. They seem to be knowledgeable and capable. I wish them luck and leave them, a happy Orion and his pretty Artemis.

Although the season is now officially open, I do not look seriously for moose on the way in. It would be anticlimactic to find one so quickly. Also, some of my equipment for the rather challenging task of processing a moose into meat is in the storage boxes at camp. I do eyeball the clearings in each place where the Stillwater widens and slows, the swamp-grass openings where moose often stand in the water and search with their long noses for just the right tidbits. Each time I check a clearing without seeing a moose, I am relieved.

The horses have settled into an easy, fast flat-footed walk, the pull of the grade having its effect. The three pack horses are lightly loaded, beneficiaries of our earlier trip to set up camp. The ride in is relaxing, for the trail is good and I know it well. I backpacked up this trail with David just before he turned six years old, a strong little guy who carried a ten-pound pack, the packing task helped by a dog named Friendly who carried his own food and another ten pounds of our stuff in his packs. This has been the trail for many other family trips and a couple other solo ones. It is not, however, devoid of change. The terrible fires of 1988 licked their way down this valley, so I pass through bands of forest that were burned. The regeneration is remarkable. The places that suffered the hottest fire have the thickest regrowth of baby pine. But it is still sad to see huge spruce trees now turned into bare, black shadows of themselves.

I am seven miles up the valley and nearing camp when I meet the only other people I see on the way in, a string of dudes followed by a pack outfit. The lead rider is a middle-aged woman who smiles and says "hello." She is followed by a half dozen more women, then a male wrangler who looks familiar but whose name I don't know. Bringing up the rear after the pack horses is Wanda, the guide and outfitter for the trip. She recognizes me and stops to talk, her face a small, animated disk under the felt brim of her big hat. "Dan, I think your tent blew down. The wind ripped through here last night, and it looked at least partially down when we went by."

"I'm not surprised. I don't really trust that pole set. Quite a crew you have here."

"Bunch of women from back East, wanted a fling in the mountains without their men. Snowed on 'em the first night, but they've had a ball."

"Seen any moose?"

"A couple up by the Wounded Man trail when we first came in. No big bull."

"Take care, Wanda."

"Have a good one, Dan."

The news about the tent worries me, so I press Major into a running walk and we cruise quickly to the campsite. One of the tent's internal poles has slipped, but I can see at a glance it's quickly repairable. The sun is now shining, the valley, with the dudes gone, mine.

There is much work to do, but I relish it. First, I will unsaddle the horses. The saddles will go onto a tarp, each upside down (easier on the saddle trees) and piled with my riding saddle on top, then covered with another tarp. Two horses will be hobbled and turned loose to graze, the other two picketed to a highline, which I will quickly construct between trees with a sling rope off a pack saddle and a cinch around the tree on each end to protect the bark. Then will come organizing my gear and cutting firewood, some in short lengths for the folding steel stove in the tent. For an outside fire there is a shallow pit to dig, the sod laid carefully by to be pressed back in place when I leave the site.

It all goes quickly, the physical exertion feeling good after confinement in the saddle. I have brought a pretty sumptuous camp. Since much horsepower will be required if I succeed and must pack out a moose, it has only seemed logical to use that same packing capacity to have a fine camp. So instead of my backpacking tent, a cocoon into which I could crawl wet and tired at the end of a hard day, I've brought my big wall tent. Inside is the woodstove and a table made of the inverted plywood boxes. I have a folding camp stool. Soon there is a strategically located stack of stove wood near the head of my bed so that I can reach out during the night, open the stove door, and pitch in a stick to rejuvenate the fire. I have everything I can need and am glad of it, for there have already been early wet snows up here. My camp must be both support system and haven after a hard day's work.

I take a short rest on top of my sleeping bag, doze, my dream a hazy replay of the trail up the valley as it looked between Major's ears. Then I awake with a start, shocked that I have wasted precious daylight during moose season when I have a permit in my pocket and a camp in paradise. I retrieve my folding saw from the wood pile, return it to its case and strap it around my waist. Before I leave camp I switch the horses, hobbling the two that were on the highline and tying the other two in their place. I take time to carry the grain sack around, giving each a couple mouthfuls, which they munch. Then I sling my rifle over my shoulder and head up the trail.

I look less for moose than for sign of them. Moose are not above using the convenience of Forest Service trails when they want to move quickly up and down the drainage, but in a two-hour circle around camp I see none of their cow-sized tracks. Their absence is certainly not because of hunting pressure. Only five permits are given for a huge area that contains this primary drainage and many smaller ones along the mountain front. The one other moose hunter in this valley seems to have been the woman at the trailhead parking lot whose guide and outfitter were packing up to leave as I saddled my horses. I talked to them briefly. The guide said they would camp just a couple miles up. They left right behind me but never caught my fast-walking horses.

We stereotype moose as critters that spend all their time in the marshy clearings, but the truth is that they spend a lot of it running the high ridges in dense timber. That, apparently, is where they are now. I return to camp just before dark, light a lantern, fire up the woodstove in the tent, fill a small pot with chili from a can, and set it on the stove, then, beside it, my coffee pot. Later, after the food, coffee in hand, I find even the large tent confining and go outside to build a small fire. The big white tent, filled with the light of the gas lantern, illuminates the entire clearing, so to better see the stars I duck into the tent and kill the lantern. The Milky Way is a stunning highway of stars. The argument of Huckleberry Finn and Jim comes to mind, how so many stars could be made, and Jim's contention that perhaps the moon laid them, for he had seen a frog lay "most as many."

. . .

The clearing is large enough to give me a panorama above, the air so clear each star looks close enough to reach out and touch. To the north, straight down the valley, I find the Big Dipper, its lip pointing faithfully toward the North Star. Once I was camped in a similar clearing high in the Sierra Nevada Mountains of California, a Marine officer charged with teaching two companies of men the skills of mountain warfare and survival. The men were from New York and New Jersey, mostly Black and Puerto Rican, good Marines but initially as intimidated by this high, open, wilderness environment as I probably would have been by theirs. The howl of a coyote the first night in camp terrified some of these muscular Marines, who would have defended without question our camp against humans with guns.

My classroom was an aspen grove. The elevation was very high, 9,300 feet if I recall correctly, for the timberline is higher farther south. Occasionally a band of sheep would visit, milling through the men, followed by sheep dogs and the Basque herder, his coyote rifle slung muzzle-down over his shoulder. Once I described the simple matter of finding the North Star via the Big Dipper. I drew blank stares from the troops. I asked whether they were not told about this in boot camp, and they said they probably were, but that they did not recall for sure. "Okay," I said, "anyone who wants to see the Big Dipper and the North Star come over to my tent at twenty-two hundred tonight and I'll show you."

I really did not expect any of the Marines to take me up on this, since I left it voluntary, knowing the tenets of Marine leadership—you do not mess with people's chow, pay, or liberty (time off). The evening was their time during this part of the training, their time to sit in small knots in front of their tents and exchange stories. So I was surprised that night when approximately fifty men strolled over into "officer country," the little knoll on which our tents were located. I showed them the Big Dipper, showed how approximately four lengths out from the two stars that formed the side of its cup opposite the handle, in the direction the two stars pointed off the lip of the cup, you could find without fail the North Star, the star that never lets you down. They were positively tickled. They watched the stars for two hours, an explosive cheer accompanying the fall of each of the many meteors they witnessed. One said to me, "Captain, Sir, you got to understand most of us ain't never seen stars like this." Since that night I have never taken for granted the privilege of seeing our stars in the western sky.

It is strange to sit alone by a campfire in a clearing in a mountain valley, telling stories to myself. There have been many campfires. I remember tiny ones, kindled with the "heat tabs," the little cubes of solid alcohol fuel with which we warmed C-rations in the military. In the hilly back country around Quantico, Virginia, in the cold and humid February wind off Chesapeake Bay, we would get into sheltered places and kindle a few sticks over heat tabs to make minifires that warmed the hands and helped the stories flow, making the noon break a good time.

There have been many campfires with Emily and the boys on pack trips, one in a camp very close to where I am now. There were discussions about whether life existed somewhere out in those stars at which we stared. We were here just before the Fourth of July in 1988 and watched one of the fires that combined later with others into an inferno that tinder-dry summer, watched it grow from a lightning strike in a patch of pine across the valley, never large enough during the time we were there to be a threat.

And there has grown in our lives another tradition involving campfires and friends, a "spring bear hunt," the quotation marks being necessary because we have never gotten a bear and are not trying very hard. In the group that goes on this spring ritual there are one or two who actually hunt, one or two more (myself included) who go as far as buying a bear tag but spend their time enjoying camp instead, and a couple more who come to fish and b.s. The tradition started with one friend and myself, grew and continued after the friend moved to Alaska, a fluctuating group that has not always been stag, for Emily and another wife have come, too.

. . .

Around the campfire on these outings, lubricated by a particular drink, the stories flow. (The drink is this: take a Sierra cup and pack it with snow, always available in spring in the mountains, at least in the timber on shady north slopes. Mix into the snow equal parts of Yukon Jack and unsweetened grapefruit juice. Serve.) Now, alone on the Stillwater, I remember one of the stories and I laugh out loud.

Roger told it. I guess I can, too, for the statute of limitations has certainly run out by now. When Roger was a boy back in the Fifties, he and his dad took a Model A pickup out looking for a deer. Roger has never been a very enthusiastic hunter, but went as a matter of course. His Norwegian father, like many of his countrymen, really preferred mutton to venison, had worked with sheep before becoming a town dweller. But times were a little tough for the family, and a mule deer would keep the larder stocked.

They asked permission to hunt on a ranch owned by folks they knew, then spent a fruitless day searching the coulees finding absolutely nothing. As the afternoon waned they had to face the fact that they had been skunked. Roger's dad steered the old pickup back on the two-track dirt road over the rolling hills toward the ranch house. Suddenly, at a low place in the road, they drove up on a single sheep, a ewe.

Roger's dad stopped the pickup and stared at her for an instant. Then he said, "There's some mutton. Yust get out and knock her in the head."

Roger thought he was kidding. Any such illusion ceased when his father grabbed the 30-30 carbine, stepped out of the vehicle, and neatly shot the ewe behind the ear. "I was horrified," Roger told us. "I suspected my old man had gotten close to the edge of the law a couple times, but I couldn't believe he'd shoot a man's sheep, especially the sheep of a man who had been nice to us and whose house was only a half-mile away."

But there it was, the sheep dead as a doornail and his father beckoning to him. "Well, don't yust sit there, Boy, help me pitch her into the back." They dropped the tailgate of the pickup and swung the ewe into the bed. Then Roger's father covered it with a tarp.

"I was beside myself," Roger said. "It was bad enough we'd done this, but the old man wouldn't even hurry. He just got back into the pickup and casually drove back toward the ranch house. My greatest fear was that as we passed the ranch house, the only way we could get back onto the county road, someone would hail us and walk over to see if we had any luck hunting. Well, I started thinking we just about had it made, because we were right abreast of the house and no one was out in the yard. Then, you wouldn't believe what the old man did. He turned into their driveway! I asked him what the hell he was doing. He turned and looked at me as if amazed I would ask such a stupid question. 'Well, we have to stop for coffee.'"

Roger had been raised with the Norwegian necessity of stopping for coffee, but this blew his mind. With a dead, poached sheep in the back of the pickup covered only by a thin tarp the old man was going to park next to this house and go in for coffee! "Yah," elaborated his father, "They'll think it's funny if we don't stop for coffee. We'll yust stay a little while. I haven't had a cup since breakfast."

The ranch wife welcomed them and did the customary thing, busily assembling not just coffee but oatmeal cookies and lefse spread with butter and sugar. "It was my favorite stuff, but I could hardly force it down, managing just enough to keep from hurting her feelings. We sat there with the whole family, the old man joking and telling stories, the kids, who I knew from school, enjoying it all, me so sick to my stomach with fear that I thought I was going to throw up. I thought someone would at least ask if we got any deer, then, if we said we got one, ask to go see it. But I guess deer were no big deal to them, because no one ever did. Maybe they figured if we got a bragging buck, we would have said so."

So they visited in the ranch house for nearly an hour, everyone having fun but Roger. After his dad drained the third refill of coffee he announced his regrets at having to leave so soon. Finally, the ewe still undiscovered, they motored slowly away from the ranch. By the campfire on the bear hunt Roger told us, "I never did go hunting with the old man again."

It has turned cold now on the Stillwater. I have pulled my coat over my down vest and find myself reaching toward the depleted pile of firewood I have gathered for outside purposes, odd small pieces I had not wished to saw to stove length. "Better save it," I tell myself. "Tomorrow might be a hard day." It is not so bad to be alone by a campfire, I decide, with good stories to recall. I go into the tent, stuff the little stove full of wood, shut down its vent, and turn in.

.   .   .

Two days of hard hunting follow. Each day the tiny travel alarm rings long before daybreak. Each day I rise and cook a big breakfast over the woodstove in lantern light, make my noon sandwich, and set out, either on foot or horseback. I see no moose and no moose tracks. I could hike the timber, but am not attracted to that because there is so much of the timber and so little chance of stumbling onto a moose. Far better, it seems, to look for tracks on the logical trails and crossings where I have seen them all the many times when I had no moose permit and was not looking for them.

On the second day, riding Marauder to spare Major, I spot in the timber to my right above the trail a shiny black form and think for a moment it might be the back of a moose. But that illusion disappears when the animal throws up its head and identifies itself as a black bear. I have dismounted. Marauder grazes quietly, never seeing the animal, and it never sees us either. A little rain has fallen during the night, just enough to green up whatever the bear intently eats, for he grazes voraciously. He feels winter coming and needs to add the fat that will see him through a long sleep. I lean over Marauder's back and watch the bear with binoculars, an unexpected bonus.

It is that night when I begin to think the two trackless days will extend into a third, my last full day to hunt, that I may never see a moose on this long-anticipated trip. True, the season extends for some time, so weekend forays up the canyons will still be a possibility, but there will be no time, no leave available from school, for another fully equipped expedition. So when chores are done by lantern light, the horses grained and secured for the night, I cheer myself by cooking a first-rate meal on the woodstove in the tent. I split and fry Polish sausages made of elk and pork but so lean they scarcely make the necessary juice for frying the thinly sliced potatoes I throw in with them. I cook a can of corn and slice a big piece of Emily's homemade brown bread. I pop open a can of beer to wash it down. No meal in a French restaurant, no wine in their cellar, could combine just the way all this combines and be so fine a meal. Afterward, after cleaning things up, I pour a nip of brandy from an unbreakable backpacking flask I have brought and crawl into my sleeping bag thinking that even if I never see a moose, me, myself, and I will have had a good time.

But my serenity lasts only a little while into the night because past midnight sometime all hell breaks loose. A sudden blast of wind and snow rips down the valley, and one side of the tent caves in. I hastily pull on my boots, then, clad only in underwear, wage a running battle with the wind and the tent. I have too few hands to both hold up the pole and tie off the guy ropes that secure the side of the wall tent. It is touch and go for half an hour. I get one thing secured only to have another come loose, the wind roaring the whole time. I am like a single sailor on deck in a storm trying to secure the sheets. Finally I get it done. The rest of the night I sleep fitfully, awakening at every gust.

But when the alarm jingles all else is quiet except for the gentle water music of the Stillwater River. Outside there are two new inches of snow. This could be the break I need. I hastily eat and, feeling lucky, saddle Major and put a pack saddle on Emily's Sugar so that if I am successful I can bring part of the meat back to camp. I wait a nervous twenty minutes until light just cracks over the mountain wall on the east side of the valley across the river. Then I quickly walk out to the main trail, indecisive, trying to decide what course to take. That issue is readily decided since there are fresh moose tracks in the new snow on the main trail, up the valley a hundred yards from camp.

So I ride rapidly south following what turns out to be two sets of tracks, a small one and large one, a cow and calf, not legal for me but exciting anyway, for moose are no longer phantoms. I catch them at Roosevelt Lake, a lake in name only, really just a sunken marsh surrounded by timber deadfall. I dismount and watch the two of them. They seem to see me, but apparently mother moose has read the fish and game regulations and knows she is safe. At one hundred yards away she looks absolutely immense. It is sobering to think of what a task I will have on my hands, working alone, if I am successful.

In another half mile I see more tracks. The snow has been the signal to the ridge-running moose that their lark up high has ended, that is time to get serious about the business of feeding in the marshes and staying fat before winter. I tie Sugar and Major at a trail junction and ease left into the timber toward the river. I hunted this two days ago, marveling at the beauty of the trout pools in this stretch where the river is separated from the trail by a thickly timbered tract. I have marked it mentally for future fishing. I circle quietly, find nothing, then shortcut back toward the trail through the timber.

When it happens it is so fast that only a blurred second goes by. There is in the dark timber an antlered moose, not a trophy but the legal game I want, and then it is down and I do not remember dropping to one knee or the report of the powerful rifle or the recoil on my shoulder. I walk cautiously up to it and feel that tinge of remorse felt by all good hunters, and also the humility and thanks. It is not only Native American hunters who respect and thank the animals they eat, who revere them, who wish to take them with as little suffering as possible. John James Audubon knew this, as did Aldo Leopold as did Teddy Roosevelt, hunters all, hunters and lovers of the things they hunted.

So I sit twenty paces from where the moose lies and lean back on a tree and try to quiet my thumping heart. I have drawn, I realize, a dividend on my investment, a premium from this big and beautiful but not always friendly environment in which I live. This is an entry on the other side of the balance sheet, opposite from eighteen years of working two jobs for modest pay, for ranching in the dark all winter around the edges of my other job. To have come to this valley with my horses, to camp by a clear river and hunt moose is a great privilege. Close to home and performed with equipment I already own, the hunt has cost me peanuts, not the thousands of dollars a nonresident guided hunter would expect to pay. Sitting leaning back against the tree, I know I am a very lucky man.

But I can't stay sitting long. There is a staggering amount of work to do if all this wonderful meat is to land safely unspoiled in the freezer at home. (It would be both illegal and immoral to waste any of it.) I find a route out of the woods to the trail, a route I'm certain the horses can negotiate. How lucky this is, to be able to take the horses right to the moose. (I shudder at the thought of shooting a moose in a marsh.) Then I trot down the trail a quarter mile to the horses, untie them quickly, and return with them to the moose. I tie Major and Sugar to trees nearby, the two of them eyeballing the downed animal cautiously. Then, before it begins, I gulp down my noon sandwich.

I start at exactly noon. At exactly four p.m. I am ready to head back for camp, and I feel as tired as if I had run a marathon. In that four hours I have: field dressed the moose; cut it into two parts; skinned each half as it lay in place; split the quarters apart by sawing down the spine; wrapped both hindquarters in cheesecloth and suspended them as high as I can on two spindly trees (we are in a burn, and the thin remaining trees are fire-damaged and weak); and loaded the two front quarters into Sugar's panniers. Montana moose (Shiras moose, to be specific) are not nearly so large as their Canadian or Alaskan cousins, and this was a young bull, perhaps three or four years old; but coping with his mass alone, on the ground, with no one to hold anything while I sawed, has been exhausting. It has been a lesson in the true meaning of the term "dead weight." I estimate the hindquarters to weigh well over a hundred pounds each, the front quarters nearly that much, and the rule of thumb is that skinned, dressed quarters weigh about half the live weight of the animal, which would have put the moose at around 800 pounds.

Because of the spindly trees, the block and tackle I brought has been useless. I horse each quarter up as high as I can get it, then tie it off. I can only hope coyotes or a bear will not find them, for skinned as cleanly as I have been able to do, working on a tarp laid on the forest floor, the quarters are beautiful meat. The other concern is that they cool quickly, but I'm quite convinced they will; they are hanging so air can circulate around them, and that air will drop to well below freezing in a couple hours.

While I'm hefting the hindquarters I remember the story about my friends Roger and Marcus, back when we were all foolish enough to let a six-pack accompany some tasks that really required a more sober concentration. Marcus had butchered, skinned, and split down the backbone the carcass of a huge crossbred steer and now had to quarter it. "Wrap your arms around that front quarter, Roger," he said, "and I'll just cut her loose." Roger was a coach, always in good shape, at the time making frequent use of the weight setup in his basement. He did a bear hug on the front quarter and said he was ready, probably not stopping to think that the quarter weighed considerably more than he did. The instant Marcus sawed the quarter loose, it was as if a hammer pounded Roger to the ground, where he lay helpless and kicking, pinned by the front quarter of beef.

"Well," Marcus said, "it's obvious those weights haven't done a damn thing for you." After letting Roger suffer a moment longer he helped lift the quarter off his friend and into the back of the pickup truck. "Since you aren't up to the job, I'll hold, you cut this one loose." So Marcus did *his* bear hug on the other front quarter, anxious to show up Roger, who took the saw and cut it loose. Marcus also slammed to the ground, pinned by the quarter, cussing, and it was now Roger's turn to laugh, telling Marcus while he squirmed that the scene reminded him of a cartoon where some critter got hit by a safe pitched out of a third-story window. This was a another campfire story, told many times, one that tended to get just a bit better each time.

My plan is to pack the front quarters of the moose back to camp on Sugar and hang them there to cool. By then it will be nearly dark. Early in the morning I will secure and clean up my camp, saddle all the horses, then pack the empty plywood boxes onto Marauder's Decker saddle. I will lead him back up the trail, the four miles to the moose, and manty the hindquarters into the plywood boxes. They will protrude from the boxes' open tops, true, but the boxes will still give the manties form and make them easier to sling. Then I will return to camp with Marauder, load the front quarters back on Sugar, load the valuable things that must come out from camp on the young mare, and head home. Then, later, Emily and I will return on a day ride, feasible, though a long sixteen-mile round trip, and retrieve the camp.

It all goes exactly that way. When I ride up from camp the next morning, the moose quarters are undisturbed. The manties (canvas-covered bundles which sling to the pack saddle) I make around them are very heavy. The big black gelding will handle them with ease, but slinging them to him by myself is a challenge. Once done, the rest is easy. The horses are flawless, impeccable, and I am proud of them and of my packing job, for I scarcely adjust a knot on the entire trip home. The sun shines, the fledgling snow now gone. Red buck brush and golden aspens garnish the green of the pines as I lead the horses at a brisk walk down the trail.

I enter the tunnel near the trailhead where the trail is squeezed between a granite wall and the frothing river, and this time I do meet a packstring. It is Wanda again, riding her pinto horse, heading upriver with a hunter. She sees me well in advance and gathers her horses in the one place on this stretch wide enough to pass with confidence, notices the weight of the packs and the moose horns riding between Marauder's manties, and as I pass, because the roar of the river makes words useless, smiles and throws me a thumbs up.

We whip into the trailhead at a running walk. I *am* Chaucer's monk, returning after a hunt with my hounds and my "dainty horses." I have gone to the wilderness and no, not conquered it, but melted into it as no one can who merely looks at it through plate glass. We will eat its bounty through the winter, every bite containing the tang of the wilderness, and that bounty will be tonic against the long, dark days.

In twenty minutes I am in the pickup headed home. I top a ridge and reach for the new cell phone (a recent concession to safety on my long commute). It just might work here, so high. I dial home and get a crackly voice of Steve. All is okay, I tell him, and I will soon be home. Through static I hear a garbled sentence and make out its last word, " . . . moose?" And I return, hoping he will hear it, "Yes, moose."

18

Weaning time · Discovery in the hills

He thumbs his glasses lower on his nose and studies intently and simultaneously both the knob that balances the livestock scale and, beyond, the calves he is weighing, visible through the window behind the balance beam. He ratchets the knob until the scale balances, then pushes the lever that prints out the ticket. After writing the rancher's name on the ticket, he places it in one of the small stacks in front of him.

Ed, the cattle buyer, is in charge of this controlled bedlam at his small stockyard on one of the many shipping days he will superintend during weaning time, when calves are taken off their mothers and brought here, weighed, and purchased. He writes what for most of these ranchers is their yearly paycheck. Like his father before him, Ed (more properly a broker than a buyer) contracts calves from ranchers during the summer, pays them a small down payment per head at that time, then arranges and supervises the shipping day, when the calves are brought in, unloaded, weighed, paid for, then shipped out again to their feedlot destination. Ed makes his living by the commission he receives on these calves and by ranching himself.

With the help of his wife Karen, a retired teacher and an accomplished rodeo performer, Ed wisecracks and teases, knowing the importance of injecting a little levity into the rather solemn business of buying a rancher's production for an entire year. Keeping the mood light is a task very difficult this particular year, because prices are sharply down. The cattle business is subject to a multiyear cycle of high and low prices. When prices are high, herds are expanded until eventually there are too many cattle, and prices drop. This is somewhat predictable, but not preventable. This year there is added salt for the wound, because calves are also averaging considerably lighter than the year before, the summer's grass having been mediocre.

So the checks Ed writes out today are smaller than nearly everyone hopes for. Thus, in the crowded scale house, decorated with pictures of subjects ranging from a multihorse team pulling a combine to a calendar photo featuring an undressed cowgirl, each rancher in turn has his moment with Ed. When prices are high and weights good, Ed can be a good-news guy, and the rancher might even smile at the amount of the check (though probably while looking at his boots so that no one notices). But today, Ed must be the opposite. "I can't take those six lighter heifers, Joe. They just won't fit the contract."

And Joe leans back and sighs and says, "Well, the contract said they'd slide in price if they were too big, but it didn't say anything about them being too light."

"Well, I know," Ed says, "but the contract was for a 550 average and this buyer just won't accept those tailenders, because they only average just over four." He gives Joe a moment to digest. Then he drops the other shoe. "And those three steers with the frozen ears. Buyers won't take them any more either. They figure if it was cold enough to freeze their ears when they were born it probably hurt their feet, too, and they won't hold up in the feedlot."

"Funny how it never bothered them when prices were good."

"That's true, Joe."

"Throw 'em all back on the truck, then, and I'll take 'em to town." The prices in Billings, now with prices on this downhill slide, will not be as good for these rejected calves as those of the contract, made when prices were better. There is just enough tension between the two men that everyone else in the scale house finds another direction for his attention, reading the clippings about the cattle market on the bulletin board or strolling back to the coffeepot and fishing for a doughnut.

In times like these there is a bit more peering over Ed's shoulder as he works the calculator, a bit more checking of Ed's figures when he totals it all and subtracts the down payment he has paid earlier, and it is not distrust but worry that causes this. It is contemplation of the yearly appointment with the banker to pay off some debt and incur more debt in order to operate through the next year. It is wheels turning about whether the haystacks will last through the winter and, if not, what the stuff will cost and whether the calf check justifies buying plenty of hay now before prices rise or instead gambling on the weather. It is a year's worth of work and worry concentrated on this one day during this one transaction.

For us it started well before dawn. Since the haul to the stockyards is a short one, everything can be accomplished well before noon, so Emily took a morning's personal leave from school. After breakfast we saddled Major and Sugar and loaded them into the horse trailer. I fired up Elmer's 1949 Chevrolet cattle truck for its once-a-year task, and we drove to our corrals across the river. Marcus was already there with his horse and trailer; Rick would soon arrive with his stock truck. We neighbors gang up to haul each other's calves on our appointed days, and we had enough outfits today to get the calves to the yards in one pass.

The herding to the corral was brief. I had let the cattle down onto the hay meadows several weeks earlier to clean up the last of their fall feed, so the push into the corrals was only a quarter mile. Once there we tied the horses, removed the bridles, and loosened the cinches. Then the work in the corral began, cutting the calves off the cows, sexing the calves—steers in one compartment, heifers in another—finally selecting a dozen good heifers to keep as replacements. All this was done to even more than the usual din of bawling, for the mother cows have been through this before and seem to know that this separation from their calves is weaning time and is permanent.

Once the corral work was done we loaded our trucks and trailers as rapidly as possible and headed to the stockyards. Elmer and his neighbors, not having this closer destination available, would always truck their calves to Billings, hoping to hit the market on a good day, and there are years in which we do this as well. After unloading they would watch the sale ring for a while, then go to dinner at a cafe, the check picked up by the man whose calves had been trucked.

The unloading of our calves is quick and routine today. There is a chute for trucks and another, with a properly sized gate, for trailers. The calves trot by the buyer and the brand inspector, the buyer counting and making sure the quality of the animals is acceptable, the brand inspector quickly checking the brand to make certain it is that of the seller. Montana has strict rules about such things—one does not take livestock across a county line without a permit or brand inspection, and horses, whether branded or not, must also have an inspection, the paper certifying this accompanying the horse.

These rules date from our frontier past with its shady cloud of rustling and the swift, vigilante justice that grew to combat it. There was in our history a silent march of men from the center of our state to its eastern borders. The vigilantes traveled by rail on a special train with just a couple of cars, unloading their horses at selected stops, disappearing in the direction of a particular reputed rustler, then coming back to the railhead. Led by Granville Stuart, an acquaintance of both Teddy Roosevelt and the famous Marquis De Mores (who were among those urging vigorous action), the vigilantes were members of the fledgling Montana Stockgrower's Association. It is said that over sixty men had been hanged by the time the expedition ended. There is still rustling today, but like everything else it is more high-tech, and the punishment for it considerably less "efficient."

For all their fault as money-makers, cattle are truly liquid assets. On almost any given business day they can be sold at prevailing market prices, and all sales are cash. And so, I, too, have my minutes with Ed's calculator and checkbook and, like the others, know I face a bank appointment in a posture less favorable than I would like.

Thankfully, the ground is still bare, and if it stays that way, enough fall feed remains that I can go a couple weeks before feeding begins. Before spring I will count and recount every bale of hay in every stack and hope to squeak by.

On the loop home Emily helps me load the replacement heifers for the trip to our corrals at the house, where they will take up residence, bawling for several days for their mothers who will be confined in the corral across the river for twenty-four hours lest they make rash forays across fences, seeking their calves. Then Emily, due soon back at school, heads for the shower. The whole valley is filled with the bawling of mother cows because several of my neighbors have also weaned today. I look east at the bare brown hills. There is a heavy cloud cover, but the cloud bank is still well above the mountains, which look dark purple in the absence of sun. The stud colt looks at me from his corral compartment and nickers.

I look again at the hills, then at the stud colt, then walk to the tack room for his halter. There is no good reason to ride him now. I am tired from the work with the cattle and would really rather sit in the house for a while and read the paper. Perhaps it is the heavy, humid clouds, the wet smell of early snow to come that does it, the hills still bare for me and the stud colt but perhaps not for long. I curry the colt, throw on his blanket, then lift on the saddle, which still smells of Major's fresh sweat. I cinch up, then turn the colt around twice and swing up on him. He freezes under my weight. I back him up two steps, tell him "whoa" again, hold him in suspension for two seconds, then let the slightest tightening of muscles ripple through my legs and telegraph to the colt, and that is all he needs. We are off like the wind.

There is nothing to check in the eastern hills. There are no cattle there, none even anywhere en route. Fences can wait until spring. But still we go there, the colt and I, his muscles strong and fresh and tireless under me. At the gate to the hills I press him sideways, reach down and open it, pull it toward me, and give it a fling, leaving it open, never getting off, a great luxury I can enjoy only now with the range devoid of cattle. We take the easy route up the road, Magnus's old wagon road, Elmer's

Jeep road, Nora's nemesis. Topping a saddle we scatter a bunch of mule deer and, just a little farther up the trial, do likewise with a flock of sharptail grouse that rise noisily almost from under the stud colt's nose but do not make him flinch or acknowledge or break gait.

We are soon on top. We circle to the salt trough, again for no earthly reason, since it need not be replenished until spring, though the deer will make good use of the half block that remains. Then we ride straight south until we reach my neighbor's gate, then turn 360 degrees and head back north. If the stud colt questions these meanderings, he gives no sign. There is a little rise at the head of Indian Coulee, a minibutte, that forms the highest elevation on our ranch. We often take guests there to see the panorama. It is right where I think Magnus drove the wild horses a hundred years ago on the day he looked down at the deserted agency buildings and decided that this was his place, that he would build his ranch here.

The stud colt may not like standing on that high place, the wind whipping the bunch grass around him, but he does as I wish. We face due west. Perhaps ten seconds pass before it hits me, before I realize what I am seeing. My normal view is of miles of foothills in a 180-degree arc to my south and west, foothills running to the base of the Beartooth range, no major edifice of man visible between the mountains and me. The pioneers built in the valleys, not up exposed to the wind. When homesteaders had to build up in the foothills on an open 160 acres they found a coulee or a depression in which to build their dugouts. They built for survival, not for a view. All the houses are down in the valleys, and from here I can see our own and those of several neighbors. But the only building visible high in the panorama has been our own brave homesteader's barn across the river, left there when the homesteader sold out to Magnus and moved his house down into the valley out of the wind where he no doubt wished he had built it in the first place.

That is, until this moment. Three miles to the west, massive even from this distance, there is on the hilltop between the mountains and me a brand-new house. It must be huge to look so large from here. It must also have been erected at an incredible speed, for I was up here hunting for an antelope only weeks ago and there was nothing at that time.

Then, a conversation in the scale house that occurred while I was dealing with Ed comes to mind. Busy figuring along with the buyer, I had only half listened. Someone asked Rick, who lives several miles west of me, who built "that great big house."

"I don't know," Rick said.

"You don't know your neighbor?" the other man teased.

"No, no one knows him. Some say he's a lawyer from Florida. The only people who have seen him are the ones who run the store, and that was just once. And of course the contractor who built the house."

The rancher questioning Rick then said something about the wind and the winter soon defeating anyone foolish enough to build on top of that ridge, but Rick replied, rather solemnly, that he did not agree. "People like that can buy insulation as thick as they want, and, besides, if the weather doesn't suit them they just won't be here for a while—they'll just head for the house in Hawaii. They aren't living here for the same reasons we are. They aren't here to make a living. They've already done that somewhere else."

And now from the hilltop, mounted on the stud colt, I see the house and it all gels. I do not blame a wealthy man for wanting a palace. But his hilltop edifice is as ugly to me as a K-Mart in the middle of a wilderness meadow. It is a wart on my landscape, a lump, a boil. And I cannot help but feel that something from me has been stolen.

A combination of the gloomy day, the dismal cattle prices, and this new, unwelcome addition to the panorama conspire against me. It is as if an evil angel sits on my shoulder and whispers into my ear a breathless monologue of things that I do not want to hear. And it goes something like this: *Can't you see that you've had your time? Can't you see that your culture has had it now for a hundred years, as long as the Crows had it and a lot longer than the Lakota who came from the east and laid claim to it? Can't you see that invaders are coming? Can't you see that they will defeat you not with force of arms as the Army did the Plains Indians but with money, money earned lawyering in Florida or doctoring in Massachusetts or programming in Silicon Valley? And just as your people once told the Indians that they were barbaric, these people will consider what you do to be primitive and of no value. And as your culture took arms from the Indians these newcomers will take arms from you, will consider it more humane to castrate your wild game than to eat it, will talk of the environment while bulldozing a ridge in front of their decks for the sole purpose of improving their view. And to them the country they conquer will be uninhabited land, devoid of civilization, for you and your culture count for no more than the Crows did for the early whites. They will not come to introduce themselves as your neighbors. You are invisible to them.*

I try to shake this critter off my shoulder for the rest of my ride, combating it with some good arguments, some feeble ones. I remind myself that many fine people have moved in recently, that rural areas get inbred in outlook and need an occasional infusion. One such is a retired drug-rehabilitation and probation officer from the Bay area. He helps us with cattle, enjoys the things we take for granted, wants to be one of us. But countering that recollection is my gaze toward the northwest, toward dryland wheat fields that I have heard a developer wants to convert to a subdivision with many houses. I have heard the protestations of the ranchers who would live below this new, hilltop town, the man whose barn and house would be split by the thoroughfare of their commuting, and others worried that their irrigation water would become tainted with sewage.

My salvation, today, if I have one, is the stud colt. He is perfect. No lesson in training has been forgotten. We have reached it together. I cue him left or right with merely a twitch of my calf muscle against him and the slightest movement of the reins, so subtly an onlooker might think the turn was made with no direction from me. Handling him is the antithesis of the horsemanship of western movies, that of non-riders told by directors to create animation by yanking the reins and jerking the bit. We plunge down into Indian Coulee, eschewing the trail for the dry creek bed that runs down its bottom, the colt taking a skidding, controlled slide down the steepest portion, which is so steep that his proud head appears to be far below me. Farther down into the coulee in the deep timber, the wind is gone. All is hushed but for the crunching of sandstone and gravel under the hoofs of the stud colt.

Just as we reach it, its grey trunk horizontal in fallen splendor across the trail at the bottom of the coulee, the tree that once contained the remains of that Crow who was left here by departing relatives, it begins to snow, huge, triple flakes, falling so densely through the firs that in moments the trunk of the fallen pine is white with them. We have stopped. A little time passes, how much I do not know, but the colt gives a shake of his head and I see that his neck is white with snow and that my legs are, too, and I release an ounce of pressure on the reins, telling the colt that he may step out for home.

WINTER

19

A lone sentinel · Coyotes · Patience

On a morning so cold the house has made strange creaks and pops through the night; on a morning so bitter that the slightest breath of breeze feels like BBs hitting my face; on a morning the frozen crowbar I carry stings through the insulated leather gloves so that I must switch hands frequently as I carry it; on such a morning he sits the high cottonwood branch motionless but for the turning of a penetrating eye to watch my progress toward the creek. What warms him there sixty feet above me, exposed to every stir of this thirty-below air? His feathers, black and white, seem too sleek to preserve him, but there is no shiver in his body nor vapor visible above his hooked beak. He plays a game of nerves with me, this bald eagle, this bird of America, for I must get to the place in the creek, a place close to his tree, where the water flows swiftly over shallow rocks. There, if the ice is thin enough, I can again bash a hole through which the cows can drink.

The eagle has been here for two weeks, ever since it turned truly cold. For a couple days there were three others with him, another adult and two juveniles, their white markings not yet painted on, their feathers still rough. The creek is too frozen for fishing; they feed instead on what the coyotes left of the yearling mule deer doe they trapped by the creek a week ago, chased, surrounded, dragged down, and killed. Alerted by the barking of Buddy from his kennel, I got to the kitchen window in time to see the last of it. They had already killed her and were playing with various portions of her dismembered anatomy, chasing back and forth in the calf pasture like lethal schoolboys. I understand how the doe's loss of life was a gain of life for the four coyotes and a gain, too, for the eagles, but I wasn't completely prepared for the tale told by the sign in the snow when I walked over later that day. One would have thought the doe was hit by a speeding car. Her skin had been completely removed, tubelike, in the way that trappers skin small animals, and it lay in the snow fifty yards from the rest of the scene. The stomach and its frozen contents lay fifty yards in another direction, and those remains of the doe still connected were on the ground at the end of a blood smear on the snow twenty paces long.

Had I been a dedicated coyote hunter or a sheep man protecting his flock, I could have waited in the moonlight to ambush the coyotes as they returned each night, announced by Buddy, to feed on what was left. But being neither, I let the coyotes be. During daylight, the eagles took over. Odd, what times we live in, when we thrust our subjective human judgments on creatures of the wild. My son has had a terrible time trying to convince college roommates that bald eagles eat carrion. Saturated by only one picture of eagles feeding, that of the birds swooping up salmon from a river, they can imagine no other scenario and flatly refuse to believe that the noble symbol of America could eat dead and rotting flesh. I have told Jon to remind them why Ben Franklin voted instead for the wild turkey as our national symbol. Not only delicious to eat, he told Congress, the turkey was smarter than the eagle and did not have the latter's propensity for eating carrion. Old Ben was a more astute observer of the eagle than even some *National Geographic* film makers.

But never mind that. The fact that he eats carrion makes me like the eagle neither more nor less. Like all of us, he just has to survive. I value this one for his beauty and am glad he is here. And I must admire any creature that can sit high on a tree limb at thirty below, motionless, except now for a subtle swiveling of his head as I approach the watering place in the creek. Finally, he has enough, needs more elbow room, and lifts on massive wings out of the tree and into the air. I have observed him before and know he will not go far, just south a quarter mile to roost in another cottonwood tree and return when I have done my work.

I have tied a scarf around my neck before launching out, and I push it higher onto my face. The hole I made yesterday is frozen with thick transparent ice. Through it I can see water shooting past, and with the crowbar I am able to make a hole two feet wide. Ice chunks broken off by my blows drop into the crystal water and sweep away. The replacement heifers have noticed my progress to the creek and have followed me. Now, one by one, they begin to drink. This chore done I walk swiftly back to the house, carefully breathing through my nose rather than mouth, afraid to dump too much of this icy air directly into my lungs. In the house I will warm myself briefly before venturing out to the next task.

. . .

It is Saturday, and that is the reason I can wait until broad daylight to chop ice for the cows. The retreat of the sun toward the year's longest night has pinched away my light on both ends of each day, so that on school days I leave in darkness and return to the ranch in twilight. Winter has set in, although it did not do so immediately after my last ride on the stud colt. The thick flakes that fell on Indian Coulee that day did continue, did dump a foot of wet snow on us so that feeding the cows had to begin early after all. But in mid-November we got a reprieve, a chinook which took the snow and bared the ground.

Steve's brothers returned on Thanksgiving for a reunion replete with this combination: the fragrance of Emily's turkey slowly roasting; stalking big, rutting whitetail bucks along the river bottom (for the generous Montana deer season extends through Thanksgiving); and, during breaks from the hunting, football on television.

Each time we can have one of these, our favorite get-togethers, there is awareness that with life as it is, such reunions must become increasingly infrequent. I noted my developing role as more senior huntsman than hunter, but did not mind. (Besides, I had my moose and could rest on my laurels.)

Christmas plans have begun to roll, too, the choir at church dusting off copies of "Jeg Er Saa Glad" and "Today There Is Ringing" and our scores of Handel's *Messiah*. As director I think of myself as the Fiddler Jones of the Stillwater valley. For those who do not know him, Fiddler Jones was one of that assembly of ghosts in Edgar Lee Masters' *Spoon River Anthology* who speak one-by-one in poems from beyond their graves. Jones begins his poem with these lines:

The earth keeps some vibration going

There in your heart, and that is you.

And if people find you can fiddle,

Why, fiddle you must, for all your life.

Which is to say, that in rural communities the issue is not whether you are well-trained for some civic task that needs doing or that you are especially suited for doing it, but that you *can* do it, and if you *can* do it, then you must, because if you did not, perhaps no one would, and something very worthy might not happen or might die. And so I direct the choir. But I take much solace from Fiddler Jones. He is one of very few happy ghosts in Masters' rather dreary assembly, one of the few who says he has no regrets.

After Thanksgiving, the preliminary bout was over and winter came in for the main event. It snowed, and then, more serious for us, it turned cold and stayed that way. We do not live in a part of Montana whose winters are particularly severe on average, but they are very erratic. We do not usually have the set-in cold of northern Minnesota, and the cold we have comes with extremely dry air, so that our livestock can usually survive outdoors through the worst of it. But there is little consistency from year to year. Stockmen crave an "open" winter, one in which the ground is bare a good share of the time, which lets the cows pick what natural feed remains, supplementing the hay they are fed. But ranchers know, too, that the mountains must get their snowpack to ensure irrigation water through the summer, and also that at least one big, wet snowstorm toward spring seems necessary to get the green times rolling.

For every open winter there are a couple tough ones when the snow makes big drifts on the lee sides of the sheds, and the cows spend much time humped in the cottonwoods with their rear ends to the wind. Tire chains for the four-wheel-drive pickup come off the nails on the shed wall and onto all four tires. The cows turn voracious. Only by eating can they protect themselves against the cold, and twice as much feed is required to keep them in condition. On our ranch the firewood pile diminishes alarmingly; we hustle more of the stuff, for we never have time during fall to assemble our total winter requirement.

This winter is starting out somewhere between the extremes, but now, after a solid week of early, deep cold, seems leaning decidedly toward the bitter. On the morning of the eagle I step into the back porch and my glasses turn instantly to thick frost. I take them off quickly so that I can see. Emily has stoked up the fires and fixed breakfast. I have put making the water hole as first chore of the morning, since water is so critical to livestock when it gets extremely cold. Animals dehydrate very quickly in our dry cold conditions. Pneumonia can be the quick result with cattle; colic, the big killer of horses, the quick result with them.

After breakfast, my toes no longer tingling, I launch out again, this time to the shed where the diesel pickup has been plugged in all night. I turn the key to light the glow plugs, wait with my fingers crossed, hear the agonizingly slow starter turn. I let it crank as long as I dare, and an instant before I quit, one cylinder thumps. I wait, try again, get two cylinders, then finally, reluctantly, the engine gives me three before coughing into life. One hurdle conquered.

The pickup must be loaded before I feed, since last night, Friday, I indulged in my little party routine, celebrating the end of the week by taking the night off from putting on my normal load of hay. On the other weeknights I always load the pickup by the red illumination of the taillights so that the load is ready to feed off long before daylight the next morning. Friday nights I indulge in this little R and R, knowing I can use the daylight of Saturday morning for stacking this particular load. But today I wish I had followed a sterner work ethic, because it is very cold. Never mind. With insulated coveralls pulled on over everything else, the work goes quickly; I stack the forty-five bales on the red pickup as quickly as I did years ago when I was king of the stack and kept up with two loaders buzzing over smooth irrigated fields. The work warms all but my face and my toes.

My hands never get cold, perhaps a legacy from Norwegian fishermen, and until I was about thirty my feet never got cold either. But on a winter drill with the Marines, when I was the commanding officer of a reserve unit camped in snow caves in a Beartooth valley, I did something very foolish. I pulled my insulated leather boots, which had been soaked, then frozen, onto my feet in the morning, relying on my feet to warm the boots—not terrific logic—and, of course, the reverse happened. Frostbite lightly touched my toes, not enough to require any sort of treatment, but enough to confirm the old belief that a part of your body once bitten by frost is ever after more susceptible. So, in mixed metaphor, my toes are now my Achilles' heel.

The replacement heifers, their thirst satisfied, can see me from their pasture, and they stand by the fence bawling. I leave the gate open behind me as I drive through. If it were less cold and the heifers were less hungry, I would never do that, for replacement heifers in December are as lively and flighty as girls in junior high school, and the whole bunch could be out the gate before you could blink. But today they glue themselves to the sides of the pickup, crowd it so tightly that when I stop it to climb on the rear and throw them their three bales I must push between two round bellies and make myself a path. Normally they would skitter aside, but today their purpose is too singular.

Then I drive the circuitous mile on the snow-packed highway to the gate across the river, where the main body of cows will remain until calving time. The tire chains thump and jingle, so I drive slowly. Through the leafless trees on the cottonwood bottom, the cows have heard my pickup. Yes, it is true, they know the sound of whatever pickup or tractor feeds them, can distinguish it from the sounds of other vehicles on the road. I have heard them bawling, a half-mile away as the crow flies, from the first moment I fired up the pickup, starting on cue with the engine's first cough into life, heard them all through my loading of the hay. When I arrive the cows are lining the fence in the hay meadow across the river like a string of huge blackbirds perched side-by-side on a telephone wire.

Now I must feed off the entire load, so I put the pickup in low range and granny gear, then adjust the "Norwegian autopilot," the piece of shock cord that stretches from the gearshift knob to the steering wheel. The pickup is now at walking speed. I step out, close the door, and swing onto the rear of the pickup. I find a secure place to stand, and grab a home-made tool also ethnically named by my boys: my "Norwegian tomahawk," a sharp triangular sickle section from a mower, welded to a steel handle opposite a hay hook. With one side of the tool I hook a bale and yank it toward me. I grab it by the strings, hang it part way over the edge of the load, and pop the strings with the sharpened sickle section. Then I push the bale over the edge of the load in twenty-pound flakes. Soon the cows are strung out behind the pickup like the tail of a kite, eating greedily. Most cows seize upon the first hay to be dropped, but there are a few that always follow right at the tailgate of the pickup until every bale is fed, perhaps certain that the tastiest morsels will be dropped last.

As I feed I detect some slippage in the four chained wheels under me, and that is a worry. Yesterday the wind blew very hard, drifting and crusting the snow. The pickup has chewed its way along with the help of the chains and the additional traction provided by a ton and a half of hay stacked in its bed. Now, however, its ballast diminished, the wheels start to chatter under me and, sure enough, the vehicle hangs up spinning just as I feed the last bale. I vault over the side and jump in behind the steering wheel, jamming the outfit into reverse. I almost back free, then spin out again and begin to settle deeply into a drift. I inspect and discover that a rear wheel has shed a tire chain in the snow. With much fishing, I retrieve it. Out comes the folding shovel from behind the seat to clear a space on either side of the bare tire. Soon I have the chain back again. I am working frantically against the numbing cold, my heart beginning to thump, for it is no day to be stuck out in the snow.

With the errant chain back on and the pickup heater blasting, I pause a minute and tell myself to cool it. There is no use getting angry, for winter can only be handled with patience. It is bigger and stronger than you are, and it will, in time, pass. I rock the pickup back and forth, and soon, fully chained, get the pickup free and sprint toward the gate, the grill showering snow onto the windshield.

. . .

On the way home I recall the story of Karl, a rancher up the creek known for his hysterical and sometimes violent temper. Like me, he got his pickup, a nearly new one, stuck in a drift even though it was chained up all around. He roared the engine, first in reverse, then in forward, the engine screaming, the chains chattering, but all to no avail. Fuming and cussing, he pulled out the throttle (pickups had throttles then), popped the clutch, got out and walked to the house, leaving the pickup spinning its wheels. This it did for more than an hour, tires smoking, until, finally, it simply died. The vehicle was completely destroyed, of course, the transmission seized, the drive lines shot.

But then, this particular man, this Karl, was known for feats of temper that make those of us who simply yell and cuss feel like bashful schoolboys by comparison. One summer, when he was baling hay, the baler refused to tie the strings, and, of course, heavy rain clouds were coming. He tried to fix it, then pounded on it, heaping curses on the baler, the clouds, and probably life in general. At the peak of his anger he turned his back on the baler and walked a quarter mile to the house. He picked up an axe. He then coldly and deliberately walked back to the baler and proceeded to chop its tires into bits. This act is admired in these parts as the ultimate exercise of bad and violent temper, not because of the act—we have all been *nearly* that mad at a baler— but because of how long Karl was able to *hold* the anger. A half mile of walking, and who knows what else? He probably took time to sharpen the axe.

Guys like Karl exist so that the rest of us can compare ourselves with them and pat ourselves on the back for being so sane. So with the GMC's radio playing, the car guys on National Public Radio joking about automatic transmissions, and the heater working so well it combines with the body heat of my exertions and the melting snow on my coveralls to steam the windows, I return to the house, my mood salvaged. They told us in the military that armies in combat operating in winter conditions spend fully ninety percent of their time and effort simply maintaining: keeping people sheltered and fed, keeping vehicles running, machines working, and so forth. The ten percent of capacity left over is what remains for fighting, and great initiative is required to use that in a focused fashion. The army that is able to do so, wins.

. . .

Ranching in winter is much the same. You do not plan your days. You work until it is too dark to do any more, and you just solve problems as they arise. So after I warm up in the house I will begin to work on thawing one of the heated self-waterers. I am confident, for this waterer has frozen before but always responds to a treatment with Emily's blow dryer directed down around the intake tube. The other waterer, that of the heifers, froze days ago, and it has a history of staying frozen until a good chinook. I kick myself every winter for not having taken a day during summer to dig it out and fix it properly, but in summer I am too busy with hay and irrigating to get it done, and bitter winter days are far from my thoughts.

So, again, I tell myself to have patience. The darkness that envelops me all week will eventually break, and so will this bitter cold. I walk to the house to have a cup of coffee and to round up Emily's hair dryer.

2 0

Requiem

*I*t is on another cold morning, on one of the last school days before Christmas vacation, after a night of snow that has blown in drifts against the arena fence, that I go out for my predawn chores and notice that by the time I fill the grain bucket at the tack room and rattle the metal gate, the stud colt has not yet come to greet me. He has not appeared out of the darkness at the gate and thrust his muzzle into the grain bucket. Most of the arena is dimly illuminated by the blue glow of the vapor light. Thinking first of escape, I look to the other gate, but see it is closed. Then, in the shadow cast by the steel machine shed, I see the colt lying in the snow, see that he is moving, and before it strikes me as strange for him to be lying there, I see his hind leg kick out, then pull back and push him into a roll. He gets up covered with snow, but does not stretch or shake. His back is humped and his tail is kinked, and immediately after getting up he looks for a place to lie down again. I sprint to the back door of the house, open it, and yell to Emily, "Call Bill—the stud colt has colic." Standing in the kitchen in her nightgown, she asks no questions, but gives a little flinch as if something has hit her and darts toward the phone.

I quickly pull on extra clothing, substituting a down vest and insulated coveralls for my work coat, and return to the colt, lead rope in hand. He is down again. I snap the lead onto his halter, get him up, and commence walking back and forth in the snow of the arena, trying to keep him on his feet. Traditional wisdom has it that a colic can turn worse if a horse is allowed to roll, that a colic beginning as an intestinal blockage can become a twisted intestine if the horse rolls in pain. This theory (and I know there are others) demands that you keep the horse up and walking. Besides, until the vet comes, what else is there to do? So we trudge in the darkness on a path we quickly make in the snow, and soon headlights cast moving shadows of leafless cottonwoods against the metal machine shed. Bill quickly checks the colt's vital signs, which are good, and gives him a drug for pain. We pow-wow and make a quick decision in favor of Bill's heated clinic in town for further assessment. So he walks the colt while I fire up the pickup and hitch it to the horse trailer. Although it is still dark and there is no light in the trailer, the colt steps into it readily.

In town, in a heated, lighted room with concrete floor and medicinal, clinic smell, the stud colt sedated against the pain, Bill again checks vital signs. His assessment and analysis come quickly. An anal examination does not tell him for certain whether there is a torsion of an intestine—a twisted gut—but he is concerned that there might be. He tells me I must weigh whether surgery is an option, and he spells out the details. The nearest full-fledged surgical facility is in Bridger, the town where I teach. Ray, the veterinarian, a tough, skilled, workaholic is well-known to me, his wife a former colleague, his son and daughter past students of mine. I have seen Ray's impressive surgical facility, the padded room with hydraulic table that rises when the horse has been sedated and laid down.

Bill estimates the cost of the surgery, which is considerable. The stud colt does not have a huge market value, and the surgical procedure could well cost as much as he is worth in dollars and cents. (His worth to me, a worth intrinsic and personal, is another matter, of course, but how much can I afford to consider that?) The kicker is

this: if indeed the colt has twisted a gut, he is likely doomed without surgery, although in a very few cases, such torsions untwist themselves. Conversely, survival on the surgical table in these cases is only fifty percent. From what Bill is saying, chances that the colt has a twisted gut in the first place are, perhaps, also around fifty percent.

I try to factor all this and do it quickly. At this point in my life I have never lost a horse to colic, although I have had several close calls. Each case has eventually responded to painkillers to keep the animal relaxed and mineral oil to soften the blockage causing the colic. Bill is acting on that front even as I make my decision. He is inserting a plastic tube down the colt's nostril and into his stomach, ready for the mineral oil. For this, and for all Bill must do to him, this spirited handful of horse, this stud colt that has so challenged me, stands with the dignity and calm of a king.

The telephone rings, and Bill's wife, his assistant, indicates the call is for me. I walk toward the phone, noticing out the window that the yard around the clinic is now bathed in bright daylight. I have had no sense of the passage of time since I walked outside and found the colt in the snow. Emily is on the line. She has called my acting principal, Roger, the same friend who inadvertently took me to the funeral home after the skiing accident and whose father fed him mutton during deer season. Roger has told her to relay that I should just do whatever I need to do, not worry about school, that he will see to it my classes are covered.

I return to the colt's side. Bill is listening again, his stethoscope pressed tightly to the flank and stomach of the horse, moving it frequently, then walking to the animal's other side and listening again. There is the slightest hint of hope in his voice when he stands straight and removes the instrument from his ears. "Well, I *am* hearing a little gut noise now." He does not have to explain the importance of that to me. Two great enemies in colic cases are an inactive gut and the length of time it is inactive. An intestinal tract that quits working can soon begin to die, particularly if a torsion has cut off the blood supply.

I decide to hang fire on arranging a surgery. Bill continually monitors not only the colt's gut sounds, but also his pulse (it has been much elevated but has descended with the effects of the drugs) and the color of his gums. We will go through a cycle of sedation with him, see if his heart rate immediately elevates again when the drugs wear off, see if his pain returns, see if his vital signs stay good.

We are well into the morning when I look up from the stool on which I sit, my fingers absent-mindedly running through the soft hair on top of the Border Collie's back, the clinic dog that has come to be petted, when Bill returns and says he will do another rectal check on the horse. I hold the stud colt's lead rope. Afterwards, as Bill removes his glove he looks me in the eyes and says, "I'm just afraid we have a torsion here," and I can no longer stand the decision I made earlier. I reverse it, tell Bill I want to head for the surgical facility and inwardly curse myself for not making the decision sooner. Bill is quickly on the phone. Then he tells me, "Ray is on his way to another emergency but should be done with it by the time you get there. Meanwhile, you can hope for a 'trailer cure.'" He is referring to a phenomenon we have discussed earlier, that some colics mysteriously cure themselves during trailer rides, the animal's exertions to compensate for the motion of the trailer sometimes breaking a blockage. But we both know that if the colt's gut is twisted, chances of such are exceedingly slim.

So then we are on the road, the gravel shortcut to Bridger. The day is cold and brilliant, the Beartooths to our south shimmering with snow. Past the church, a coyote speeds across the road in front of us. I drive as fast as I dare, constantly eyeballing the left mirror for the trail of vapor the colt's breath makes high out the side of the trailer in the cold winter air, for that tells me he is staying on his feet. Several times I skid to a stop, jump out and check him, then drive on.

It is not the first fast trip the stud colt has taken in my trailer. He took a long one, even before he was born, housed in the belly of a great old mare I had driven a long way to buy. We bought two, actually, from a breeder in Ohio, a younger mare and Angie, the colt's mother, a rare prize, a grand old lady of her breed with foundation horses just three generations back. Roger and I allowed just one day of personal leave combined with a weekend, setting out after school on a Thursday, driving all night. It was an insane winter trip, the kind only those who have suffered cabin fever and those who truly love horses can understand. Roger got out at Sioux Falls to visit his son, and in the same city I picked up my son David, who made the round trip with me to Davenport, where the man with the horses met us part way, then up into Minnesota to briefly see my parents, then back to Sioux Falls to again exchange David for Roger.

The entire trip back west, from Iowa to Montana, was made in the teeth of a winter gale so vicious it kept the truck and camper heeled over like a sailing ship at sea. We stopped and staggered into a Perkins all-night restaurant in Rapid City, South Dakota. It was surrounded by highway patrol cars. Roger was wearing a black knit watch cap and looked an awful lot like Jack Nicholson in *One Flew over the Cuckoo's Nest*. Neither of us had shaved for a couple of days, and our eyes must have looked like spitholes in the snow. Over pancakes Roger asked, "Are they looking at me like I just escaped from somewhere?"

"No," I laughed. "But every cop in South Dakota must be in here."

"No," Roger said. "That's impossible." He sipped his coffee. "No way in hell South Dakota could have so many. They must have borrowed some from North Dakota and Nebraska. Must be some kind of a convention."

When we got Angie and the other mare home, I couldn't resist, even though Angie was heavy in foal and I was tired. I threw a saddle on her back and rode her, just a hundred yards or so, and I felt in the stately mare a gait and way of going that Elmer or Magnus would have died for. I told Emily, "Now, here's what I'm ordering. This mare must have a sorrel stud colt with blaze and stockings behind." And that spring we looked out one morning and both gawked at the rare luck of getting exactly what I wanted, for beside old Angie strutted a sorrel stud colt with blaze and hind socks and a look on his face as if he were already well along toward conquering the world.

The memories make me briefly smile. After an hour we hit town. It feels strange to pass right by the school without stopping, to see the familiar cars parked there and, looking out at me, the windows of my classroom. At the clinic I park and unload the colt. I look for the miraculous trailer cure and for one brief moment think I've been given it, for the colt walks easily the first ten paces. Then he cramps and his tail kinks anew.

The veterinarian's daughter, home from college on vacation, comes out with news that Ray's other emergency continues, that he will come as quickly as possible, that he says to keep the colt moving if we can. She volunteers to help me walk the colt, so we take turns some, but mostly walk together, she keeping me interested in stories of her life at college. There is little snow here at Bridger, the south wind having blown the snow off the ground around the clinic, peeling it down to brown, frozen gravel. Much time passes. The colt walks easily part of the time, with difficulty sometimes. Occasionally, as if to shake off this curse by pure exercise of will, he arches his neck, stands tall, and moves ahead of us as far as his lead rope will allow in a shuffling shadow of his running walk.

Ray comes, finally, his other emergency having been as involved as this one is. He gives the colt only a quick glance, then speaks terse instructions to the young woman veterinarian, an intern, who is with him. She disappears. We walk the colt into a rear entrance of the clinic. The colt's shoes are loud on the concrete floor. Ralph has installed ice shoes on him for me, shoes with tips of hard-surfacing welded onto their caulks, for I have decided the colt's elite days are over and that he will work all winter and help me calve toward spring.

Ray, like Bill, examines and re-examines. His stethoscope flits over the colt's body, his fingers part the lips to reveal the gums, his syringe reinstalls soothing drugs into the colt's system. He leaves and returns several times, as does his assistant. Once while Ray is gone I recall a chance meeting I had with him at a fast-food joint on the outskirts of Billings. I was headed a hundred miles east, after school, to buy alfalfa seed from a farmer. It would be late at night before I returned. We were both too hurried to even sit down, so we had a brief visit, standing, each with a hamburger in one hand and a cup of coffee in the other. Ray, hearing what I was up to, asked when on earth I had time to plant the seed once I bought it. "Oh, at night, after school. My tractor has good lights."

He looked at me, shook his head, and said, "Aadland, you're crazy."

"I guess so," I said. "And where are you headed, Ray?"

"To Hardin. I spend two days a week down there to be the vet for the racetrack."

"Wait a minute, Ray. You hold down one of the busiest vet practices in the territory there in Bridger, and you commute down to Hardin two days a week to take care of the race horses? And you call me crazy?" He saw what I was driving at and laughed. We went out into the parking lot, each to our separate pickups and separate missions.

Ray comes back into the concrete room and goes over with me what is involved in a surgery for a twisted gut. "Imagine," he says, "an inner tube of a truck tire filled with water, terribly heavy and impossible to grip well. Imagine this being accessible to you only through this opening you have cut. Now, imagine this heavy, slithery affair being completely twisted over 180 degrees so that you must somehow wrestle it back to the way it was before. Everything has to go just right before it will work."

Then Ray does another complete check of the colt. Again, it is a glance out a window, at the windswept hills and buttes and, farther off, the Pryor Mountains, that shows me the passage of time, for the sun now has the slant of a winter afternoon. After this check of the colt, Ray looks at me with tired eyes through his glasses and says, "Dan, this colt is not a good surgical prospect. I'm almost certain we have a torsion, and I'm afraid his condition will not stand surgery. It is likely that some of the gut tissue has begun to die." And I am not surprised at this assessment because it explains his stalling, his reluctance to begin the extensive preparations for surgery. He is too good a man to take my money.

And I say to him, "Then we'd better do what we have to do."

He asks whether I wish to be briefly alone with the colt, but I say, "No, that's okay." We have always been pretty much alone together, the colt and I. No one else has ever ridden him except Tex, and that only because I had a broken leg. I reach out and lay my hand on his withers, working his mane deeply into the spaces between my fingers. He has grown so very tall. His sorrel coat is shiny, and even now, after all this, he is very beautiful. He seems to me much braver than I can be. And if I could talk I would say, "My friend, this is a mountain I do not think we can climb together." Then Ray and his assistant take him away.

Ten minutes later they slowly walk back to the pickup where I stand and wait. Ray is carrying the stud colt's halter and lead rope. He hands them to me and I lay them gently in the bed of the pickup box. We exchange brief words of encouragement to each other, reaffirm that we have done the right thing. If Ray's eyes are a reflection of mine we are both in sorry shape indeed. The woman vet at first seems composed, but then she turns her back to us.

I drive through downtown Bridger, all three blocks of it. At the bank corner a knot of my students, newly released from school, spot me and look surprised, no doubt assuming it was illness of mine that kept me from classes. I manage to return their smiles and waves. Then I head south on the highway. I have no stomach for a return by the same gravel route and will instead go the way I usually do by car, south on the paved highway, then over to Red Lodge and home. I drive past the sawmill where I have many times bought rough-cut fir for various ranch projects. It is closed now, the machinery idle. On each side of the highway there are sugar-beet fields blown bare of snow, what is left of the beet tops piled in brown clumps for the cattle, little islands of dead vegetation surrounded by frozen dirt. I make it a mile down the road, maybe two, before the road in front of me seems to tilt and wave and nearly crash, and something in me explodes, and I hear in the cab of the pickup strange, awful sounds that can not be coming from me although I know that they are.

I am very startled by this sudden, choking grief, and I am glad there is no one here to see it. I know that I should stop the pickup, know that I should not be driving, but I continue anyway to speed down this highway that has become blurred and sur-real, the horse trailer behind me bouncing lightly on its springs. The beginning attempts to argue my way out of this only anger me. I turn on the tape player. The strains of "Air on the String of G" by Bach begin. It is one of the world's greatest and saddest and most powerful pieces of music, and I cannot stand it. Its great reservoir of feeling combined with mine could break what fragile dam remains, would be too much to stand, too much for the confines of the vibrating cab of this pickup truck, so I twist the switch to shut it down.

There will be a time, I tell myself, after the passage of some days or weeks, when I can tally it all and figure why the death of my stud colt seems to have catalyzed every grief and stress and loss I have ever known. The words of friends come back to me, those who have said, "Dan, you can't keep doing this." They mean the two jobs with the stretch of sixty miles between, but I know others with similar work loads, and I have never felt abused by mine.

But I know the tally is considerable. There are the happenings of life that are ordinary but still take their toll: a near-miss on the highway some weeks ago, one of many in my years of commuting, but particularly frightening. I could not see. The bug-spattered windshield turned into a brilliant opaque sheet in front of me when hit by the low morning sun, and the horn of a fuel truck when I was nearly on its bumper told me how close I was. A head-on collision between the truck and my little car would have been a mere chip-shot for the truck, and I probably would not have survived. There is the recent departure of several good friends, the progress of "empty-nest" syndrome as the boys leave home one by one, the sheer fatigue of a life style offering too little time for sleep. And, of course, there has been this smothering, yearly descent of darkness that masks my home and ranch from me much of the time during winter, that sends me out to fix a fence by the headlights of the pickup.

And then there has been the truly heavy stuff. The death in my small school over the years of an inordinate number of students, most to vehicular accidents: funerals in gymnasiums with students looking to me for more strength than I have. There are more psychologists' catchwords: midlife crisis; post-traumatic stress disorder (you were in Vietnam weren't you, Dan—why do you think you were unscathed by it?).

But as I speed the pickup south toward the mountains through the late afternoon shadows that have begun to darken the valley, I cannot dwell on any of it, for there seems no room in me for anything except this searing grief, and attempts to "count blessings" fall flat. I invoke a good friend's maxim, one I have often quoted to others: "A man will not die in winter who is expecting a colt in the spring." I remind myself that the stud colt was bred to four mares, two of them mine, that these colts will soon come. But even this fails. Everything around me just says, "loss, loss, loss." And I look to the Beartooths, past Whitetail Peak, to the ridges made cloudy by the snow blowing off them, and I know that above and behind the peak the snow drifts are deep on high Sundance Pass.

21

El Sol

*I*n the winter afternoon that the stud colt died, I was traveling south up the valley of the Clark's Fork of the Yellowstone River on my half-circle route toward home. The valley here is broad and flat, very fertile, but drier than the one farther west where our ranch is located. The Clark's Fork Valley is also warmer than that of our home ranch because it opens to the south into Wyoming through a large break between the Beartooth Mountains of the Absaroka range to the west and the Pryor Mountains to the east. Strong south winds blow up this valley much of the time. Although they chill you to the bone in December, the average temperature brought by these winds is warm by Montana standards. So with irrigation water taken from the river, sugar beets grow well in this valley, and farther down, fruit trees that would never survive on the ranch, for the growing season is some weeks longer than ours at home.

The river was named after Captain William Clark, the partner of Meriwether Lewis, of the famous expedition that bears their names. Clark explored near here in 1806, and his sergeant, Nathaniel Pryor, left his name on the mountains to the east. A year earlier a French explorer named Larocque had done a somewhat more thorough canvas of this region than Lewis and Clark did, but since he represented the Canadian government and wrote his journal in French, he has never been well-known to us. And, nearly three-quarters of a century later, a gallant and brilliant Nez Perce chief named Joseph led men, women, children, and a huge band of prized horses on a forced march from Idaho, east through Yellowstone Park on the headwaters of the Clark's Fork, then turned north down this valley following the identical route (though in the opposite direction) I traveled daily on my drive home from school.

During my many years of commuting between school at Bridger and our ranch near Absarokee, I often thought of all these earlier people, but most of all of "The Children of the Large Beaked Bird," the Absaroka, better known to us as the Crow Indians. This valley of the Clark's Fork of the Yellowstone was a common wintering ground for them. As I drove along the highway I would often think of their lodges, pitched in the cottonwood groves for protection from the wind. Inside there would be buffalo robes on the floors of the tepees and a warm fire and a plentiful supply of the dried meat that would sustain them through the winter, at least in good years.

In tougher times when winter came too early, and the snow drifted deep around the tepees, and the wind howled through the villages at night, the adults must have lain awake, wrapped in their robes, worrying. They did not worry about paying mortgages on their land or about whether their cows would calve well, but about their supply of meat and the availability of firewood, for which they already trudged far in the snow each day to find. They worried about their horses, which were growing gaunt. Daily they were spending much time peeling the bark of young cottonwood trees, stripping it into thin, strawlike strings, poor nourishment but better than nothing for the horses that were so important to them. During Decembers such as these, I wondered as I drove home from school whether the Absaroka participated in the same vigil I did more than a century later.

This vigil involved the setting of the sun, and it requires some explanation. At our latitude and position in the time zone, the path of the sun sinks lower as winter comes, and sunset comes steadily earlier until, in early December, it sets at 4:30 in the afternoon. (That is the official time on flat ground—the sun settles behind the Beartooth Mountains some minutes sooner.) At that point it holds constant for a couple weeks. True, the days continue to shorten, but only in the morning, the sun continuing to rise later each morning, cheating the day only on the one end. And so, even before the shortest day of the year, the sun begins to grant an apparent reprieve, for after sundown holds constant at 4:30 for two weeks, it actually begins to edge later. Thus, the retreat toward the shortest day is not a symmetrical one, not a perfect hourglass, but contains a preview in the afternoon of the better and longer days to come.

As a commuter who had a ranch at home, I was keenly aware of these changes. Every minute of daylight that remained when I pulled into the ranch was precious to me. In the fading light I could quickly eyeball the condition of the livestock and begin any presupper chores before deep darkness set in. Throughout the year I would notice every change in illumination along my commuting route, both coming and going. I would notice just when a particular barn caught the morning sun, notice that the light had walked up or down the wall (depending on the season) a tad further when I passed it the next morning. My friends were sometimes surprised at my fascination with this—it took changes measured in the half-hour before they seemed to notice much.

In the fall when the days were still long, lengthened by daylight saving time, I could visit with my friends a few extra minutes at the end of the day over a last cup of coffee without feeling desperate to head home. In spring, when long days returned, my drama rehearsals kept me after school. But during winter, with the fading of the light, preferring to correct my papers at night when other work was done, I sprinted from the school every day exactly at four.

As you head south from Bridger on Highway 72, before reaching Belfry there is a place where the valley is open and presents a fine view of the Beartooth front, a rugged line of mountains broken by canyons where creeks emerge. Where one such canyon splits the high ground there is a particular notch in the skyline, and this notch

or depression was central to my December vigil. It was precisely in this notch, at 4:15, that the sun settled for those two weeks of earliest sunset each December. I would watch this as winter deepened. In late November the sun would be hovering some distance above the mountains when I made my turn at Belfry and, of course, in a path descending to the west of the notch. Only during winter's shortest days did it set far enough to the south to hit the notch, and I knew, when it started doing so, that the dark days had bottomed out. I knew, too, that when I returned to school after Christmas vacation, the sun would again be missing the notch to the west just slightly, that it would be just a finger's width above the horizon when I checked it while driving through that open place in the valley. And although the worst of winter weather might yet remain, *my* winter would be then on the mend.

It was during those very shortest days that I thought most of the villages of the Absaroka. Did these brave people also come close to despair at these shortest days? Did they watch the sun settle into that notch as I did, watch it hover there a few seconds in cold fire, then plunge below the mountains leaving the snow briefly pink? Did the quick darkness come for them as well with the same sinking of spirit?

. . .

And so, back to the day that the stud colt died. I am leaving the veterinarian's clinic, bouncing over the railroad tracks in the red pickup pulling the empty trailer. At the bank corner where the group of students throw me friendly waves, I glance up at the clock. It reads 4:03. I am, coincidentally, leaving Bridger at my accustomed midwinter time. On a normal day it would have taken that long to get to the car, scrape the windshield, and pass the bank downtown.

Now fast-forward to a place up the valley near where the view of the Beartooths fully opens. The shadows are long and dark. As I break out from the valley hills to the view of the Beartooth Mountains, the sun settles in the crevice, white light penetrating thin clouds, its disk touching into the accepting notch. It will be gone, I know, in an instant. But it is not. Hovering there while I scarcely breathe, still lighting the valley, stubbornly refusing to go, the sun gives me one precious, unexpected, extra minute. It is not much. It is everything!

Epilogue

Last fall I decided to plow a large dryland field high on the west side of the valley above the old homesteader's barn. We would very much like to preserve the barn, but are not certain how to do so. It is made of huge logs hewn square by hand. Next to it, across the foundation of the old house (which was moved down into the valley), sits a shelter belt of trees, ash and some sort of elm, the elm now finally having died, the ash still partially hanging on. All the yet-living trees have many dead branches and in winter look like skeletons, then surprise us in spring with sprigs of new green leaves sprinkled among the dead branches. We have heard that the homesteader and his family packed water to this shelter belt for many years to get it established.

The field right around the barn was my first farming project. Elmer, a better rancher than farmer, had seeded this field fully forty years earlier with a seed mix designed for dryland pasture. Emily remembers seeding the field with the then-new truck. She alternated between keeping her mother company on the seat of the truck and the more exciting location next to her dad in the back, where he filled the air with flying seed by cranking hard on the handle of a spinning broadcast seeder. The pasture that resulted was very good for many years, but nothing lasts forever, and

Elmer had quit farming. So when Emily and I took over the ranch there was much rejuvenation to be done.

When I plowed the field around the barn, working mostly at night, I called Mrs. Moloy, a lady in her eighties, one of the two little girls who was raised on the homestead. "Alice, I'm plowing up by the barn, and I'll bet I can tell you exactly where your

garden was. It was right on the west side of the shelter belt, wasn't it?"

She was puzzled at first, needing to get her bearings. Then, "Well, yes, Dan, it was right there, and it was a wonderful garden. But it's been fifty years. How did you know?"

"Well, it's tough plowing up there, because it's been so long since the field's been done. But when I got to where your garden was, my plow sunk six inches deeper and the engine of the tractor quit lugging so hard, and the soil was black and beautiful. So I wanted you to know how nice the soil was and how much good your garden has done me, and how much it helps my mood every time the tractor gets to that spot." She was tickled. We had a good visit. Then I asked, "If this works okay, some day I'll plow the upper field too. Do you think it's worth it."

"Oh, my, yes," she said. "The last time it was farmed was in the early Forties, when Elmer farmed it for us. He came down to the house for a glass of water, and he said that was the best soil he'd ever plowed."

So, after many years of planning on it, last fall I did finally plow the upper tier above the barn, thirty acres or so. The furrows of Elmer's plow were still visible, especially in late afternoon when the sun slanted across them. You could also feel them rise and fall under you when you drove a pickup across that field. Other than that, it was hard to tell the acreage had ever been farmed. Sagebrush was invading. The plants were still relatively small, but they were troublesome, their woody stems intertwining with the plowshares and forcing me frequently to get off the tractor and laboriously knock off the soil accumulated by the sage plants that twisted themselves around the shares.

Then, over winter, I let Mother Nature work on the plowing for me, breaking down the soil by freezing and thawing, so it would disk better in spring. April found me up there again, high above the valley, pulling the disk back and forth. It was a nice change to work high on the western side of the valley. At the northwest end of the field I could peek over the ridge farther west into another valley, that of the West Rosebud River, and see the ranches in the valley bottom running up toward the village of Fishtail and beyond, all the way to the mountains, a view so fine I would deliberately turn the tractor in a larger-than-necessary loop to indulge in it as long as I could. The view east was also fine, for now I looked across the valley toward home. Our ranch house and buildings were hidden by the cottonwood trees. The east valley wall viewed from so far away looked steeper than it really is, the timber draw we know as Indian Coulee easy to pick out since it is the only coulee on our ranch that has so many trees.

It is funny what perspective can do, how much more clearly some things can be seen from a ways off, and this is true with time as well as distance. Four winters have passed since the year of the stud colt. Four times the buck brush has turned blood-red and the quaking aspen bright yellow, and four times they have sprung back into life again. Four crops of calves have been born bawling for their mothers and four sets of foals as well, their impossibly long legs like tipsy stilts as they struggle up, working delicate noses along their mothers' sides. Four times brave crocuses have briefly bloomed before the year's final snow.

We have in the hills many cacti of the prickly pear variety. Flat and spiny, this cactus hugs the ground, ready to inflict a bite you will not forget should you be so careless as to sit on one. It grows in the rocky places where there is little soil, in gravely ground that does not hold moisture, often between flat slabs of shale. And in such places, once a year, the cactus makes great beauty with its yellow flower as bright as sunshine.

On the ranch we are surrounded by beauty. And yet, when the perspective is just wrong, when we are so close to the ground that we see only the spines of ranching, the struggles, the debts, and the endless succession of physically taxing jobs, there is a danger of becoming blind to the beauty. Then it is good to climb the ridge and see the ranch spread out in front of you below the Beartooths under the big sky.

I have taken early "retirement" from teaching, missing my fellow teachers and the daily audience of students, captive listeners to my stories. In return I get winters during which the ranch is never hidden from me by darkness. I have been riding a colt, a sorrel gelding with a blaze face named Little Mack. He is the son of the stud colt and a mare out of old Mona, our first broodmare and Rockytop's mother. The colt has the same perfect gait, the endurance, the wind, and the drive of his sire, but he is more tractable. His attitude, if it could be in words, would be something like, "Dan, you're no kid anymore, so as long as you let me cruise out I'm glad to help you with whatever needs to be done." Our first ride out of the corral was a flight across the east range, down to Beaver Creek, up into the neighbor's and home. Like his father the colt did this, held to a flat walk and running walk, loping only a short distance, in just over forty minutes. He shows every sign of becoming the very best horse I have ever known. Maybe someday we will cross Sundance Pass. But still, sometimes, I think of the stud colt.

I have heard it said that ranching is not an occupation but a way of life. It has never been free of its thorns. Ours today simply come in different forms from those against which Magnus and Elmer struggled. It takes more than toughness to endure. It takes never losing sight of the beauty.

About the Artist

I might have looked far and wide without discovering an artist who combined academic credentials and renown in the art world with immersion in the culture this book represents. But I did not have to, for Nik Carpenter of Bridger, Montana, met these requirements in spades and was a boyhood friend as well. Nik knows Montana ranching and Montana ranchers, and his work in oil, charcoal, pen and ink, and conté rendered here reflects that.

Most of the art was created specifically for this book. I did not ask for direct portraits of the real people mentioned in this work but for representative types, so Nik used his ranching neighbors as models. Pieces that do depict the actual individuals described in the text are the portrait, from an old photograph, of Magnus on horseback at the beginning of "The Ranch" section, and, in the color insert: the painting of Elmer with his team, Dan and Daisy, also from a photograph; the picture of the farrier, Ralph Hughes; and lastly, that of St. Olaf, my father's little Lutheran country church on Red Lodge Creek, for which the actual church served as a "model."